The Dilemma of
American Immigration

The Dilemma of American Immigration
Beyond the Golden Door

Pastora San Juan Cafferty
Barry R. Chiswick
Andrew M. Greeley
Teresa A. Sullivan

With a foreword by Governor Bruce Babbitt

Transaction Books
New Brunswick (U.S.A.) and London (U.K.)

Library of Congress Catalog Number: 83-543

ISBN: 0-87855-481-5 (cloth), 0-87855-935-3 (paper)

Printed in the United States of America

Library of Congress Cataloging in Publication Data
Main entry under title:

The Dilemma of American immigration.

  Includes index.
  1. United States—Emigration and immigration—
Addresses, essays, lectures. I. Cafferty, Pastora San Juan.
JV6493.D54 1983   325.73   83-543
ISBN 0-87855-481-5
ISBN 0-87855-935-3 (pbk.)

Contents

Foreword

Over the last decade, immigration and refugee issues have once again moved to the top of the public policy agenda. Despite important reforms during the past fifteen years, public confidence in our immigration system has been steadily eroded by the tide of recent events. Highly publicized accounts of increasing illegal immigration from Mexico and Central America, the arrival of thousands of Cuban and Haitian "boat people" on Florida beaches, and the near administrative collapse of the Immigration and Naturalization Service have contributed to the growing perception that U.S. immigration policy is hopelessly out of control.

While it is questionable whether the situation has reached the state of crisis proclaimed by many alarmists, we are clearly in need of a careful, objective reexamination of our immigration and refugee policies. However, the succession of blue-ribbon panels and special task forces created in recent years to explore the issue has demonstrated that this is easier said than done. Immigration occupies a very special place in our national life, both past and present. Whether one is a believer in the melting pot or a confirmed cultural pluralist, it is impossible to probe the foundation of our immigration policies without exposing a whole range of deeply ingrained, fiercely defended, and often conflicting values and attitudes. The profound influence that successive waves of newcomers have had on the economic growth, political institutions, and social character of our country make a dispassionate, balanced treatment of the issue exceedingly difficult.

The analyst's job is further complicated by the fact that immigration policy is inextricably linked to other social and political issues, and is of concern to an ever-widening spectrum of interest groups, each with a stake in the debate. Organized labor points to the impact of illegal immigrants on wage rates and unionization efforts; state and local officials worry about the demands of recently arrived immigrants, both legal and illegal, on costly social services; farmers claim that without foreign labor crops would rot in the fields; Hispanics are concerned about the possible civil rights implications of efforts to crack down on illegal immigration; religious groups seek to reduce the vulnerability of migrants to abuse; northeasterners decry the "unfair subsidy" that the presence of Mexican workers represents for the Southwest. From bilingual education to rising health-care costs to population growth, an increasing number of controversial issues can be connected to immigration.

This fierce competition of economic and political interests characteristic of the debate over immigration policy has led to some strange and unfamiliar alliances. There is no "liberal" or "conservative" position on immigration. The AFL-CIO, environmental groups, the Ku Klux Klan, and some social reformers argue for more restrictive policies. Hispanic groups, conservative farmers, the ACLU, and other social reformers support more relaxed measures. In this confusing political environment, it is little wonder that policy makers have been unable to agree on which direction our immigration policy should take.

Any successful reevaluation of our immigration and refugee system must begin by sorting all of this out, peeling away the rhetorical excesses and misunderstanding to lay bare the basic values and interests that have shaped American attitudes toward immigration. This book successfully traces the fundamental continuities and shifting attitudes in the immigration debate through the events of the past 200 years. We have come a long way since the exclusion acts of the 1880s and the national origin quotas of the 1920s, but as the authors remind us, many of the concerns expressed today seem hauntingly familiar. Despite changing circumstances, much of the battle over immigration continues to be fought over the same old ground. If, as appears to be the case, similar themes appear over and over again, our past experiences offer important lessons for the present.

A great deal of the current controversy, especially over illegal immigration, also springs from competing theories or assumptions about how immigrants behave and limited empirical information regarding the ways in which they affect our economic, political, and social institutions. Combining the tools of their separate disciplines, the authors have skillfully tackled these complicated technical arguments surrounding the immigration debate. In a straightforward manner which the layperson can appreciate, legitimate concerns are distinguished from groundless fears as the authors carefully explore the information that we do have and the ways it is used by those on various sides of the issues.

After sifting through all of the evidence and weighing competing values and interests, we must inevitably make some difficult choices and begin the process of formulating specific, workable policies. The authors have here presented a comprehensive series of recommendations. Some of these measures have been suggested before; others are new. Taken together, they represent a direct challenge to examine our own preferred prescriptions and ideas. Though it is unlikely that everyone will agree with all of the recommendations, they are thoughtfully developed and deserve careful consideration.

The United States has been attempting to define a suitable immigration policy for almost a century now. That we have not succeeded is no surprise. Immigration remains one of those intractable social issues, forever open to redefinition and debate as economic conditions, social conventions, and political attitudes shift in one direction or another. There may be no definitive solution to the immigration puzzle. But we must always insist that our immigration and refugee policies reaffirm our commitment to dominant American interests and values while reflecting an awareness of the realities of a changing world. Coming at a time of particularly rapid and complex change, and widespread uncertainty about our basic national goals and purpose, this sensitive and informative book is welcome indeed.

Bruce Babbitt
Governor of the State of Arizona
Tucson, Arizona

Preface

Immigration may well be the thorniest and most ethically problematic issue confronting America today and in coming decades. The ancestors of 99 percent of the population came to this land within the past 400 years—in terms of human migration, an infinitesimal span of time. With few exceptions, we are a nation of recent immigrants. And it is only in the last quarter of this span of 400 years that substantial legal barriers have been imposed on immigration, first against the entry of East Asians and then half a century later against southern and eastern Europeans.

These barriers, based on prejudice against people who seemed different from those already here, were eventually rejected as inconsistent with the spirit of tolerance inscribed in our founding documents and praised as the American virtue. By 1965, the same social and political thought and processes that had led to the expansion of civil rights for native ethnic and racial minorities, including the outlawing of race and sex discrimination in work, housing, and political life, led to amendments that liberalized the immigration laws. Moreover, there was a new awareness of the importance of emerging Third World nations, whose populations were discriminated against in U.S. immigration law. Nevertheless, the 1965 legislation did not return immigration to the open-door policy that prevailed in the nineteenth century.

Recent discussions of immigration have created a popular image of the U.S. as beleaguered on all sides by potential immigrants—people seeking employment who will enter illegally if they cannot do so legally, or who will make spurious claims of persecution in their homelands if there is no other way to enter. It is noteworthy that this unease with immigrants is a continuous element in American history. In a 1753 letter concerning German immigrants to Pennsylvania, Benjamin Franklin wrote: "Those who come hither are generally the most stupid of their own nation . . . it is almost impossible to remove any prejudices they may entertain." But he went on to write: "I am not against the admission of Germans in general, for they have their virtues. Their industry and frugality are exemplary. They are excellent husbandmen and contribute greatly to the improvement of a country" (Bennett, 1963, p.5).

Not only the native-born, but even the immigrants themselves, express unease concerning the next boatload. During the recent influx of Vietnamese boat-people one of the authors overheard the following exchange between two middle-aged women with very strong East European accents: first woman (looking up from her newspaper): "Why should these people want to leave their own country and move here?" Second woman (in reply): "I don't know, but we have enough of our own problems without them."

To varying degrees we all share this "gangplank" or "next boatload" mentality. We are grateful for the freedom and affluence of America, yet ambivalent at the prospect that a later group of foreigners will not only share them, but also may depreciate their value to us. Now that we and our immediate relatives are here, it is easy to see that the gangplank should be raised. Our unease regarding new waves of foreigners has existed in every generation since the first settlers along the eastern seaboard, although it undergoes periodic upsurges and declines that are related to business conditions and political and social development.

The unease is an authentic ambivalence. Even in the most intensely restrictionist period the United States has never completely cut off the flow of immigrants. Americans feel guilt about restricting immigration. Those who currently argue against further immigration do not argue that the largely open-door policy that once prevailed was wrong or contrary to U.S. interests, but rather that the situation has changed and that this change has justified the position they are forced to adopt. But almost no one advocates a completely open border. It is nearly universally accepted by Americans that some standards for admission are needed. This is accepted even by those whose ancestors—or who themselves—might not have been admitted under the standards. Although Americans still see this as a country that provides a haven for the "wretched refuse" of the earth, we want to be highly selective of who actually is admitted to its bounty, and we hold many different views about the appropriate number of immigrants and selection criteria. Too guilty to end immigration, too fearful not to limit it, Americans have from the beginning of the republic, and particularly in the last century, been caught in the inconsistencies seemingly inherent in an effective and satisfactory immigration policy.

America's unease regarding immigration—that we are a nation of immigrants fearful of further immigration—may well be insoluble in principle because it has to do with who we are and who we wish to let join the family of Americans. America's creed—that we are a nation of refuge—is powerful and moving, but it does not provide a practical, decisive rule governing how often, to whom, and under what conditions we are to offer this refuge.

We are deeply moved when we hear of Indochinese drowning in the South China Sea on the way to freedom. We are moved at the reports of tiny Haitian boats braving hurricanes and the naval patrols of other Caribbean nations to escape. Some memory of our own ancestral past throbs when we hear of the Mexican mother about to give birth desperately struggling across the border so that her child can be an American citizen. Yet despite the pity we feel for the individuals involved, we are nervous about the shiploads and crowds and masses the individuals represent, and what impact they will have on us when they get here.

Are there enough jobs to go around? Is there enough land, enough fresh water, enough energy to share with immigrants? Can these foreigners share our political ideals of freedom? Can they be assimilated into our culture to become good Americans, or will they change American culture in a way we will not like? Will they use social services paid for by us? Will they merely enjoy the economic benefits of America while continuing to owe allegiance to another nation, friendly or otherwise? Those who came before have asked these questions since before the republic began. To be a nation of immigrants is to expose one's country to an extraordinary risk of great harm as well as an extraordinary chance for great benefits. While one can point to many accomplishments of immigrants, not all nations have been happy with their experiences. The West Europeans, for example, have developed reservations about the ultimate economic, social, and political impact of their darker skinned immigrants from the West Indies, Africa, South Asia, and the Middle East. The Japanese, who have had a history of discriminating against twentieth century Korean immigrants, were loath to accept Indochinese refugees, allegedly because of fears that these foreigners could not become Japanese. Mexicans at first welcomed foreigners from a country on their northeastern border, but these entrants became rebellious and through force of arms severed their territory from Mexico to join the more powerful neighbor.

To let in new immigrants is to bet, in effect, that they too can become useful, productive, and loyal Americans, even if they are not just like us. We cannot make such a dangerous bet without wanting to hedge. Somewhere between the bet and the hedge are to be found the nation's immigration policies—the statutes, court decisions, programs, and protocols by which the United States has vacillated in the last century between its impulse to let in more immigrants and its fear of doing so.

In this book we explore American immigration experience and policies. We look first to the past for the patterns that the country has established in dealing with this issue. We then turn to some specific suggestions for future direction as the United States struggles with the latest, acute immigration issues that it must face in the decades immediately ahead. On some issues we favor following policies of the past; on others we propose radical departures.

We represent among ourselves a good bit of the diversity and heterogeneity of the American population that has fueled the immigration debate. One of us is an immigrant, one is the child of an immigrant, one is the grandchild of an immigrant, and one is a fifth-generation American. According to the ethnic classification schemes now popular with the Census Bureau we represent three distinct ethnic groups. Two of us are southerners, and two northerners. We differ in religious identity and in the intensity of religious practice. Among us there is at least one Democrat and at least one Republican. We are sufficiently independent-minded to resent both the label "liberal" and the label "conservative," which have at various times been appended to one or another of us. Two of us have had extensive public policy experience in the federal government; all of us have some research experience overseas as well as extensive U.S. research experience on the myriad issues relevant for understanding immigration policies. Among us are a demographer, an economist, a historian, and a sociologist, who, as realistic social scientists, recognize the economic and social problems, and opportunities, that immigration continues to present now as it did for past generations. This recognition, and our dismay at the reception of social science research on immigration, are responsible for this volume.

It would be naive to assume that we, or anyone, could present a technical solution to what is ultimately a problem of values and economic and political self-interest in various groups in the population. Immigration policy must always be made by a process of balancing values and interests and making choices. What we have done here is to explore the values and interests and to explain the principles by which we have made our balancing decisions. Although this may not provide an all-embracing solution to America's immigration problems, it does provide a rational basis for dealing with them that should command widespread support.

There is no dearth of literature on immigration. We have chosen to emphasize in this volume our shared vision that a dramatic overhaul of American immigration policy is in order. For purposes of clarity in making this important point, we have tried to avoid footnotes, overly technical discussions, and some of the cumbersome paraphernalia of our craft. However, we have tried to include citations to the most important studies that have influenced our position; our selected references include the works we found most helpful. Where data appear without attribution, they are the results of our own analysis of readily available public data. The data available in the Annual Reports and the Statistical Yearbooks of the Immigration and Naturalization Service and in the Census of Population have been invaluable.

We are deeply grateful to the Revson Foundation and to its president, Eli Evans, for their confidence and enthusiasm about this project and for providing funds. We are also grateful to Mitchell Sviridoff and Siobhan Oppenheimer-Nicolau, formerly of the Ford Foundation, as well as to the Ford Foundation itself, for encouragement and for additional funding. This study is not necessarily representative of the views of these individuals or of the foundations. We have had complete independence in designing the research, reaching the conclusions, and drafting this report.

An outstanding staff at the National Opinion Research Center facilitated our work. Notable among them were William C. McCready, Director of the Cultural Pluralism Research Center, and Mary Kotecki, the Center's former Administrative Assistant. Christian Jacobsen contributed the analysis of the geographic impact of immigrants. Lewis Gitlin offered important assistance at every stage, but his analysis of historical and legal issues affecting immigration deserves special mention. During the writing of the manuscript, the research assistance of Robert Tomei, David Smith, and David Eubanks was particularly useful. Vivian Tillman kept us organized throughout. Susan Campbell and Suzanne Erfurth provided editorial assistance and prepared the book's index. Chris Lonn and the word processing department worked long and hard in getting us from manuscript to typeset copy. Finally, we must acknowledge the useful conversations we had with a number of colleagues, including Harley Browning, Carmel Chiswick, Robert Gordon, Douglas Laycock, Silvia Pedraza-Bailey, and Aristide Zolberg.

P.S.J.C.
B.R.C.
A.M.G.
T.A.S.

Part I
IMMIGRATION AND THE
AMERICAN CAULDRON

1
Introduction: The Policy Setting

Immigration is an issue of continuing concern for Americans. We are torn between the belief that America, land of opportunity, will offer even greater opportunities in the future for us and for others, and the fear that the opportunities that attracted our forefathers are no longer unlimited (Bustamante, 1976; but see Ehrlich, Bilderback, and Ehrlich, 1979). Over the past two centuries, Americans have vacillated between welcoming immigrants and keeping them out. From time to time a major reform of immigration policy is enacted, and we assume that the issue has been resolved and turn our attention elsewhere. For awhile in the late 1960s and early 1970s, it appeared that we were at such a point. In 1965, major amendments were made to the 1952 Immigration and Nationality Act (the McCarran-Walter Act), itself largely a recodification of the 1924 Immigration Act and subsequent amendments. Many felt that we could put aside the issue of immigration. Indeed the U.S. Bureau of the Census removed from the 1980 Census of the Population the question on parents' nativity that had been asked in every decennial census since 1870.

But by the mid-1970s, it became apparent that the U.S. faced new immigration problems. For example, by the time the 1980 Census was taken, the Census Bureau found itself engaged in a number of lawsuits and controversies on Capitol Hill over whether and how aliens were to be counted. Illegal aliens were a special concern. To many, the most important immigration issue was the continued illegal entry of thousands, if not millions, of persons along the southern border of the United States. But there were other issues as well: the admission of one-half million refugees from Indochina since 1975; 14,500 immigration violations of various types by persons from various countries of origin; Haitian entrants, both legal and illegal, who sought asylum as "economic refugees" and feared, perhaps rightly, that having done so they would be persecuted if they returned to Haiti; and in 1980, a new Cuban refugee population, the "freedom flotilla."

Foreign policy issues always threaten to become immigration issues; witness the admission of Soviet dissidents and the attempted expulsion of Iranian students during the hostage crisis. President Jimmy Carter's emphasis on human rights abroad served symbolically to reinforce our own commitment to protect the persecuted by offering asylum. The Refugee Act of 1980 helped to clarify and expand the grounds of persecution that would justify refugee status.

And because immigrants are human, with all sorts of human problems, many immigration problems become social problems as well. The health of refugees is a concern, and so is the medical care provided at public expense to illegal entrants. Some observers are most concerned with crime—crime by the immigrants, crime against the immigrants (especially against the illegal ones, who are afraid to report the crimes), and the strengthening of organized crime by an influx of potential recruits. The alleged connection of immigrants with the smuggling of illegal drugs is a related concern. These fears were fueled by reports that Fidel Castro had sent prisoners from Cuban jails as refugees in the summer of 1980. That over 800,000 Mexican nationals could be apprehended while illegally crossing the border in recent years suggests that large numbers eventually do penetrate. It is suspected that where there is flouting of the law, as there is with illegal entries, corruption must be widespread. Indeed, the FBI ABSCAM investigation revealed that the Congressmen and Senator who were subsequently convicted had been bribed to introduce private immigration bills, that is, special legislation to permit the immigration of an individual.

But the public's major concern, especially in a time of slow economic growth, high and uncertain rates of inflation, growing budget deficits, and high unemployment, is the economic impact of foreign-born workers on the United States. Commentators claim both that new immigrants will take all the jobs and that they will thrive on welfare, and the contradiction is rarely pointed out. Others argue that the immigrants take only the jobs that no one else wants, and are told that those are the jobs that native-born minority groups want and need. In both domestic and foreign policy, many issues can be related directly and indirectly to immigration. It has been said, only half in jest, by more than one commentator that Mexico would let us have its oil if it were carried into the country by illegal aliens.

As a result, the 1970s saw the rise of a variety of new interest groups concerned with immigration problems. With United States birth rates remaining at low levels throughout the seventies, Zero Population Growth (ZPG) turned its attention to the 20 percent of American population growth attributable to immigration. ZPG was concerned not only about the numbers of aliens admitted legally and the numbers of illegal entrants and overstayers, but also about the fertility rates of the immigrants. A new interest group, the Federation for American Immigration Reform (FAIR), reflected the environmental concerns that had been so significant in the liberal politics of the seventies. FAIR pointed out that resources in the

United States were limited, and said that increasing numbers of immigrants could strain those limits. Like ZPG, FAIR was especially concerned with the entry of illegal aliens.

That some "liberal" groups should seem to take a stand against immigration is not so startling. As in the debates during the nineteenth century and during the period immediately after World War I, there are "liberals" and "conservatives" (as well as nativists) in the coalition favoring more restrictive immigration policies and "liberals" and "conservatives" in the coalition favoring less restrictive policies. Immigration, unlike most other issues, appears to cut across the neat liberal-conservative dichotomy so dear to ideologues and political commentators.

In 1978, Congress responded to these concerns by establishing the Select Commission on Immigration and Refugee Policy (SCIRP). The SCIRP commissioners included eight members of Congress, four cabinet officers, and four presidential appointees. Its chairman was the Rev. Theodore M. Hesburgh, President of Notre Dame. SCIRP conducted public hearings across the nation, commissioned its own research, and talked to government agencies and scholars in the field. In February 1981 SCIRP submitted its report, which recommended some increases in the number of immigrants admitted, sanctions against employers who hired illegal aliens, and an amnesty for illegal aliens in the country as of January 1981 (Select Commission on Immigration and Refugee Policy, 1981). But few expected the SCIRP report to settle the controversies or to lead to immediate congressional response. For one thing, the recommendations could not be defended by SCIRP's research because the commission did not fund research on some basic issues, including illegal aliens and the economic impact of immigrants.

Most Americans were aware of the continuation of immigration and had reservations about its magnitude: 80 percent of those questioned in the Roper Survey of June 1980 reported they felt that immigration laws should be tightened (Roper, 1980). Both major parties included statements on immigration in their 1980 presidential platforms, but the statements were as vague and uninformative as the English language permits. Very few campaign statements were made, beyond Ronald Reagan's cryptic comment before a Mexican-American audience that the undocumented workers needed to be documented. After he was elected president, Reagan proposed amnesty for illegal aliens and a temporary worker program for 50,000 Mexicans. But during the campaign, immigration was a topic that was too sensitive, too complicated, and too hot to handle.

In the following months, several pieces of legislation were drafted. One, the Immigration Reform and Control Bill of 1982, passed the U.S. Senate, but died in the House of Representatives. Among its provisions were an annual ceiling of 425,000 legal immigrants to the U.S. (except refugees), the imposition of civil and criminal sanctions on employers who knowingly hired illegal aliens, and an amnesty to illegal aliens who had entered the United States before January 1, 1980. The bill also included provisions for a temporary worker program. However, its reception was mixed at best, and it produced outcries both that it went "too far" and that it did not go "far enough."

Our purpose here is to analyze in a systematic manner the various issues and arguments regarding immigration and immigration policy. By clarifying the issues and organizing some of the recent research findings— our own and those of other social scientists—we hope to inform public discussion. We believe that raising the level of the debate from emotionalism to rational discourse on costs and benefits, who gains and who loses, will allow a more rational and productive immigration policy to emerge.

Contemporary Immigration to the United States

In 1980, the United States granted permanent residence visas to 505,000 aliens; of this number, approximately 45,000 were refugees. In addition 125,000 Cuban refugees were "paroled" into the United States, as were smaller numbers of Southeast Asian refugees and refugees from other countries. Another 3 million were admitted for temporary stays, including 250,000 foreign nationals on student visas. An unknown number of illegal aliens were present in the country; estimates of their number range from the 6.5 to 9.5 million suggested by FAIR to the "3.5 million to less than 6 million" suggested by demographers at the U.S. Bureau of the Census (Siegel, Passell, and Robinson, 1979). Some of these illegal aliens were legal entrants who overstayed their visas, others had entered with fraudulent visas, but it is believed that by far the largest group entered the United States in a clandestine fashion. Some of them would stay in the U.S. only a few days or weeks before returning to their homes; others would stay, by plan or by happenstance, for the rest of their lives. A small group of temporary workers (about 6,000 in 1980) entered the United States for short periods to harvest crops. Other small groups of temporary entrants were the temporary workers admitted because of their distinguished ability or merit (professionals and artists) and persons who commuted to work every day from their homes in Mexico and Canada.

But numbers alone do not tell the story. U.S. immigration has always been characterized—and caricatured—on the basis of the largest group of recent immigrants. Thus in 1830 "they" were German and Irish; in 1910 "they" were Jews and Slavs and Italians; in 1980 "they" were the Mexican illegal aliens and the Cuban and Indochinese refugees. Another form of the caricature has been the purposes for which "they" have come: "they" want to earn money and send it home; "they" are aristocrats who would be killed at home but who won't know how to work here; "they" are rich or poor, lazy or industrious, religious or atheist, skilled or otherwise.

The most important hallmark of American immigration, and the one that defies stereotyping, is its heterogeneity. Correspondingly, the most important mistake made in immigration analysis is the assumption that "they" are all alike in some respect. "They" do not all speak Spanish, or accept jobs at the minimum wage, or live in major cities. American immigrants include most of the world's nationalities. They come as economic immigrants, as refugees from natural or political disasters, as investors in the U.S. economy, and as family members of U.S. citizens or permanent residents. Some are social misfits who could not find a place in their own countries and may not find one here. Some are unskilled in their own countries. Some are skilled at home in a trade or craft, but cannot practice that skill in the United States because the field is more technologically advanced here, because the technical aspects differ sharply (e.g., law), or because the trade union or occupational licensing laws exclude them. Some have training and skills that can be readily marketed in the U.S. Some are highly skilled indeed and will make significant advances in science or medicine while in the United States—35 of the 150 American Nobel laureates in the past 79 years were naturalized citizens of the United States.

Many approaches to immigration policy have failed because they oversimplify this heterogeneity. The immigration problem is not simply a problem of undocumented workers, or of Mexicans, or of refugees. Immigrants are not just unskilled workers who are glad to take low-paying jobs, nor are they all foreign physicians who work in inner-city hospitals. Historical events, journalistic practices, and fads in academic scholarship all tend to shift the spotlight from group to group among the immigrants. Undocumented workers are the issue until a new influx of refugees comes; unskilled workers are the problem until the American medical profession warns of a coming "glut" of foreign doctors. Every new international crisis has its immigration ramifications. Because different aspects of immigration are presented from time to time as being "the" immigration problem, the government is encouraged to handle immigration policy piecemeal, managing each crisis as it arises, and finally arriving at a policy that is more often than not inconsistent, incomprehensible, and incompetent. The false impression is conveyed that immigration is out of control, but in truth it is the policy-making process that is out of control.

Our Objectives

It is flattering but fallacious to think that all the world would like to come to the United States. But many indeed would like to emigrate here, and they are willing to put their names on long waiting lists to do so, to risk their jobs and what limited freedom they may have by applying for exit visas, or to risk their lives crossing the border with the assistance of "coyotes" (smugglers), who frequently prey on them. We have, intentionally or not, effectively advertised our prosperity, our freedoms, and our way of life through Voice of America, through affluent American tourists and servicemen, through word of mouth communication with friends and relatives already here, and through the mass media. Movies often portray an affluence and lifestyle that even most Americans do not experience. It is not surprising that many would like to take us up on the chance to pursue the American dream. And so, while not everyone wants to come to the United States, there are enough potential immigrants that some restrictions are necessary. The question is not whether to limit immigration, but how to limit it and at what numerical level.

There is an element of déjà vu in current newspaper editorials, letters to the editor, and statements from lobbying groups in the immigration debate. Some of the comments could have been written sixty years earlier. As in the 1920s, many of the attacks on immigration are strident and full of fear.

Recent research on the descendants of the earlier immigrants shows that most of the restrictionists' fears were illfounded. Rather than forming a disadvantaged class, turn of the century and early twentieth century immigrants have done very well in the United States. Indeed, they often earn more and have higher levels of education than those whose ancestors came decades earlier (see, for example, Lieberson, 1980; Chiswick 1977b, 1979, 1982a, 1983a, 1983b). Was the restriction on immigration in the 1920s a necessary condition for the immigrants' success? Or were the restrictionists wrong? If they were wrong in 1920, are they wrong today, or have circumstances changed so much that a stronger case can be made for restrictions? These are the questions to which we address ourselves in the first part of the book. Above all, we have tried to avoid the pitfall of regarding immigrants as an indistinguishable mass. Instead, we have tried to highlight the problems and benefits that different kinds of immigrants bring with them. We have thought about the issue of restrictions in terms of the mix of immigrants as well as the total number of immigrants, but we have tried to keep uppermost the question of how to develop a rational set of policies.

Any brief review of public policy problems, whether domestic or foreign, shows that immigration impinges on virtually every area of concern. In the second part of this book we have outlined the consequences of current immigration policies and pointed to some unanticipated outcomes. Many of these consequences have been highlighted in the immigration debate, including the effect of immigration on transfer payments and on ethnic relations within the country. Other issues, such as the response of foreign governments to our immigration policies, have received less attention.

In the final part of the book we present the outline of a new immigration policy, based on a point system, provided with a set of criteria for admitting refugees, and administered by a new commission for immigration. We advocate a temporary worker program as well as provisions for the temporary admission of students, tourists, and businessmen. Finally, we discuss the significance of naturalization in the current climate, and we explain our reasons for rejecting a number of proposed solutions to immigration problems.

No revision of immigration policy, no matter how extreme, can resolve all of the issues or satisfy all of the competing interests. What we can offer are guidelines for a contemporary policy. American immigration policy need not erase the words of Emma Lazarus from the Statue of Liberty, but it should adapt them to the times.

2
Continuities in the Immigration Debate

The tensions in creating and implementing American immigration policy have existed in this nation from the beginning. The national motto, "e pluribus unum"—out of many, one—refers not only to the federal system unifying the states but also to the quest for an identifiable "American" resulting from diverse roots and customs. Michael Kammen, in his book *People of Paradox*, demonstrates that the inconsistencies inherent in the American system existed from the very beginning:

> And so it was that American colonial history, which had begun with a quest for purity and homogeneity, ended with a sophisticated rationale for pluralism and heterogeneity. What had happened was not really so paradoxical as it may seem, for the so-called melting pot had been a boiling cauldron all along, from Jamestown to James Madison. There is a very real sense in which the American nation emerged not in response to provincial disunity, but in response to a historical problem of long duration: how best to control unstable pluralism, how best to balance the areas of compulsion and freedom in American life (1972, pp. 73-74).

Martin Dooley recognized the same problem of the quest for unity in the midst of unstable pluralism, as reported by his literary creator in 1898:

> An Anglo-Saxon, Hinnissy, is a German that's forgot who was his parents . . . I'm an Anglo-Saxon . . . th' name iv Dooley has been th' proudest Anglo-Saxon name in th' county Roscommon f'r many years . . . Pether Bowbeen down be th' Frinch church is formin' th' Circle Francaize Anglo-Saxon club, an' me ol' frind Dominigo . . . will march at th' head iv th' Dago Anglo-Saxons whin th' time comes . . . Rooshian Jews . . . they'd be a tur-r-ble thing f'r anny inimy iv th' Anglo-Saxon 'lieance to face. Th' Bohemians an' Pole Anglo-Saxons may be a little slow in wakin' up to what th' pa-apers calls our common hurtage, but ye may be sure they'll be all r-right whin they're called on . . . I tell ye, whin th' Clan an' th' sons iv Sweden an' th' Banana Club an' th' Circle Francaize an' th' Pollacky Benivolent Society an' th' Rooshian Sons of Dinnymite an' th' Benny Brith an' th' Coffee Clutch that Schwartzmeister r-runs an' th' tur-rnd'ye-mind an' th' Holland society an' th' Afro-Americans an' th' other Anglo-Saxons begin f'r to raise their Anglo-Saxon battle cry, it'll be all day with th' eight or nine people in th' wurruld that has th' misfortune iv not bein' brought up Anglo-Saxons (Dunne, 1898, p. 55).

But times, we think, are different today: the call for unity has been swallowed up in the present clamor for preserving an individual's culture and values and the national search for roots. Mr. Dooley's unity is scorned as "anglo-conformity" (although he would be the first to question what about it was "anglo"—let alone conforming). There are new problems, new issues, new limits that we must face.

Nevertheless, if we concede that the restrictionists can make a good case for their position today, we are forced to take seriously the restrictionists in ages past. At all times the restrictionists have counted among their number some of the best minds and some of the most public-spirited citizens of their respective eras. It is only in historical retrospect that their motives have been suspect. Indeed, the restrictionists were often at great pains to distinguish their arguments for restriction from those of previous generations. The argument today, as in the past, is that immigration until now, or until very recently, has been a good thing for our country, but now it must stop, or be sharply curtailed. The restrictionist, in other words, does not draw the line one hundred, fifty, or even twenty-five years in the past; he draws the line in his own time. However, even though he may be cast in the role of villain by immigration historians, the restrictionist has been honest in speaking about one side of the dilemma, namely, the fear of immigration that lurks in all of us. On some occasions, at least, the restrictionist position represented the wiser social policy. Surely at some times in the country's history it has been easier than at other times to absorb large numbers of immigrants.

We do not wrestle with issues of immigration in a theoretical vacuum of philosophical debate between "restrictionism" and "antirestrictionism;" but in the practical order, where there are concrete political, social, and economic problems for both the United States and the sending countries. There will always be a component of restrictionism in American immigration policy. It is not a question of whether the restrictionists in any given era are right or wrong. The immigration issue is so enduring and to some extent so intractable that the terms of the debate must always to some extent be the same. In this chapter we review the continuities that have marked the immigration debate as well as their current restatements.

Economic Issues in Immigration

One of the most durable objections to the continued entry of immigrants is fear of their impact on the economy. Three distinct themes can be considered under this heading. The first is the fear of cheap labor—the fear that immigrants will take the jobs of the native-born and so contribute to lower earnings amd greater unemployment.

A second economic argument is in some ways the opposite of the first: instead of fearing that immigrants will take jobs, we fear that they will not take jobs and will require support at public expense. Regulations against the admission of paupers were among the earliest immigration restrictions, but the growth of the public income transfer system has made people more aware of a potential problem.

The third economic argument against immigration is that immigrants will somehow "plunder" the United States, whether by sending their earnings home or by retiring to home countries with their life savings and Social Security. (For data on this point, see Kraly, 1982.) This fear has become more pronounced with concerns for the value of the dollar on foreign exchange markets. Historically, this concern was milder and took the form of ridiculing immigrants with their savings-and-loans, their currency exchanges for sending remittances to their home countries and their frugal consumption habits. But these attitudes reveal an underlying sense that political power is closely tied to economic power, and that immigrants who are not fully committed to the United States do not deserve to share in its prosperity—even if they have worked for it.

To discuss these economic fears in more detail, it is necessary to determine to what extent they are legitimate.

Cheap Labor

Among the most vocal opponents of immigration have been America's workers, including their union leaders. This historical opposition is not surprising, although it is ironic: popular support for the restrictive quotas of the 1920s stemmed partly from the belief that the socialists and anarchists among the immigrants were responsible for the growth of unions and the increased number of labor disputes. But labor's opposition is not surprising because most immigrants are workers. They come with few assets other than their eagerness to work. As a result, the immigrants are in direct competition in the labor market with earlier immigrants and native-born workers. In more recent decades, with greater differentiation of workers by skill level, labor's concerns are more likely to be specific to particular skills. This is understandable. Physicians and nurses would regard the immigration of a large number of foreign-trained physicians and nurses as an economic threat. Similarly, native-born unskilled workers would be threatened by the immigration of unskilled workers.

Much of the immigration debate that has fueled the fear of cheap labor fails to recognize that a differentiation of skills is relevant. Opponents of immigration generally use arguments that apply to the immigration of unskilled workers as if all immigrants were unskilled. The problem is confounded by another assumption (usually implicit) that every job taken by an immigrant is taken away from a native-born worker—that is, that the economy is a zero-sum game, and immigration must necessarily cause unemployment. (For quotations to this effect by high-level government officials in Democratic and Republican administrations, see, for example, the *Los Angeles Times*, 1979, and *U.S. News and World Report*, 1974.) As our discussion below shows, these arguments are at best only shadows of the truth.

Income. The total output of a country, and hence the income of its population, is produced through the combined effects of inputs referred to as "factors of production." These factors of production include land, capital, and labor. Labor is best thought of not as a homogeneous factor but as a set of factors for different skill levels. As a general principle, the overall income of the native-born population of a country should increase with immigration. An increase in the labor supply of a category of workers due to immigration would depress the wages of native-born workers with similar skills, that is, those who are close substitutes in production. It would, however, raise the return to other factors of production, including other workers, land, and capital. The increased income of other factors of production arises from the principle of complementarity: the extra output of an extra unit of capital is greater if the stock of labor working with the capital is larger. As an example, a bulldozer with one driver can move a certain amount of earth a day in a road-repair project. The productivity of the bulldozer will be greater, however, if there are additional workers involved in the work it is doing—to direct traffic around the work area, provide relief drivers, repair the machine on the spot when it breaks down, and so forth. (The arguments in this and the next few paragraphs are developed in detail in Chiswick, 1982d.)

Because the increase in the incomes of the other factors of production is greater than the decline in the income of the factor that is a close substitute for the immigrants, the overall income of the native population increases. But increased income for others is cold comfort for the native-born workers whose own incomes decline.

In the contemporary world, groups adversely affected by a change in public policy or external circumstances lobby long and hard for either protection or compensation. That is, in the terminology of the Washington bureaucracy, they want to be "held harmless." The held-harmless principle is at least partially accomplished through the income transfer system. Some of the income loss would automatically be mitigated by the increase in income transfers that are targeted to low-wage workers and their family members. These transfer programs include Food Stamps, subsidized school lunches, and, for some, subsidized housing. In addition, for single-parent families there is Aid to Families with Dependent Children (AFDC) and in half of the states two-parent families may also be eligible if one parent is unemployed (AFDC-UP). The family may also be eligible for Medicaid, which finances health care for the poor and medically indigent. Regardless of other income or assets, if unemployment occurs the worker may be eligible for unemployment compensation benefits. These programs did not exist in the earlier periods of large-scale immigration. AFDC and unemployment compensation are the products of the middle 1930s, while Food Stamps, subsidized school lunches, Medicaid, and AFDC-UP, as well as the broadening of eligibility under AFDC, are all products of the mid-1960s. The Food Stamp program did not achieve its nationwide scope until the mid 1970s. Although the social welfare programs were instituted for other reasons, the social insurance programs of the Great Depression and the income transfer programs of the Great Society were instituted in periods in which the number of immigrants, particularly low-skilled immigrants, was very low relative to the size of the U.S. population. (For a description and analysis of the income transfer programs, see Chiswick, 1977a.)

Suppose, as happens to be the case, that public policy does not permit a differentiation in the receipt of public income transfers between citizens and legal resident aliens. Suppose also that the held-harmless principle is adhered to so that transfers are increased to make low-skilled native workers no worse off than before the immigration. The low-skilled immigrants will also be substantial recipients of these transfers. Since the taxes to pay for these net transfers are paid by high-skilled native-born workers and the owners of capital, the income of the native population can be reduced as a consequence of immigration. That is, although the principle of complementarity raises income of the native population before taxes are paid and transfers are received, after paying net transfers to the low-skilled immigrants the native population may have incomes lower than before the immigration.

The economic fear that low-skilled immigrants may be beneficiaries of income transfers in an amount sufficient to lower the income of the native population is not without foundation. One response is to have an immigration policy that favors more skilled workers. This has two beneficial effects. The direct effect is that it increases the relative number of high-earners among the immigrants, thereby decreasing the relative number of immigrants eligible for the income-contingent transfers. The indirect effect is that, through the principle of complementarity discussed above, the larger the proportion of high-skilled workers among the immigrants, the higher the earnings of low-skilled native workers. This reduces the number of natives eligible for these transfers and the magnitude of transfers per recipient. Indeed, this discussion suggests that the skill composition of an immigrant population may be more important than the number of immigrants in determining their long-run economic impact.

A variation of the economic argument regarding "cheap labor" is the fear that employers will "split" the labor market by having a lower paid immigrant labor force working alongside the native-born labor force (Piore, 1979). The presence of the labor market "split" would intimidate the native-born workers, make them fearful for their jobs, and chill efforts to bargain collectively or to improve working conditions. As usually formulated, this argument assumes that employers will exploit the ethnic antagonisms among their workers and will seek to hire new immigrant workers as different as possible from their current workers (Bonacich, 1972, 1973). This appeared to be the strategy Upton Sinclair described in the packing houses of Chicago at the turn of the century. Ethnic differences may not be required for this stategy; the difference between "old" and "new" workers may be sufficient to induce a "split" labor market. Yet, if the antagonisms become too intense, worker productivity may fall, to the detriment not only of the workers, but also their employers. Moreover, coalitions do form among seemingly divergent groups of workers when this is in their overall economic self-interest.

Unemployment. In analyzing the effect of immigration on unemployment, it is important to distinguish between taking a particular job slot and depriving a native worker of a job. Since at least the 1880s the argument that there is a "fixed" number of jobs in the American economy has been used to oppose immigration. If that were true, the measured unemployment rate in 1982 would have been 75 percent, not 10 percent, given the population growth of the preceding one hundred years. In general, the argument that immigrants create unemployment is fallacious. (By measured unemployment, we mean the percentage of the labor force who report that in the previous week they have not worked even one hour for pay or profit, but they have looked for work within the past four weeks or they were on a temporary job layoff.)

To understand why immigration does not create unemployment, consider what happens when an individual takes a job. Immigration critics have focused on the point that a particular job cannot simultaneously be held by a native-born worker and an immigrant. But the fact that the immigrant worker is productive, with wages to spend, means that his economic impact is far greater than merely occupying a job slot. Consider what he does with his earnings: he may hoard them, spend them, or decide on a mixture of the two.

Suppose the immigrant hoards his money. Then natives gain the benefit of his production and give little pieces of green paper in return. This has a deflationary effect; it is as if the Federal Reserve System reduced the money supply by the amount hoarded. Natives as a whole have greater consumption, workers allocate themselves among jobs in the labor market, and the rate of increase in the price level is lower than it would have been otherwise. As long as there is some flexibility in wages, and workers can change jobs, no long-run unemployment is created. If the immigrant does not literally hoard his wages—say, in his mattress—but rather banks them in a thrift institution, then his investment has employment-creating effects.

Suppose that the immigrant spends his wages. There is no deflationary effect, but there is an increase in the aggregate demand for goods and services by the amount of the immigrant's earnings. This is not inflationary because output has also been increased by the magnitude of the immigrant's earnings. Employment is generated because workers produce the goods and services purchased by the immigrant.

In either instance described here, immigration per se does not result in a net loss in jobs to natives, even if immigrants take particular job slots that native workers would otherwise occupy. There are, however, three circumstances in which immigration would result in increased measured unemployment, although they are not the circumstances generally meant by those who argue the unemployment-generating effects of immigrants.

The first way that immigrants can raise the measured unemployment rate is if they themselves are unemployed, that is, if they are without work but are looking for jobs. The effect that their unemployment will have on overall unemployment rates depends upon how numerous they are and on the extent to which their unemployment rate differs from that of natives. In 1969, a year of tight labor markets and very low unemployment, adult male immigrants in the U.S. for less than five years worked three fewer weeks during the year than native-born workers with the same demographic characteristics. This implies that the immigrant unemployment rate was higher or the labor force participation rate was lower by a combination of 6 percent of the labor force. The work-year of those who had been in the United States for five to nine years was only one week shorter than that of the native-born, implying that the immigrant unemployment rate was higher or the labor force participation rate was lower by a combined 2 percent. There was no difference in the number of weeks worked between those who had been in the United States for more than ten years and the native-born. A similar pattern occurred in 1975, a year of very high unemployment, although the intensity of unemployment for those in the U.S. less than 5 years was greater in the recession. (For a detailed theoretical and empirical analysis of the employment and unemployment of immigrants, and the source for the data in this and the next few paragraphs, see Chiswick, 1982b.)

There are differences in length of work year by country of origin. Other things being the same, Cuban and Mexican immigrants worked fewer weeks in 1969 than British immigrants, by one week and two weeks respectively. Immigrants from Southern Europe and the Balkans also worked one less week; the small group of immigrants from other Latin American and other countries worked 1.5 fewer weeks.

Shorter work years are not necessarily proof that the immigrants were looking for work, but a direct examination of unemployment rates shows similar results. In the 1970 Census reference week, the last week in March 1970, immigrants in the United States for up to five years had a significantly higher unemployment rate than that for the native-born; for immigrants in the country a longer period of time, there was no difference in unemployment rates.

It is important to note that both shorter work years and higher unemployment rates are short-term characteristics of immigrants that virtually disappear after the first five years in the country. The greater unemployment among the recent immigrants is common to all recent labor market entrants, including youths entering the labor force after leaving school and women entering or reentering the labor force after a period of childrearing. As with these other recent entrants, the unemployment of recent immigrants after their initial entry into the U.S. labor force is likely to be associated with voluntary job change. That is, much of the unemployment arises from the immigrants' acquisition of labor market information through the voluntary experience of alternative jobs, moving on to better jobs as preimmigration skills adjust to U.S. labor markets and new skills specific to the U.S. are acquired. Evidence for this comes not only from the decline in unemployment with the duration of residence, but also from the greater upward occupational mobility of immigrants during their early years in the U.S. compared to the native-born (Chiswick, 1978b; North, 1978). Upward occupational mobility is generally associated with voluntary job change.

Some of the higher unemployment and smaller number of weeks worked may arise from layoffs and discharges. As new entrants to the U.S. labor market, recent immigrants have fewer skills specific to their employers or workplaces, and, because their employers had less information about them, more hiring errors are likely to have been made. It is likely, however, that voluntary quits far outweigh layoffs and discharges. If this were not the case, no upward occupational and earnings mobility of immigrants, particularly recent immigrants, would be observed in the data. Yet, the smaller number of weeks worked among recent immigrants in the recession does suggest greater layoff rates for recent immigrants (little training specific to their employer, and low seniority) and more difficulty in finding jobs.

The second way in which immigration could lead to unemployment is if there are wage rigidities. Wage rigidities, whether instituted by the minimum wage, a union contract, or social convention, can result in unemployment from any change (including immigration) that depresses the market wage for the affected group below the wage floor. Under these circumstances, more workers would offer their labor services than there are job slots. The imperfection is caused by the wage floor: any action that increases the labor supply or decreases labor demand for workers receiving wages at the wage floor creates unemployment. There are two possible solutions. The first is to eliminate the wage floor. Such a solution is politically unacceptable to many persons. This is shown, for example, by the stability over time in the ratio of the minimum wage to average manufacturing wages, and by the spread of coverage of the minimum wage to almost all segments of the economy. This arises despite evidence that the minimum wage reduces job opportunities for low-skilled workers, particularly youths (Rottenberg, 1981). In addition, many wage floors are beyond the reach of government policy, especially if established by union contract.

Another way to address the wage floor problem is an immigration policy that minimizes pressures against the wage floor. For example, considering the federal minimum wage as a wage floor, a policy that favors skilled workers would raise the wages of low-skilled native workers, expand their job opportunities, and reduce their unemployment. This could be especially favorable for native-born youths and minority group members.

The third way that immigration affects unemployment is through the frictional unemployment of native-born workers. This is the temporary unemployment that arises when workers adjust to a change in the relative wages and job opportunities in the labor market. (Frictional unemployment of immigrants has been discussed above). Frictional unemployment is socially efficient because through this process workers identify and gravitate to what have now become their best employment opportunities. Because immigration changes the supply of labor, it affects relative wage opportunities. Some native workers will quit their current jobs in search of now higher-paying jobs. Some employers will lay off workers in sectors where workers' productivity has fallen below the market wage. Given the change in labor market opportunities, both workers and employers invest more in information about the labor market with one consequence being temporary or frictional unemployment. Frictional unemployment among native-born workers arising from a cohort of immigrants will tend to be short-lived, lessening as workers find their best employment opportunities.

Even if immigration is a slow, continuous process rather than a process of large, discrete "waves," there is an adjustment process and frictional unemployment, but it is less intense as the relative changes in job opportunities are more easily anticipated.

Summary. The fear that immigration brings "cheap labor" to disemploy native-born workers is without foundation as a general proposition. Depending on the composition of the particular cohort of immigrants, a lowering of wage rates for some groups of native workers will occur and some temporary unemployment may arise. However, immigration can lead to increased output, increased employment, and an improved economic climate for the native population as a whole. With appropriate income transfers limited to the native population, these benefits of immigration can be shared by the native population. As with so many other issues concerning immigration, a failure to recognize the heterogeneity of the immigrants themselves and of their effects on the native population leads to erroneous conclusions.

Immigrants and Transfer Payments

A second major economic fear is that immigrants are attracted to the United States principally because of its welfare provisions. The hypothetical improvement of the economic climate through the employment of the immigrants is of little interest to the critics who share this fear, for their darkest suspicion is that many immigrants will prefer not to work.

For immigrants who entered the United States from the "welfare democracies" of Western Europe and Japan this fear is clearly irrelevant. As welfare recipients, many of them would have done better had they remained in their home countries. The fact is that most immigrants come to work and they actually do work, although the transition to the U.S. economy may produce some temporary dislocation. Most studies have shown that immigrants are not disproportionately represented on welfare rolls (Simon, 1981; Blau, 1982). The exceptions to this generalization are discussed below.

Immigrants are not entitled to all transfer payments. For example, they are rarely entitled to unemployment compensation during their early years in the U.S., even though that is when they are most likely to be unemployed. All states require employment in the year prior to the onset of unemployment (generally defined as the first four of the most recent five calendar quarters). Moreover, benefits are linked to past wages, and unemployment must arise from a layoff or from a job quit with "good cause." Although immigrants can receive Food Stamps, Medicaid, and AFDC on the same basis as natives, recent legislation limits the access of new immigrants (other than refugees) to Supplemental Security Income (SSI), the federalized welfare for the aged, blind, and disabled, during their first three years in the U.S. Because Social Security benefits, including Medicare and disability insurance, are based on work experience in a covered job in the U.S., recent immigrants would not be eligible for these programs. Most direct federal educational benefits are limited to citizens.

Although, in general, immigrants do not migrate to the U.S. for the explicit purpose of receiving income transfers, and although recent immigrants may not be eligible for some transfers, this does not mean that transfers have no effect on the size and composition of the immigrant population of the United States. The knowledge that transfer payments are available if an immigrant is not succesful reduces some of the risk of immigration, particularly for those whose economic prospects in the U.S. are less certain. The transfers also affect reemigration decisions (that is, an immigrant's leaving the U.S. to return home or go to some other country). When there were few or no income transfers and jobs were lost during a widespread (cyclical) decline in economic opportunity, many immigrants returned to their home countries. During the early 1930s, for example, emigration among the foreign-born exceeded immigration. With the availability of public income transfers, reemigration is less likely to occur.

The major exception to the generalization that recent immigrants tend not to receive substantial transfer payments is refugees. Economic immigrants, that is, persons whose migration decisions are based primarily on the search for higher paying jobs, often have the time and resources to plan their trips to the United States. Some economic immigrants gain entry to the U.S. only because of their high-level or scarce skills, and they have jobs waiting for them. Refugees, in contrast, are often forced to leave their homes in great haste and without bringing any assets. Rather than being selected by their energy, ambition, desire to move, and by having labor market skills that are more readily transferable to the U.S., they are selected by their ethnic origin, their social class, their political views, or their fear of being caught in the literal or figurative crossfires of political instability. As a result, refugees often require more assistance in becoming adjusted socially and economically to the United States; unlike economic immigrants, they are also more likely to have young and old dependents who also require assistance, and they are less likely to have relatives who are already established in this country.

As has been discussed above, however, immigrants can increase the burden of the income transfer system without receiving the payments themselves (Chiswick, 1982e). This would happen if the wages of low-skilled native-born workers declined or their unemployment increased as a consequence of the immigration of low-skilled workers. If high-skilled immigrants were admitted, after their brief period of adjustment there would be no additional transfer payments needed for the direct and indirect impact, and there would be more taxpayers available to share the tax burden.

At least part of the charge that immigrants are a drain on the public purse is indirectly a criticism of the administration of the welfare system. Although immigrants may not constitute a major drain on the welfare system, this drain is concentrated in a few areas where low-skilled immigrants are concentrated. Despite considerable federal assistance in most welfare programs, some programs are still the responsibility of the local and state governments. Thus, although these levels of goverment have no direct influence on the admission of immigrants to the country, they are expected to finance some portion of the welfare programs (e.g., AFDC and Medicaid, other medical care, unemployment compensation), whether it is the immigrants themselves or the adversely affected natives who use these services. The impact of Cuban refugees on Dade County, Florida (Miami), is a case in point. Efforts to disperse Indochinese and Cuban refugees in order to spread the impact more widely have been unsuccessful. Subsequent internal migration has resulted in the Indochinese gravitating to California and the Cubans gravitating to Southern Florida, their respective first-choice residences (Gordon, 1980).

Remittances and Commitment

Americans have long had the expectation that immigrants will become permanent residents and, eventually, citizens. This is not the expectation of many other countries, where citizenship is hard to acquire by any means other than birth. While it is expected that most immigrants to the U.S. will become American citizens, and it is not very difficult for a resident alien to do so, it is very difficult to become a Japanese or Swiss citizen. In many Western European countries it is expected that foreigners will not become citizens, and that the majority of foreign workers will be temporary. Such immigrants are discouraged from becoming citizens. In some countries, they are prohibited from doing so. It is expected that some substantial portion of their wages will return to the country of origin (immigrant remittances), either as they are earned or as savings when the worker returns home. However, in the United States the practice of earning wages with the intent of returning them in some fashion to the home country is sometimes seen as an economic threat.

In the case of the immigrant who sends a portion of his wages home, some portion of the salary is spent for maintenance and immediate consumption in the United States. This expenditure increases demand and has the potentially beneficial employment results discussed earlier in relation to all immigrants. The portion he sends home will also ultimately be spent on goods and services. Some of these goods will have been produced in the

United States, and will directly increase the demand for U.S. goods. Others will have been produced in another country, but presumably that country also buys U.S. goods. As a consequence of the outflow of U.S. dollars in the form of immigrant remittances, exports of U.S. produced goods and services increase. In the extremely unlikely event that the relatives in the home country bury the U.S. dollars in the ground (literally or figuratively), the remittance has a deflationary effect and the U.S. benefits from the immigrant labor and does not have to give goods and services in return. In short, the sending of remittances does not eliminate the beneficial effects of immigrant workers.

But the most serious fear of the public is that the temporary worker, who has not committed himself to the American political system by permanently settling and investing in this economy, is "ripping off" the U.S. economy. Sometimes, by extension, it is argued that the usual public amenities or "social overhead capital" of American life—schools, public highways, libraries, parks—should not be available to immigrants because they and their ancestors have not worked for it. Lying at the root of this contention is the belief that only citizens are "real" taxpayers.

In fact, of course, the immigrant pays taxes too. These include sales taxes, property taxes (indirectly through rent if not directly), Social Security taxes, and income taxes. Most social overhead capital is paid for by the taxpayers as it is consumed through user-fees (e.g., highway and bridge tolls) or through taxes (e.g., school buildings) as the bonds used to finance construction are retired, rather than when the social overhead capital is constructed (see Usher, 1977; Chiswick, 1982d). Thus, immigrants also contribute to the financing of the extra social overhead capital constructed and consumed because of their presence.

Solutions to Economic Problems

There are two types of fears regarding the economic impact of immigrants—real and imagined. The imagined, like many irrational fears, may be impossible to lay to rest, although a public that is better informed regarding the consequences of immigration is less likely to harbor such fears. Once the legitimate fears are appropriately identified, they must be addressed if we are to fashion a realistic immigration policy. Some economic groups may lose in earnings, employment (particularly where there are wage floors), or tax burdens, while others gain.

One solution to this is compensating the losers directly or indirectly. If lower income workers lose, they can receive greater income transfers; if it is the higher income workers, they can pay lower taxes. These transfers among the native population are in principle feasible if the immigrants themselves are not large recipients of the income transfers. If certain localities are paying disproportionate sums for the medical care or schooling of immigrants, a reallocation of federal aid may be warranted.

A second alternative is to recognize the reality of losses but not to compensate the individual because the losses are generally widely shared, as are the larger economic benefits. The inefficiencies and inequities of attempting to finetune compensation might outweigh the benefits. A substantial bureaucracy would arise to determine who is adversely affected and by how much. Additional resources would be devoted by private groups to try to influence the compensation decisions.

A third alternative is to restrict the immigrants—either the destinations within the U.S. to which immigrants may go or the jobs they may take. Such measures have been taken before, but only indirectly. Recent research found that turn-of-the-century legislation limiting the number of hours women could work could be attributed to efforts to reduce female immigrants' job opportunities (Landes, 1980). Natives in many occupations and unions have succeeded in restricting the employment of aliens; through a presidential executive order, aliens are barred from most federal civil service jobs (Carliner, 1977). But these "solutions" are generally costly to the society as a whole. Efforts in the past decade to force a wider dispersal of the impact of Indochinese and Cuban refugees have not been successful since secondary migration has resulted in the Indochinese and Cubans gravitating toward the states and areas that they had preferred in the first place. The restrictions prevent immigrants from working where they are the most productive, thereby lowering the income of the immigrants and reducing the favorable overall impact on the native population. The only beneficiaries are natives who prevent immigrants from competing with them in the labor market. In addition, explicit restrictions against aliens raise serious civil liberties issues.

The Economic Benefits of Immigration

Just as many groups have historically opposed immigration for economic reasons, many others have encouraged it. These groups include some employers and trade associations, various state and local governments, and some educational institutions. Immigration may be encouraged because it provides a supply of workers with particular skills or because it provides an abundant supply of workers with a range of skills. But immigration may also be encouraged because it provides constituencies of various types: consumers for certain goods and services (including students to fill otherwise empty classrooms), inhabitants to increase relative political power, and countrymen to provide larger ethnic enclaves (for political and cultural reasons) within the United States.

But like the analysts who fear continued immigration, the analysts who favor immigration have often used facile reasoning and misleading analogies. Some of these have some basis in fact. For example, it is true that the United States will experience a decline in the size of the available youth labor force in the next few decades because of the precipitous decline in U.S. fertility that marked the late 1960s and the early 1970s. It is also true that low-wage, unskilled jobs have become much less attractive to most native workers, partly because of the increased educational level of the labor force and partly because of the existence of alternative income supports. But the two conclusions often drawn from these facts are not necessarily true: (1) that the United States will "need" continued immigration, and (2) that the immigrants will only take jobs that native workers will not take.

The "Need" for Immigration

The United States will not "need" continued immigration. If there is a relative decrease in the supply of labor at a particular skill level—let us say, low-skilled youths—the relative wage for workers with that skill will increase. The market price for the final product, whether it is a good or a service, rises relative to other prices. The sector in which these workers are employed contracts both in terms of employment of that skill level per unit output and in terms of total output. The converse occurs if the relative supply in the skill category increases. These consequences may not be the ones that Americans "want," but the concept or term "need" does not apply. There is no "need" for a given number of workers with particular skills, because adjustments occur through changes in relative prices, changes in consumption, changes in relative wages, changes in production techniques, and changes in skill levels.

As an example, the relative decline in the size of youth cohorts in the coming decades will not create a "need" for low-skilled immigrants to fill jobs in the occupations in which youths are concentrated. Rather, in the absence of increased low-skilled immigration, the relative wages of youths (and low-skilled labor in general) will rise, thereby raising the cost of "youth-intensive" goods and services, such as newspaper delivery, babysitting, grocery bagging, and fast food meals. In response to the higher costs of youth labor, employers will attempt to substitute other factors of production, including adult workers and capital, for youth labor. Adults with cars or trucks will replace youths for delivering newspapers, the use of babysitting cooperatives and older babysitters will increase, and fast-food restaurants will become more automated as will supermarket checkout counters. In addition, consumption patterns will change in response to the higher market prices. More newspapers will be purchased at stores and at bus and train stations, or delivered through the mail, rather than being purchased through home delivery. Parents will use babysitters less often and will consume more leisure/entertainment at home. For example, higher babysitting costs will encourage the purchase and use of video cassette recorders and computer games, at the expense of going out to the movies. Consumers will eat less often at fast-food restaurants and more often at home and at other kinds of restaurants.

The relative decline in employment in the youth-intensive sectors, however, will not be as large as the relative decline in the youth cohort. As the relative wages of youths rise, a larger proportion of youths will seek employment. And, in this instance, because of the restricted employment opportunities for youth (in part due to minimum wages and other legislative measures that have artificially raised the cost of employing youths) a decline in the size of the youth cohort will raise the *proportion* of youths who are actually employed. The rise in the wages of youths will also attract others who are close substitutes in production into the labor market—such as retired persons and adults with little skill or physical impairments.

If the situation were, rather, a "shortage" of workers with a particular skill level (say, physicians), an additional response would materialize. As the "shortage" increased, wages would rise and, unless the higher wages were considered transitory and the training period were long, more native workers would acquire the required skills. Immigration can, however, shorten the adjustment period.

The term "need" is not relevant in an economic analysis of immigrants in the labor market. It does arise in the politics of the issue, as employers of a factor that rises in price, and consumers of goods and services that increase in price, allege harm, to themselves and to the society as a whole. While they may well be correct regarding the harm to themselves, the harm to society as a whole is less obvious. Those who own businesses or machines, or who have skills that are profitable if there is an abundance of low-wage labor, will understandably favor a policy of increased low-skilled labor to offset a declining youth cohort. It is in this political sense that arguments are made that we "need" continued immigration because some demographic groups will constitute smaller proportions of the labor force, because there are "dead-end" jobs that are not being filled, and because of the inevitable delay while the labor market and product market adjust to a different skill mix of labor.

"The Jobs We Don't Take"

The second allegation that is often made is that aliens, especially illegal aliens, only take the jobs that native workers will not take. This generalization is on the whole false; to the extent that it is true, it reflects only a temporary situation for some skilled immigrants, particularly refugees, and a permanent situation for some of the unskilled immigrants. The popular belief that all or most immigrants take "unwanted" jobs again ignores the heterogeneity of the immigrant group: not all are unskilled workers. Skilled workers who immigrate typically experience a pronounced but temporary downward occupational mobility, but with increasing length of residence in the United States, their occupational levels rise. Even among unskilled immigrants, many are in jobs not unlike those of low-skilled native workers (Chiswick, 1978b, 1980b; North and Houstoun, 1976).

Data on illegal aliens apprehended in 1975 indicate that three-fourths of those working in the U.S. for at least two weeks were earning more than the federal minimum wage (North and Houstoun, 1976). Of these jobs, 20 percent were in relatively well-paid industrial work. These data need to be interpreted with caution; it might be that enforcement is selectively invoked against the illegal aliens with the highest paying jobs, and it is undoubtedly true that many illegal aliens as well as legal aliens work at low-level agricultural and service jobs. But these data do indicate that even among a relatively unskilled portion of the immigrant stream, there are many who are receiving wages in excess of the legal minimum wage.

It seems more reasonable to assert that many immigrants are willing to begin with low-level jobs in the hope that after they acquire experience and training relevant to the U.S. labor market they (or their children) will experience the upward mobility so long a part of the American dream. It is probably unrealistic to believe, as some European countries apparently do, that large numbers of immigrant workers can be permanently relegated to do the menial work of the country. Although there are workers who may accept this temporary role for themselves, most strive for upward social and economic mobility for themselves and their children.

Studies using data from the 1970 Census of Population and other data sources indicate that the upward mobility of immigrants is quite impressive (Chiswick, 1978b, 1979, 1982b; Featherman and Hauser, 1978; Martin and Poston, 1980). Adult male immigrants have been compared with native-born males of the same age, schooling, place of residence, and ethnicity. (The data that follow are from Chiswick, 1979.) Although recent immigrants have lower earnings than the native-born, their earnings rise sharply with the duration of residence. Economic migrants in the U.S. eleven to fifteen years have about the same earnings as the native-born, while economic immigrants in the U.S. for more than fifteen years have higher earnings. Among whites, for example, immigrants in the U.S. for twenty years have earnings 6 percentage points higher than those of the native-born. The earnings parity at eleven to fifteen years and the higher earnings after fifteen years are not characteristic only of white immigrants; the same patterns are found when Mexican, black, and Filipino immigrants are compared with native-born persons of the same race or ethnic origin. Perhaps even more startling is the finding that the native-born sons of immigrants have earnings 5 to 10 percentage points *higher* than those of their counterparts with native-born parents. These findings are not unique to the post–World War II period. A recent reexamination of 1909 data for white men collected by the Dillingham Commission (1911 report) reveals similar patterns existed in the U.S. at the turn of the century (Blau, 1980).

If it cannot be argued that we "need" continued immigration for the growth of the economy, can it at least be argued that continued immigration can be economically beneficial? Certainly the analysis above has implied that motivated, productive, and especially skilled immigrants can be of great benefit to the economy. Indeed, it was shown above that immigrants increase the overall income of the native population as long as the immigrants do not themselves receive substantial amounts in income transfers.

A word of caution is required, however, regarding attempts to justify the admission of immigrants for particular industries that might otherwise shift their production abroad, or disappear altogether. The two arguments most commonly advanced in the context of international trade to provide protection or subsidy of particular industries are the "infant industries" and "national defense" arguments, neither of which is relevant in this instance. The infant-industries argument asserts that because of "start-up" costs an industry that is new to a country requires a short period of protection until it is firmly established and its products can be fully competitive with the products of other countries. That is, after a brief period of assistance it will be fully competitive in the international market. The argument does not relate to protecting established industries that want immigrant workers because they are losing their competitive advantage. Those who might be tempted to advance the "national defense" argument probably would not want these industries dependent on foreign workers.

Nor should the admission of immigrants be based on anticipated "need" for narrowly defined age or skill groups. Rather, as a basic principle the impact of alternative immigration policies governing the number and characteristics of immigrants admitted should be examined in terms of their overall impact on the economy and the distribution of the impact among segments of the population. An "infant skills" argument may be made, however, to encourage the immigration of workers with productive skills that are not currently available in a country. During the early days of the industrial revolution such arguments were frequently made and the immigration of such workers was encouraged. In the pre– and post–World War II period the immigration of a small number of nuclear scientists and aeronautical scientists and engineers may have substantially influenced the military capabilities of the world powers. Today, this "infant skills" argument may be relevant for some countries for high-technology workers, but it is difficult to see it as relevant to occupation-specific immigration in the contemporary United States.

Political Issues in Immigration

Fear of Disloyalty and Disunity

From the time of the Alien and Sedition Acts of 1798, immigrants have been suspected of conspiracies and treacheries. The greatest fear has been of the immigrant who is in fact a spy or at least an infiltrator. From time to time, immigration regulations have limited the entry of communists, anarchists, and violent revolutionaries, and during World War II persons of Japanese origin in the Pacific Coast States were deprived of their civil liberties and interned. Today there is a new concern about the admission of possible terrorists. All those who apply for admission to the United States must swear that they do not advocate the overthrow of the United States government by force. It is obvious, however, that the type of villain one most fears will perjure himself in his application for admission—and by the time he is deported for perjury, the damage may well have been done.

The early quota system, which gave preference to national groups already in the United States, in one sense intensified the problem of potential immigrant activism by ensuring that relatively few home countries would be represented in the immigrant stream. To the extent that new immigrant groups represent a diversity of countries, it becomes less likely that any single group can gain the political power necessary to accomplish a shift in foreign policy, to create a political dichotomy on domestic economic or social issues, or—even worse—to create separatist sentiments in a geographically concentrated foreign enclave. If a country does not have homogeneity (and the United States never has), substantial heterogeneity, in which no coalition of a small number of ethnic groups can dominate the political scene, may generate the most political stability.

Another fear of the political impact of immigrants is based upon the fact that there are relatively few democratic countries in the world. "Is it not true," ask the critics of immigration, "that these immigrants are uncomfortable with democratic ways? That they will not understand us?" The implication is that the dilution in the average level of political commitment and mobilization will harm the polity. And the political persuasions of particular groups of immigrants have always been questioned. Catholics were believed to owe their fundamental allegiance to the Pope, immigrants from monarchies were believed to prefer strong authority to self-direction, revolutionaries were believed incapable of appreciating orderly transitions of government. The expression that these fears take today tends to emphasize the possibility of communist spies and political agitators among the Indochinese and Cuban refugees and, at the other extreme, the political apathy of many Hispanics who do not participate in any political activity.

All of these are recurring and disturbing fears. A facile answer is that they are the same fears that were being voiced one or two centuries ago, and that the offending immigrants were soon assimilated politically as well as economically. The sons and daughters of immigrants of every nationality have been politically responsible; many have entered political office. And although immigrants are barred by the Constitution from becoming President or Vice-President of the United States, they have served with distinction in the Cabinet and in Congress as well as at state and local levels of government. Political fears about immigration are not compelling unless reasons can be offered demonstrating that today's fears, unlike those of yesterday, are based on reality. The most recent U.S. experiences (in the 1960s) with native-born terrorism and illegal antigovernment activity were primarily the work of disaffected youths from middle-class families, and had nothing to do with immigrants. The urban riots of the 1960s and later decades did not occur in the immigrant-ethnic neighborhoods.

However, there is a more fundamental approach to political fears of immigration. These fears are based on apprehensions about the stability and durability of the American political system. This "deep fear" is that the American system is fragile and easily subverted from within; that the American system requires a high degree of homogeneity in belief, and that this is best guaranteed by limiting the geography of birthplaces; and that national-origin groups, translated into ethnic interest groups, will be irresistible as lobbyists.

The current national debate over immigration itself demonstrates why much of this apprehension is unwarranted. All of us were once immigrants; if immigrant politics remained our principal concern, there would be no restrictionists, or we would all be restrictionists save for immigration from our "home" countries. But, more important, if immigrants could not or would not adopt American political values, there would be no American political system. The system cannot be considered without reference to immigrants; they have had too much significance in its shaping.

It would be foolish to deny the importance of ethnic associations as lobbyists. The hearings before the Select Commission on Immigration and Refugee Policy and before Congress demonstrate the diversity and viability of ethnic interest groups. But it is this very diversity that guarantees that no single group can dominate national policy: in America, everyone wants a piece of the action.

Even within a single ethnic group, it would be rare to find unanimous opinion on any piece of immigration legislation. Every group has its dissidents and its deeply divided opinions. For example, Mexican-American groups are justifiably interested in current immigration proposals; a large and continuing Mexican immigration is of particular concern to them. However, there is no single Mexican-American position; the entire spectrum of immigration opinion can be found among Mexican-American groups, from the most restrictionist, favored by those who fear an adverse economic impact on themselves and an adverse political or social reaction against Mexican-Americans, to a completely open-border policy, favored by those who believe the border irrelevant or who want to increase Chicano political power. This diversity within the Mexican-American community is similar to the diversity that is experienced in all ethnic communities when they are confronted with large immigration streams from their countries of origin. If there is such diversity within a single ethnic group, then fears of a great immigrant political conspiracy seem especially unfounded.

Still, it must be admitted that there is no final empirical answer to the question, How much diversity can be tolerated? The burden of proof may lie with those who claim that little diversity, or little additional diversity, can be tolerated. One practical policy initiative that could be followed would be to continue to draw immigrants from all over the world, and not merely from one or two countries. The most dangerous political situation may well result when there are only two significant groups—a permanent "we" and "they"—contending in the political arena. In considering major ethnic-political disputes, such as in Canada, Belgium, or Northern Ireland, the significant factor is not diversity, but polarization. Indeed, if America is true to its principles (and to its Constitution), the appropriate answer to the question may be that we can tolerate as much diversity as there are people in this country.

The Law and Immigration

A special kind of fear is associated with the influx of large numbers of illegal entrants to the country. It is the fear that failure to enforce the immigration laws of the country breeds cynicism, hypocrisy, and a more general disregard of law. Presumably, the cynicism would be greatest among those who are most like the illegal entrants and those who are most likely to have contact with them, but there would also be hostility and resentment among those who are legally admitted or who are native-born.

Most Americans favor the principle of a more stringent enforcement of immigration law, even though there is disagreement about what this means in practice. The enforcement of immigration law is a subset of the more general problem of deterrence among potential lawbreakers of all types. Some murderers are not caught, but most of us do not conclude that we can get away with murder or that the police do not really care about murder. We are deterred partly because of the serious consequences of conviction for murder and partly because of the high probability that we will be caught.

Americans need to believe that there is a good faith effort to enforce immigration laws. Such an effort would require considerably more man-power and budget than the Immigration and Naturalization Service (INS) currently has. What deserves further consideration is the consequences of apprehension as an illegal entrant. At the present time, it is usually only deportation; if a stricter penalty is imposed it is because of other violations. As two-thirds of the apprehensions are of Mexican nationals at entry or within three days of entry, the deterrent effect is quite minimal. Stricter penalties imposed on illegal entrants, particularly against repeat offenders, including fines and brief imprisonment, might have a substantial deterrent effect. It would not take long for potential illegal entrants to learn that apprehension was no longer the revolving door it has become at the Mexican border, but rather imposed relatively substantial costs on the illegal alien. If immigration law were enforced *within* U.S. borders, the problems at the international borders would be minimal, although bilateral treaties that permit joint enforcement on both sides of the border might have a greater deterrent effect and promote cooperation between the two countries.

Another development in recent years has been the substantial decline in real resources devoted to enforcing immigration law in the interior, referred to as "area control" in the INS jargon (see Chiswick, 1981). This may have sharply reduced the effectiveness of enforcement operations. An apprehension in the interior and subsequent deportation is more costly for an illegal alien. The time and other resources devoted to moving from the border to an interior location and to finding a job and residence there may be for nothing, as the process may have to begin again. Thus, while there may be little or no deterrent effect from an apprehension at the border, the larger cost to the illegal alien of an interior apprehension may imply a much greater deterrent effect.

Political Advantages of Immigration

While there is always some fear that immigrants may not assimilate into the American political system, there is also pride that they have chosen to join it. In a world in which political ideologies contend, the people who "vote with their feet" become an important validation that a political system is working. Americans are fond of noting that few immigrants wish to enter the communist states. Given a choice, we like to think, people prefer the freedoms and higher incomes available in the United States.

We also pride ourselves on the fact that many American immigrants have chosen to become one of us, to be naturalized. Although there is nothing in U.S. law that compels resident aliens to become naturalized, it is nevertheless a common expectation that they will, and about two-thirds of all foreign-born persons living in the United States are naturalized citizens. Naturalization is the sign of full political unity and commitment. Ready access to naturalization has been so intrinsic to the American immigration process that purely economic motives for immigration are viewed by many as lacking in grace. The better life in America is made up not only of economic freedom, but also of personal freedoms, including political and religious freedom and the right to be different if one chooses. Immigration policies that emphasize solely economic aspects—whether they are policies to provide temporary labor for employers, or policies to provide temporary jobs for workers—without allowing for the possibility of naturalization seem to many to be too instrumental and grasping.

Some commentators would even argue that the provision for naturalization ensures a kind of "hybrid vigor" among Americans. The American dream becomes stronger and more real for the native-born when they can watch the enthusiasm of the foreign-born. We come to appreciate what we have been born with when we see others sacrifice their homelands to achieve it.

Since the rise of the modern state, movement across national borders has been monitored and controlled. As a result, immigration is shaped and regulated by the political process, even if it is undertaken for economic reasons. If we overlook the symbolic value that immigration has for the American people, we will never fully understand the climate in which immigration policy is made.

Social/Cultural Issues and Immigration

Continued immigration is feared as a source of tension in the social fabric. The old question of how much diversity can be tolerated comes up once again. There are two aspects of diversity at issue. The first is the size of the immigrant stream: How many strangers can we absorb before we cease to be recognizable? The second aspect is the composition of the immigrant stream: Are they to be skilled or unskilled, are they likely to be family members of American citizens or unrelated to anyone in this country? From countries that have sent immigrants before, or from new countries? Sometimes the two aspects are combined. "We could absorb a few of group x," someone will say, "if only they would live throughout the community. But all the x's clump together, and none of us feel safe/comfortable/welcome when we are in x-ville." And the "x" in that statement has been, in various cities and decades, the Irish, the Polish, the Swedes, the Jews, the Chinese, and the Mexicans. The alleged problems of x-ville are the same in every generation and every city: x-ville has too much crime, too much poverty, and too much unrest.

Fear of Crime

Strict enforcement of existing criminal laws and restrictions barring the immigration of convicted felons are the answer to the worry that immigrants are or might become criminals. That this is a widespread fear is illustrated by the reaction of Americans to the young male Cuban refugees of 1980, who are without family ties in this country; though those who have been released by the U.S. authorities are not convicted felons in Cuba or in this country, they are feared as potential criminals. Fear of strangers is deep-seated in humans; from the very beginning, immigrant groups have been suspected of harboring vice and crime. Immigrant neighborhoods often had high rates of crime, and immigrants were overrepresented in the penal institutions. There are two important questions raised by such facts: Why is there so much social pathology in some immigrant neighborhoods, whereas in others there is so little social pathology? And, what measures of social control is the broader community justified in taking?

It is important to remember, first, that crime among immigrants has been concentrated among the low-skilled. Thus, family disruption, crime, and similar problems may be class phenomena rather than results of immigration. It is true, however, that the immigrant community has an added problem not shared by the indigenous lower class community—its traditional social control mechanisms may not work, or may not work as effectively as they did in the old country. This problem also affects native-born migrants, such as rural dwellers who have moved to the cities. The insight of the Chicago school of sociologists was that migrant communities experience an initial period of "social disorganization." During these transitional periods, strains on the family and community are likely to be severe.

Although it involves an extra cost item in the balance sheet on immigration, nothing precludes the host country or community from maintaining its social control system—not just the police, but also social service agencies, schools, churches, and other institutions that provide social incentives and disincentives. "Social control" does not connote merely punitive actions—it includes all actions, including approval, that are conducive to harmonious relations. This includes the efforts of private and state welfare agencies to provide services and aid the immigrants' adjustment. The current policy of using individual or group "sponsors" for refugees is an attempt to make the adjustment process easier. The emphasis on kinship ties and prearranged employment in the issuance of immigration visas serves a similar function for immigrants other than refugees.

Fear of Divisiveness

One fear that has persisted, however, is the fear that the immigrant will never want to be "like us"—that he will cling to his native culture with its strange foods, strange clothes, odd customs, and, most of all, its language. For decades, lawmakers have proposed various schemes for compelling immigrants to learn English, although most immigrants quickly learn at least the minimal amount of English required for coping in this society; at the present time, English is required to complete the naturalization process for all but the very old. Very few immigrants do not adopt at least some aspects of American lifestyles. What is the alleged harm if the immigrant does keep his native culture?

Divisiveness is nearly always the evil feared from too much cultural diversity. A proliferation of languages, religions, ideas, and customs is seen by some to threaten national unity and the will to work together. The fears in this area are focused not only on the possibilities for tension between the immigrant and the native-born, but also on the possibilities for tension among different immigrant groups. Historically, each wave of immigrants encountered some antagonism from the preceding waves. In large urban areas, where there is often a polyglot immigrant neighborhood, these tensions may be most visible. Such an area is Chicago's Uptown, which has immigrants from Indochina, Latin America, Pakistan, and a dozen other places. Schools often report minor scuffles among children of different groups—in the case of the Indochinese, often rivalry and hostility between ethnic groups that had been antagonistic before immigration.

But the more alarming possibilities, according to many observers, are the tensions between the native-born and immigrants. Denver has recently seen violence between Mexican-Americans and Indochinese refugees; the riots in Miami in 1980 and 1982 were traced at least in part to hostilities between Cubans and blacks. Although based in part on economic competition, particularly for jobs and housing, these hostilities often have broader origins. In some cases, ethnic antagonisms begun abroad are brought here—this happened among the European immigrant groups as well. In every case, someone's "turf" is being invaded by the immigrant groups, and so the perceived threat extends to family and social group cohesion, and not just to jobs: a fundamental mistrust of a different culture and lifestyle, but one that applies to all kinds of perceived differences, including economic class, religion, and racial background, and not just immigrant status or language.

This last point is not meant to minimize the fear of divisiveness. It exists to some extent in all societies, even the most homogeneous. The Japanese, for example, have objected to accepting more than a handful of Southeast Asian refugees for fear that their presence will disrupt the tranquility of the nearly 100 million Japanese. While the danger of divisiveness may be real, it is neither new nor overwhelming. And while the potential for divisiveness is the unfortunate price of a nonracist immigration policy, American culture and society are enriched through the diversity of the nation's inhabitants.

There is no simple answer to the question, How much diversity can we stand? But there has never been a simple answer to that question, and there is as yet no compelling reason to give the question special significance today. Indeed, there are people who feel that the social and cultural diversity fostered by immigration is a good thing for the republic. Others believe that the fear of diversity generates policies and behavior to compel conformity in a way that is inconsistent with the spirit of tolerance and personal freedom that makes America so attractive to immigrants, as well as to the native-born population.

Support for Cultural Pluralism

The founding fathers were masters of compromise. The Constitution represents a masterful compromise of the competing interests in the fledgling nation. But one suspects that Madison and Jay were not entirely happy in their recognition that factions and competing interests were inevitable. In our own day, there has been a veritable celebration of pluralism—not as a condition to be endured and dealt with, but as a positive good that adds yeast and vigor to the community. The so-called "ethnic revival" of the late 1960s and the 1970s reminded us of the strengths that had come about because of, not despite, our diversity.

It has been, in fact, a source of pride that most ethnic disputes in the United States have been relatively uneventful—at least, as compared with the ethnic struggles that have gone on in such places as Uganda, Nigeria, Northern Ireland, Malaysia, India, and Pakistan. The most intractable of the United States's ethnic problems has been the welfare and advancement of the two significant groups that were not voluntary migrants to the U.S., native American Indians and blacks.

Summary

This chapter brings together a number of themes that have characterized the immigration debate from its beginnings. We have reviewed the economic, political, and social/cultural fears about immigration, especially as they affect the current debate. Many of these fears are legitimate; some are phantoms. There are also important continuities in the arguments used by the proponents of continued immigration. Although we see the immigration issues of our day as being ones of particular importance, it is useful to trace the ways in which these issues have recurred and reemerged. In the next chapter, we review the legal and administrative solutions that have from time to time been devised to deal with the continuing immigration process.

3

A Capsule View of American Immigration Legislation

Today's immigration issues are deeply rooted in the accretion of two centuries of policy (Keely, 1979; U.S. Commission on Civil Rights, 1980; Hutchinson, 1981). Immigration legislation has had three distinct phases: (1) the period prior to 1875, when there were minimal legislative restrictions; (2) 1875 to 1965, when there were numerical restrictions based primarily on country of origin; and (3) the period since 1965, when numerical restrictions have been based primarily on family relationships. A brief overview of these periods will help to put our analysis into historical context.

Pre-1875: The Era of Minimal Restrictions

Despite minimal federal statutory restrictions prior to 1875, today's cautious attitude toward immigration has its roots in the character of early seventeenth century colonists. Although many settlers were "pulled" to America by the hope of opportunity, many more were "pushed" across the ocean by adverse economic and political conditions in their native lands. Those who immigrated did not so much seek to preserve European society as to escape it. While the reasons for departure varied, the colonists shared a common vision: distinguishing their society from that of the Old World. This vision often manifested itself in exclusionist sentiments against subsequent arrivals.

However, survival in the New World often depended upon mustering enough able bodies to harvest the crops and defend the settlements from the unfriendly Indians and foreign powers with designs on the colonies. The early commonwealth charters did not even implicitly ban the admission of subsequent settlers. Virginia (1609) and Massachussets (1629) both welcomed "any other strangers that will become our loving subjects." In general, fears of paupers, criminals, and those who spoke or worshipped differently were not explicitly expressed in the charters (although religious discrimination was not uncommon in subsequent legislation during the early colonial period). However, a subtle national consciousness among colonists soon became evident in the new republic. The Constitution distinguished between natives and non-natives; only a natural-born citizen could become President of the United States. Article I differentiated between naturalized and native-born citizens by stipulating the years of citizenship required before a naturalized citizen could become a Senator or a member of the House of Representatives.

Shortly after the adoption of the Constitution, concern about foreigners increased. Congress authorized customs searches away from the border in 1789 to regulate the internal flow of immigrants and passed the first naturalization laws in March 1790. These statutes denied citizenship to "white" indentured servants, "non-white" aliens, and those who lacked "good moral character." (Congress would not define "good moral character" until 1952.)

The first federal statutory limit on immigration, the Alien and Sedition Acts, was passed in 1789 and gave the President power to expel from the country anyone he judged dangerous. However, President John Adams refused to use his new power and the statute was generally unpopular; Congress failed to renew it in 1800. A March 1807 act forbade the importation of slaves after January 1, 1808, but this was an anti-slavery compromise designed by the authors of the Constitution, rather than an anti-immigration statute. Restrictive measures remained unpopular until near the end of the nineteenth century. What little attention Congress did give to the immigration issue in the first three quarters of the century was allegedly intended to encourage immigration, although it probably had a net deterrent effect. The "Steerage Acts" passed in 1820 and subsequent years improved conditions on the ships that brought immigrants to the States, but by raising the costs of transporting immigrants across the ocean the acts served to curb immigration. The legislation also marked the beginning of official recordkeeping in 1821, because the captain of each arriving ship was then required to present harbor authorities a list with specific passenger information.

Many states actively recruited immigrants, and federal legislation provided parcels of land to foreigners who, after paying minimal sums of money, agreed to inhabit and cultivate sections of Illinois and Michigan. First canal and then railroad construction provided jobs for many immigrants who moved West.

But restrictionist sentiment also began to grow during the 1830s and 1840s. A large influx of Catholics met with distinct opposition. The burning of the Ursuline Convent in Charleston, Massachussets, in 1834 became a symbol of anti-Catholic sentiment. During the late forties the wave of Irish fleeing the potato famine fueled anti-Catholic sentiment and spread fear that Irish Catholics, controlled by Tammany Hall politicians if not the

Pope, would take over the government. Political responses to these fears were not long in coming. The Native American party appeared, followed by the "Know-Nothings" and the American Protective Association. Nativist societies spread to Pennsylvania and Washington, D.C.; when local economic conditions seemed worsened by recent arrivals, several states sought to restrict immigrants' entry. In a series of decisions referred to as "the passenger cases," however, the Supreme Court ruled that such actions violated the federal government's exclusive power to regulate foreign commerce.

Nevertheless, states found other methods by which to try to influence the settling of immigrants. At the same time that midwestern states were offering suffrage to attract foreigners, eastern seaboard states eliminated the franchise for immigrants. The Know-Nothing and Native American parties demanded that citizenship, long residence requirements, and literacy be required of all voters. And the eastern regional unease about immigrants soon became evident on the Pacific coast as well. White workers, already grumbling about a standard of living they felt was too low, felt threatened by new waves of settlers looking for work in the cities and others eager to prospect for gold. Along with the workers from the rest of the American continent came large numbers of Chinese fleeing the famine in Canton.

During the 1860s and early 1870s, while the country underwent the upheaval of the Civil War and Reconstruction, the issue of immigration was inevitably juxtaposed with slavery, especially when the immigrants arrived under labor contracts designed to increase the supply of workers. Under the contracts, signed with shipowners and employers, workers who were too poor to pay for their own passage would be able to come to America in exchange for working for a fixed period of time under the contract. The system clearly differed from slavery in that the contracts were entered into voluntarily, were for a fixed period of time, and did not bind the worker's descendants. Also, unlike slavery, which was confined to the Southern states, immigrant contract labor was not regionally restricted. Distinctions grew up and were no doubt reinforced by racism and economic competition—among "coolies," "indentured workers," and various contract workers whose immigration had the effect of lowering wages and working conditions for native-born workers. Congress then forbade American trading in coolies with both China and the West Indies, but condoned more humane forms of foreign contract labor. In 1864, in reaction to a manpower shortage created by the Civil War, Congress authorized employers to pay the passage and bind the services of prospective immigrants. The 1864 Act also created a U.S. Immigration Office in New York City and a National Commissioner of Immigration, who was to report directly to the State Department. This Act was in effect only until April 1868.

After the Civil War, even the limitations on "coolie labor" were relaxed, marking a return to the prevalent nonrestrictionist treatment of immigration. The Burlingame Treaty of June 1868 specifically granted Chinese the right to enter the United States. In the following year, the Union Pacific Railroad was completed. This marked the emergence of great corporate wealth, but also a very large floating labor supply. Chinese by this time accounted for 10 percent of the California population, and racial hostility intensified. Mistreatment of the Chinese on the West Coast, along with growing efforts in the East to discourage immigration, were among the factors that led to political pressures by humanitarians and others concerned with the brutal treatment of aliens. This political pressure resulted in the Civil Rights Act of May 1870, which guaranteed equal protection under the law for aliens. Further liberal initiatives by Congress in the early 1870s included making aliens of African descent eligible to become naturalized citizens, and a "reciprocal treatment" agreement with Italy that guaranteed to citizens of one country who resided in the other the same rights and privileges as the native-born. By 1874, the Supreme Court had even upheld the right of states to permit aliens to vote.

1875 to 1965: Distinctions Based on Country of Origin

In 1876, the national political platforms set the tone for the coming era of immigration policy. Only four years earlier, the candidates had expressly encouraged immigration. During the country's centennial year, the issue of immigration was conspicuously absent from the presidential campaign. The initiative in immigration issues increasingly rested with Congress; indeed, in several cases the Supreme Court ruled that only Congress had power to control immigration. *Henderson v. Wickham, Chy Lung v. Freeman,* and the Chinese exclusion case underscored the congressional prerogative, including the right of Congress to exclude aliens. The Immigration Bureau was moved in 1882 from the Department of State, with its focus on foreign relations, to the domestic Department of the Treasury, which was a signal to the world that the nation had the right to enact regulations limiting immigration to protect its national interest. Public opinion, partly influenced by organized labor, turned sharply against continued immigration. By the 1892 presidential campaign, both political parties denounced an open-door policy in their platform statements.

1875 Through World War I

Several distinct themes emerge in the legislation of this period. The first is a series of acts, applied without regard for country of origin, designed to exclude undesirable immigrants. The second is the exclusion of contract workers—ostensibly, a universalistic criterion, but one that had the effect of differentially excluding Orientals, for whom contract labor was a far more common mechanism for immigration. The third is a growing trend toward the explicit exclusion of certain national (or racial) groups. Inevitably, these three concerns became increasingly identified in legislation.

Excluding undesirables. In 1875, Congress instituted a restrictive policy that excluded "lewd" and "immoral" aliens from entering the United States to engage in unlawful activities. Convicted felons were also barred from entering. A similar Act was passed in 1882. This Act denied entrance to lunatics, idiots, and persons likely to become public charges, and, for the first time, established a fifty-cent head tax, which helped defray the cost of processing immigrants. As interest in immigration continued to grow, Congress formed committees to study the issues. In July of 1888, the House of Representatives convened the Ford Committee, which reported that despite the 1875 and 1882 restrictions alien paupers and convicts were numerous.

A March 1891 Act clarified ambiguities in the 1882 Act by vesting in the federal government the entire process of inspecting immigrants. Polygamists and persons with "loathsome" or "contagious" diseases were added to the list of undesirables denied entry. Transportation companies were charged with returning to the country of nationality any immigrant they had borne to the United States who, within a year of arrival, became a public charge. In 1893, transportation operators were required to outline their procedure for screening passengers and were required to post bonds. In addition, the companies were compelled to circulate copies of U.S. immigration laws. The President was given the power to close immigration from countries in which cholera or other infectious diseases were present. But the Senate rejected a bill requiring overseas consular inspection to determine, among other things, each immigrant's moral character.

A 1903 codification of extant statutes augmented the excludable classes by banning epileptics, insane people, and professional beggars. This legislation also included the first political ban, forbidding the immigration of anarchists, who had become an object of public antipathy following the assassination of President William McKinley a year and a half earlier. The head tax on aliens was raised to two dollars (Canadians, Mexicans, and Cubans were exempted). Grounds for deportation were expanded: Section

1218 provided for the deportation of aliens up to three years following their entrance and called for the expulsion of any alien who became a public charge within two years of entry. Despite a move to authorize refunds of the head tax in 1905, Congress raised the fee to four dollars per person in February 1907.

The second decade of the twentieth century opened with various acts aimed at specific types of immigrant misconduct. The Narcotic Drugs Import and Export Act permitted the deportation of aliens who violated it. Those who misbehaved while in the United States, as well as those entering the United States illegally, were liable to deportation. Aliens who lived off the earnings of prostitution were judged deportable. In 1913, the Supreme Court paved the way for increased expulsions by denying deportable aliens much of the Fifth and Sixth Amendment protections afforded defendants in criminal proceedings. The court refused to hold that deportation was a criminal penalty and that a deportation hearing was part of the criminal process. Deportees were subsequently forced to rely on the vaguer safeguards of the right to due process—a safeguard that applied only to actions by the states.

Congress, aware of a new voting block of immigrants concerned with immigration opportunities for their relatives still in Europe, did not act to resolve ambiguities in their statutes. One indication of congressional wavering is the fate of bills requiring literacy of all those admitted. In the nonelection years of 1911, 1913, and 1915, Congress approved the requirement, but did not override the President's veto; and in each of the three subsequent election years it did not approve the requirement.

In February 1917, Congress overrode President Woodrow Wilson's second veto and enacted a bill that repealed all previous inconsistent acts and codified the immigration statutes, in particular, the "quality control" aspects of the legislation. The act barred people of "constitutional psychopathic inferiority," and those who had experienced at least one previous attack of insanity. Alcoholics, stowaways, and vagrants were also barred. Legislation refusing admission to women coming for immoral purposes was extended to include men coming for similar reasons. The most controversial section of the bill dealt with literacy requirements. The subject of much debate between the Congress and the White House since President Grover Cleveland had objected to it in the late nineteenth century, the literacy requirement was finally established for all immigrants. It required that all immigrants older than sixteen years demonstrate literacy in a language in order to be admitted.

During World War I, Congress tried to protect the country against those who might avoid the draft or spread unrest when it gave the President the power to control the entry and departure of both citizens and aliens during national emergencies. The Anarchist Act of 1918, a precursor to the Subversive Activities Control Act of 1950, made it easier to exclude and deport anarchists and other "politically undesirable aliens advocating radical theories." The Russian Revolution had made infamous the term "radical" in this country. "Radicals" were blamed for labor strikes and self-proclaimed "radicals" often participated in and claimed credit for violent actions. The national press spread fear of these extremists in lurid front-page stories. Immediate post-war isolationist sentiment was reinforced by June 1919 bombings of the homes of public officials, including Commissioner of Immigration Frederick C. Howe. Public outrage grew when foreign anarchists were arrested for a midday bombing on Wall Street on September 16, 1920.

Excluding contract laborers. Congressional action in 1875 barred the importation of unconsenting Oriental contract laborers. This measure could be justified because of objections to the involuntary nature of such contract labor; however, the pressure of organized labor led to further restrictions on contract labor in general. Agitation from the West Coast led to particular restrictions on Asian labor. In February 1885, Congress prohibited the importation of immigrants under contracts established prior to migration. Immigrants entering after February 1885 were in the ironic position of having to prove to immigration authorities that they would not become public charges even though they could not use a labor contract signed prior to immigration as evidence of an employment opportunity in the United States. Concern increasingly focused on the economic aspects of immigration, and in 1887 the Secretary of Labor was given specific authority to take charge of local immigration affairs in order to provide special attention to contract labor problems. In 1888, Congress passed a law allowing the deportation of alien contract laborers within one year of entry, the first expulsion legislation in ninety years. In 1903, legislation transferred the Immigration Bureau from the Treasury Department to the Department of Commerce and Labor. In 1915, the Supreme Court upheld a state government's right to refuse to hire aliens when the employment involved the common property or resources of the people of the state, the regulation of the public domain ("police power"), or various other types of public work. Concern about the economic impact of immigration would be intensified during the 1920s and 1930s.

National-origin restrictions. A new aggressive nationalism, triggered by a bomb explosion in the face of police at a German anarchist meeting in Chicago's Haymarket Square, intensified xenophobia. Conservative intellectuals on the East Coast began publicly asserting the undesirability of Southern and Eastern Europeans. In New Orleans, citizens lynched eleven innocent Italians, leading to cries of indignation from Italy and talk of war. Some sort of national preoccupation with the alien "threat" was evident in the decision of the Supreme Court to hear the case of *Yick Wo v. Hopkins*, a case that guaranteed due process rights under the Fourteenth Amendment to resident aliens.

The form that restrictions took was the limitation of immigrants from certain countries or racial groups. The concern with Asians was of long standing. Besides the various laws limiting contract or coolie labor, there was a further Chinese limit in 1884, and an Act in September 1888 banning the immigration of any Chinese laborers. A 1902 Act extended the ban on Chinese, who were permanently excluded two years later. Japan first allowed emigration in 1885. An act of Congress in February 1907 laid the cornerstone for Japanese restrictions. Despite the opposition of President Theodore Roosevelt, the Act separated Japanese immigrants from European immigrants, whose racial characteristics were more similar to those of most native-born Americans.

But Japan had recently gained world stature by defeating Russia in 1905, and Japan was important to United States aspirations in the Pacific. Not wishing to irritate Japan, President Roosevelt, using powers granted the President by the February 1907 Act, accepted a promise from Japan that no more passports would be issued to Japanese laborers seeking to emigrate to the United States. The adoption of this "gentlemen's agreement" may also have been encouraged by a desire to offset an executive order of the previous week that had denied more than temporary stays to Japanese and Korean workers who had entered the United States through Mexico. The Japanese were targets of particular antagonism: a 1913 California Act prohibited them from holding interests in agricultural land.

Although neither the Chinese, who already had been excluded, nor the Japanese, who were still covered by the gentlemen's agreement, were directly affected by a 1917 Act that created the Asiatic barred zone, the indirect consequences did affect all Orientals. The act was aimed primarily at Hindus, but it barred residents of India, Burma, Siam, and the Malay states. The Philippines had become part of the United States as a consequence of the Spanish-American War of 1889, and Filipinos were considered nationals who could migrate without restrictions; this held until the islands achieved independence in 1946, at which time numerical limits and a quota of 100 visas a year were imposed. The exclusion of Asians applied not solely to those born in Asia, but also to persons of Asian extraction who were born elsewhere, for example, in Latin America. The Asiatic barred zone cemented in the 1917 legislation was not cracked until World War II, when a token quota of 105 a year, barely above the minimum country quota of 100, was given to China, a war ally. A token quota was given to Japan when the 1952 Immigration and Nationality Act gave a quota of 100 visas a year to each independent Asian country that had previously been denied a quota. However, a ceiling of 2,000 visas a year was imposed on Asia as a whole for visas subject to these quota limits. Special post–World War II legislation permitted the immigration of wives and fiancees of U.S. servicemen stationed abroad, and under this legislation many Asian women, particularly Japanese and later Korean women, immigrated outside of the quota limits. It was not until the 1965 Amendments that the stringent restrictions on Asians were eased.

Of more immediate concern to Americans who did not live on the West Coast was the change in the character of European immigration. British, Germans, and Swedes entered the United States in record numbers, despite the relative improvement in conditions in their home countries resulting from increased industrialization and lower birth rates. Although the numbers may have been a concern, these Northern and Western Europeans were considered assimilable. Of greater concern was the increased migration from Southern and Eastern Europe. Italian, Hungarian, Austrian, and Russian immigration was greatest during the first decade of the twentieth century. Ethnic prejudices against people who had darker skin or "strange ways" made Southern and Eastern Europeans conspicuous, especially in the "great urban triangle" encompassing St. Louis, Boston, and Washington, D.C., where 80 percent of the Southern and Eastern Europeans settled. Immigrants who left the enclave or "ghetto" encountered this hostility, which in turn often discouraged their efforts to assimilate.

Advocacy of restrictionism began to spread among academic groups. W. Z. Ripley's new school of anthropology, arguing that race lines conformed to physical types, which were delineated by regional geography, became popular. Conservatives looked to eugenics as a scientific justification for restrictionism. The opposition to immigration grew as immigration grew. In 1905 and in 1910 immigration exceeded one million persons. The annual rate of immigration reached 10.5 per one thousand persons in the United States (in the 1970s the annual rate was about 0.3 immigrants per thousand population).

Perhaps the most significant work to come from the Congress during this decade was the forty-two volume report of the Dillingham Commission (1911), the first in-depth study of the U.S. immigration situation. The report, which reflected the popular prejudices of the era, was the foundation for later restrictive legislation. It gave credence to the popular belief that Northwestern European immigrants were more desirable than their counterparts from Southern and Eastern Europe.

Reactions to immigration from neighboring countries in North America were mixed. Throughout the period of the western advance on the frontier there was a continuing substantial movement back and forth across the Canadian border. Both Canada and Mexico had been exempted from the fifty-cent head tax, and were subsequently excluded from the increased head tax. The two-dollar head tax legislation also exempted Cubans. The Dillingham Commission could make no valid recommendations concerning Mexican immigration, partly because there were no statistics for southern border crossings into the United States. Mexican immigration was apparently growing, however, partly because of political instability in Mexico and partly because of increased demand for labor in the Southwest.

Except for special treatment for countries in the Western Hemisphere, restrictionism continued to grow. This was evident in a reassertion of racial superiority, coupled with a patrician fear of race suicide. Following U.S. victory in World War I, a new sense of isolationism spread across the country. Representative George Huddleston of Alabama told Congress that such a feeling was not surprising:

> After every foreign war comes a resurgence of chauvinism. It is the scum that boiled up out of the cauldron of disorder, bloodshed, and national hatred . . . and I am reminded also that the drives against aliens and against freedom of speech which have always characterized the backlash of war have not always had their origin and their entire support among the most patriotic elements of our people. They have not always come from those who are most concerned about the preservation of Americanism. To the contrary, the Alien and Sedition Laws of 1798 represented what was left of Tory sentiment in the United States, not the sentiment of the people who had won the revolution, who had fought for it at Lexington and Yorktown, but of those who cherished un-American ideals and believed that wealth and class should dominate this country and that the common people existed for no higher purpose than to maintain a privileged upper class (Congressional Record, 67th Congress, 1st Session, p. 510).

Nascent isolationism, combined with the revival of restrictionism and bolstered by the Dillingham Report, led inevitably to calls for new federal legislation.

The Interwar Period

The interwar period was marked by the passage of both numerical restrictions and national-origins restrictions. Both types of restrictions were responses to a strong anti-immigration sentiment that became widespread following World War I.

Public opinion against immigration. America's efforts to distinguish itself from the rest of the world after the war were manifest in numerous forms. In particular, great attention was paid to the international "threats" of an expanding Russian and Japanese presence. The growing "threat of anarchism" was recognized by the *New York Times*, which uncharacteristically linked the issues of violence and immigration by condemning the Bolsheviks in a 1919 editorial:

> The United States is for the men and women who believe in its institutions, who understand order and liberty under law. It should cast out this drove of foreign destructionists who have come here to bring about its ruin (*New York Times*, 1919, p. 14).

Fear of Russian immigrants grew to include any people who emigrated from the Russian sphere:

> They are coming from lands of unrest and revolutionary action and we should like to know in what spirit they are coming, whether to make use of opportunities in a free land, with respect for its institutions, or whether they are bringing their hatred and prejudices, their revolutionary spirit, their class consciousness and their contempt for democratic institutions (*Chicago Tribune*, 1920, p. 6).

But the Russian Bolsheviks could not be identified at the border, unlike the Japanese, against whom a second xenophobic movement had grown. The Japanese were resented, not for political reasons as the Bolsheviks were, but for economic reasons. Although the "gentlemen's agreement" was presumably still in effect, it did not apply to Hawaii, and loopholes in the accord often left room for the admission of relatives and "picture brides." The 1920 Census figures revealed to the rest of the country what the West Coast and Hawaii had known for years: the agreement was not effective in ending Japanese immigration.

Alarmist headlines spread throughout the West: "150,000 on Pacific Coast Gobble Up Productive Land—Fear of 'Yellow Invasion' Growing." There was an outcry against Washington's apparent inability to see the problem:

> People of the Eastern States do not understand that racial solidarity is a boastful characteristic of the Japanese people, and that this question of solidarity has a sinister aspect to the white people settled in our Western states (*San Antonio Express*, 1920, p. 1).

California Senator J. D. Phelan challenged the Japanese to "fight for it" if they wanted California.

Washington's reluctance was based in part on a desire not to disrupt negotiations with Japan for control of Yap Island in the South Pacific. Although both candidates for President pledged support of West Coast sentiment in the 1920 campaign, Californians refused to wait. By a 3-to-1 margin they strengthened the Alien Land Act of 1913 by forbidding aliens to buy or lease land in the state. The Texas Legislature passed a similar law after an "invasion" of two Japanese who moved into Harlingen, Texas (Canadians and Mexicans were exempted from the Texas law). Hostility increased after a Japanese sentry killed an American lieutenant in Siberia. Although Japan apologized for the incident, it fueled anti-alien sentiment.

Anti-immigration sentiment was augmented by several domestic problems in addition to the perception of an international threat: concern about the large number of unnaturalized immigrants already in the country, confusion and inefficiency in admitting aliens, and worry about the economic impact of immigration.

Before attending to the new influx of aliens, Congress felt that it must deal with the large percentage of resident aliens who were not yet naturalized. Representative Albert Johnson of Washington said that Congress could not draft any kind of legislation to restrict immigration into the United States from all countries until we knew what we were

> going to do with the millions of unnaturalized aliens who are here now . . . .
> I would to God that this country could hold out hands to all of these millions and say, "Come here." But we cannot do it. Can you not see the signs of trouble? Oh, it would be better that we give the half of all that we possess in means to help sustain them where they are than to bring them here. That, of course, applies to people in other countries, too, in our present condition, distress is here; discontent is here; world problems are here to make mischief right here (*Congressional Record*, 67th Congress, 1st Session, p. 501).

Processing aliens became another problem. Ellis Island in the 1920s was ill-prepared for an influx of immigrants. The Immigration Commission scurried for money and administrative help to alleviate the overcrowded, dirty conditions in the buildings and to overhaul the inefficient procedures. Panic spread in New York City when typhus broke out on the Island. Ships diverted to Boston to control the disease spread fear up the coast, and the carelessness of inspectors who admitted diseased aliens seemed to confirm the public suspicion that the immigration policy was altogether too lax. Conditions on Ellis Island were to become much worse before they became better.

Economic difficulties, especially employment problems, were also being blamed on immigration. Immigrants were simultaneously blamed for spreading unrest and strikes among workers and for causing unemployment by intensifying the competition for jobs. But the nature of the economic threat was elusive. In December 1920 the *Chicago Tribune* reported that there were 160 men available for every one hundred jobs, and that there was even a surplus of housemaids. But only a year earlier, the *Tribune* had reported a serious shortage of unskilled workers and attributed it to literacy requirements for the admission of immigrants. Farm labor remained in short supply, for many farm workers had been drawn to the cities and the war industries during the war and had not returned. The European immigrants did not work in agriculture (only about 3 percent were farmers), and the void was being filled by Mexican workers. Their northward migration, although still only a relative trickle, was welcomed in the Southwest. Few jobs were available in the industrialized cities, perhaps in part because the lengthy work shifts of the wartime years were maintained even after the war ended.

But despite doubts about the specific extent and nature of unemployment, civic and labor groups warned of its danger. The Knights of Columbus cautioned men not to move to urban areas, where jobs were scarce. A National Economic League Survey in November 1920 found that labor was "foremost" among national problems, and the American Federation of Labor cited substantial unemployment as the most pressing reason for barring immigration for at least two years.

A related but less significant economic problem was also linked to immigration: the return of wages and often of the immigrants themselves to their home countries. Many aliens sent money to their families instead of pumping it directly into the United States economy. Some of the Europeans themselves returned home to apply the training and capital they had received in the United States. The felt injustice of return migration was expressed by editorial writers:

> We exchange the skilled workman, familiar with American production methods, for the unskilled workman; working men for women; people who speak English for people who do not; people familiar with our institutions and laws for others who are not. This exchange is an expensive one for this country and constitutes a considerable gift to Europe (*New York Times*, 1919, p. 6).

Congressional response. Despite the public sentiment, Congress hesitated. The House Committee on Immigration reported favorably on a bill to prohibit immigration for four years, but the third session of the Sixty-Fifth Congress (1919) adjourned without acting upon it. When it returned, the House voted to ban all aliens, except for relatives of United States citizens, for two years. The Senate substituted a bill to limit immigration to 3 percent of U.S. foreign-born. The Senate bill overwhelmingly passed both Houses, but President Woodrow Wilson killed it with a pocket veto.

Ten weeks later, on May 19, 1921, President Warren G. Harding signed into law practically the same bill that Wilson had vetoed. This bill, the Per Centum Limit Act, laid the groundwork for the National Origins Act of 1924. The 1921 bill limited the number of immigrants from each country to 3 percent of the number of people born in that country and residing in the United States according to the 1910 Census. By this formula, close to 60 percent of the approximately 360,000 immigrants to be allowed into the United States each year were from Northern and Western Europe. The intent of the bill was to limit Southern and Eastern European immigration, as immigration from this source had been rising for the previous thirty years and Northern and Western European immigration had been in relative decline. Asian immigrants were still barred by the 1917 legislation. Immigration from the independent countries in the Western Hemisphere, including Mexico, was not subject to the numerical restrictions in the 1921 Act, and would not be subject to any numerical restrictions until the 1965 Immigration Amendments.

Emigrants left Europe in hordes, intending to arrive before the 1921 ban was effective. To prevent all of a country's yearly quota from being filled in a single day, Congress had stipulated that no more than 20 percent of a nation's yearly allotment could be used in one month. But the poorly timed departures from Europe, particularly following the enactment, brought tremendous crowds to Ellis Island. Ships that could not dock crowded the harbor entrance. Disputes developed about the order of arrival and the fate of those whose country's quota had already been filled. As a stopgap measure, a Congressional resolution admitted all emigrants who had set sail before June 8, 1921. The monthly ceiling was eventually lowered to 10 percent to relieve congestion, but boat races across the Atlantic in an effort to time arrival at precisely 12:01 A.M. on the first day of the month continued until the 1924 law was enacted imposing still more restrictions.

Monthly quotas affected the processing of aliens. The unanticipated concentration of immigrants at the beginning of every month exacerbated the already-overcrowded situation at Ellis Island. The raising of objections to the conditions at Ellis Island in the British Parliament in 1923 drew worldwide attention to the problems there. Within a few months, editorials in major United States newspapers called on the government to lighten Ellis Island's load by giving consulates abroad greater authority to inspect potential immigrants.

Court decisions after 1921 also formed part of the background for congressional action in 1924. The Supreme Court found that Japanese nationals were not eligible for citizenship because they were neither "free white persons" nor aliens of African nativity or descent, as required by naturalization laws. The court also upheld state restrictions against the owning of real property by aliens. State court decisions also reflected the growing mood of restrictionism. The Rhode Island Supreme Court forbade aliens to drive vehicles for hire, and a New York court refused to permit the handling of soft drinks by aliens.

The 1924 National Origins Act. The National Origins Act was introduced to the House as an amendment to the Johnson Immigration Bill by Representative John J. Rogers of Massachusetts. It is best known for its formula for allocating immigrant visas. Unlike the quota system of 1921, which considered the number of foreign-born residents in the United States, Rogers's amendment was based on the "national origins" of each individual in the United States in 1920. The underlying philosophy in the amendment seemed to be the desire to reflect accurately the composition not only of the population of recent arrivals to the United States, but of all residents. Critics focused on the efforts to base the formula on the 1890 Census, which would omit the recent influx of Eastern Europeans. The 2 percent quotas, based on 1890 population figures, were to be maintained until 1927, when 150,000 visas would be allocated in proportion to the national origins of the white population of the United States in 1920. These changes limited immigration opportunities for Eastern and Southern Europeans even more than the 1921 Act.

The legislative debate emphasized two issues: the treatment of the Japanese and possible exemptions from the quotas. Public opinion seemed to favor complete exclusion of the Japanese. There was a growing belief that the Japanese were unassimilable. Exclusionist sentiment grew when Congress learned of a letter Japanese Ambassador Hanihara sent to indicate his displeasure with the proposed legislation. Congress resented both the foreign involvement in what was seen as a domestic issue and also the veiled threat implicit in the Ambassador's letter. Secretary of State Hughes, who was hoping to keep Japanese-American relations from deteriorating further, pointed out that the Congress was trying to ban immigration from a country that would have been allocated a ceiling of only 246 under a proposed 2 percent rule. Congress balked at the Administration's suggestion that consideration of the section dealing with the Japanese be postponed eight months while the executive branch sought to smooth relations through diplomatic channels.

The issue of exemptions was resolved by counting all immigrants under the quota with the exception of (1) wives and children of United States citizens; (2) immigrants previously admitted who returned from trips abroad; (3) immigrants from the Western Hemisphere countries; (4) students younger than fifteen; and (5) ministers of any religion and professors. Some Japanese immigrants could enter under these exemptions, although persons of Asian origin born in the Western Hemisphere were still to be treated as if they had been born in their countries of racial origin.

President Calvin Coolidge said he would not have signed the bill if it had simply provided for exclusion of the Japanese, a measure he found "unnecessary and deplorable," but he accepted the measure, praising its "good features and comprehensiveness," on May 26, 1924. Japan was not given a quota until 1952, when it was given the minimum quota of 100 visas a year. It was not until the 1965 Amendments that immigration policy ceased to discriminate flagrantly against Asians.

Despite the apparent completeness of the 1924 Act, several additional initiatives were undertaken. Two days after the National Origins Act became law, Congress appropriated eleven million dollars to create the immigration border patrol. The border patrol was presumably intended to curtail exploitation of the free passage courtesy granted Mexico and Canada by Eastern Hemisphere natives entering the United States through its northern and southern borders. Less than a year later, immigration officers were given the power to arrest without warrant any alien found entering or attempting to enter the country illegally. In 1925, the Supreme Court again approved restrictions against the holding of real property by aliens, but also moved to protect the rights of aliens, by contrasting warrantless searches at the border, which are justified on the ground of national self-protection, with those in the interior, which require probable cause.

For the rest of the 1920s, and during the 1930s, there was a gradual softening in the severity of public opinion against immigration. During the Great Depression, departures of emigrants exceeded the admission of immigrants. Racism declined in intellectual circles as eugenics and theories of biological determinism waned in popularity. A basic familiarity with aliens was widespread. The "foreign hordes" and their children were becoming increasingly Americanized. Elder Americans, who had seen their territory "invaded" by foreigners, gave way to youth, who had grown up accepting immigrants. The expansion of education gave the immigrants' children greater opportunity; and the New Deal itself reflected a nation's belief that a person's environment was a greater determinant of his behavior than race or ethnic origin.

A few symbolic gestures were made by Congress during this fifteen-year period, including granting legal status to aliens who had entered the United States prior to July 1, 1929. As World War II approached, most immigration legislation dealt with security provisions. The 1940 Alien Registration Act was the first statutory requirement for visas for nonimmigrants. It required the registration and finger-printing of aliens; expanded the class of deportable aliens to include smugglers, those who helped others enter illegally, and those who carried weapons illegally; and facilitated expulsion of aliens. Perhaps to increase the effectiveness of prosecution of deportable aliens, the Immigration and Naturalization Service, which had been located at the Department of Labor since 1933, became part of the Department of Justice in 1940. In that same year, Congress revised the nationality laws to make Indians and Eskimos eligible for citizenship. Yet basic policy did not change. In spite of the declining proportion of foreign-born persons in the population and in spite of the improved economic conditions after the trough of the Depression in 1933, the restrictions were retained. In one of the most deplorable manifestations of U.S. immigration policy, boatloads of Jewish refugees fleeing from Hitler's Germany were turned away and forced to return to what was known at the time to be almost certain death (Morse, 1968; Feingold, 1970). Such behavior was the combined result of anti-Semitism and a mindless observation of annual quotas. Even in the early post-war period there was a remarkable insensitivity to the plight of the displaced persons in Europe, particularly those who were Jewish (Reimers, 1982).

World War II To 1965

World War II had an effect on immigration policy altogether different from that of World War I. From the newly integrated army to the repeal of the Chinese Exclusion Act in 1943, the atmosphere was right for a liberalization of immigration policy. Americans seemed united in their appreciation of democracy. The Bracero Program, which was in effect from 1942 to 1964, supplied farmworkers from Mexico to fill the void created by American workers who had joined the war effort. After the war, the December 1945 War Brides Act granted admission to alien wives and children of any U.S. serviceman honorably discharged from service in the war. In 1946 over 5,000 fiancees of World War II veterans were admitted. Toward the end of 1945 a directive by President Harry S. Truman gave refugees preferred status and allowed for the entry of 40,000 refugees. The Displaced Persons Act of 1948 permitted 205,000 persons to enter by "mortgaging" future quotas for Poland, Germany, Latvia, Russia, and Yugoslavia. The presidential campaign platforms reflected American reaction to the legislation: the Republicans took credit for the Act and the Democrats called for the admission of more, condemning the legislation as discriminatory against Jews and Catholics in particular.

In subsequent years, two trends became evident. One was a rather pragmatic approach to immigration, characterized by the extension of the Bracero Program, authorization of recruitment of farm workers both in Mexico and among illegal Mexican workers in the United States, and provision of wage and working-condition standards for legal foreign laborers. The Truman Administration established blue ribbon commissions to study both the immigration dilemma in general and migrant labor in particular.

At the same time, another trend arose, this one among conservative forces who sought greater control of aliens, and it subsequently resulted in new restrictive legislation. Aliens outside the Southwest encountered stiff job competition from returning veterans. Connecticut prohibited aliens from taking positions as pharmacists, funeral directors, or hairdressers; occupational restrictions were also passed in Michigan and Kansas.

The Immigration and Nationality Act of 1952, better known as the McCarran-Walter Act, was largely a recodification of existing immigration law. Particular attention was given in the policy debate to new features that focused on the immigrant's political ideology. In particular, the Act barred the entry of communists. Despite widespread opposition from religious and civil liberties groups and President Truman's veto, the McCarran-Walter Act became law on June 27, 1952.

The Act also defined drug addicts and those who had been convicted on two or more offenses, whether or not moral turpitude had been involved, to be excluded aliens. Priorities were established within the quotas that gave first preference to those whose special skills would be of particular benefit to the United States and then to close relatives of either U.S. citizens or lawfully admitted aliens. In addition, the procedure for deportation was specified, and the processes for admission and exclusion were modified to ensure inspection both by consulates abroad and by immigration officers at the border.

The 1952 Act was remarkably unpopular legislation. Within a few years, presidential candidates of both major parties had promised revision, and the American Bar Association, the AFL-CIO, and even the Daughters of the American Revolution had called for changes in the Act, including the end of the national-origins quota system. Although the Act retained its authority, a variety of legislative initiatives during the 1950s allowed the admission of various refugee groups and relaxed the adjustment-of-status procedures to make it easier for foreign-born persons in the U.S. to acquire resident alien status. Under these revisions, additional classes of immigrants were admitted, including illegitimate and adopted children of U.S. citizens and resident aliens, and relatives of legal residents who might otherwise have been excluded on the grounds of criminality or disease. The Fair Share Refugee Act of 1960 permitted the Justice Department to parole into the U.S. refugees who fled communist or Middle East countries. In 1961, a permanent program for nonquota admission of alien orphans was established, and the annual ceiling of 2,000 visas from Asia was eliminated. The exclusion of persons with tuberculosis and leprosy was also lifted.

Further actions in the early 1960s extended the Bracero Program, gave the Attorney General permanent power to parole refugees, provided aid for Cuban refugees, and allowed the nonquota admission of some immigrants. These actions were responses to the backlog that had developed in the processing of persons in the skilled-specialist and kinship-preference categories.

By 1964, President Lyndon Johnson, in his State of the Union Address, called for immigration reforms as part of the growing civil rights movement. This set the stage for the third chapter in the history of American immigration policy.

1965 to the Present: Family Reunification and Refugees

The national-origins quota system of the 1920s recodified in the 1952 legislation was obviously inconsistent with the domestic and international developments of the early 1960s. It was an era of intense civil rights legislation, in which race was declared an irrelevant criterion for selection for jobs, housing, and public accommodations. It was also an era in which the United States wanted to develop good relations with the newly independent countries of Asia and Africa. It was a time of rapidly increasing productivity and real income, during which Americans believed that a period of long-term economic growth had just begun, and that a more humanitarian immigration policy with less emphasis on economic concerns was warranted.

There were, however, disquieting developments south of the border. From 1945 to 1965, over 1.3 million Mexican nationals became resident aliens, and the annual rate was increasing. Youth cohorts in Mexico grew rapidly as a consequence of infant mortality rates that declined faster than birth rates. The slow growth of the Mexican economy led to forecasts of increased Mexican immigration. The "safety valve" implicit in the temporary worker (Bracero) program was closed when the program was terminated in 1964. It was also recognized that with their new political independence, the English-speaking Caribbean Islands would no longer be subject to the small subquotas for dependencies, but rather would be free of numerical limitations under the 1924 exemption to independent countries in the Western Hemisphere.

The 1965 Amendments to the 1952 Immigration and Nationality Act substantially altered the spirit and the letter of immigration law and practice (Keely, 1971). This legislation was at the same time liberalizing and restrictionist. It abolished the national-origins quota system that had been applicable to the Eastern Hemisphere, and thereby ended the severe numerical limits on immigrants from Asian countries and the less severe limits on immigrants from Eastern and Southern Europe. But it imposed numerical limits for the first time on the independent nations in the Western Hemisphere. Equally important was the change in priorities for the issuing of immigration visas within country and hemisphere limits. Kinship ties with a U.S. citizen or resident alien became the dominant rationing criterion, replacing the relatively greater emphasis on labor market criteria (skills) that had been introduced in the 1952 Act.

Under the 1965 Amendments, the immediate relatives of U.S. citizens could enter the United States without numerical limit regardless of the country of origin. ("Immediate relatives" includes the spouse, minor children, and parents of U.S. citizens; to reduce the practice of pregnant women entering illegally to give birth to U.S. citizen children, subsequent amendments stipulated that only adult U.S. citizens could sponsor their parents.) For immigrants subject to numerical limitation, a quota of 170,000 visas a year was created for the Eastern Hemisphere and one of 120,000 visas a year was created for the Western Hemisphere. This was subsequently (1979) merged into a combined worldwide ceiling of 290,000, which was reduced to 270,000 when the Refugee Act of 1980 removed the refugee category from the preference system and created a separate program for refugees. To prevent any one country from dominating the immigration stream, the 1965 Amendments included an annual country ceiling of 20,000 visas for those subject to numerical limitation for the Eastern Hemisphere, regardless of the size of the country's population, the number of immigrants already here, or the number otherwise eligible for visas. Because the growing Mexican immigration was tending to "crowd out" immigration from other Western Hemisphere countries, the country limit of 20,000 visas a year for those subject to numerical limitation was extended to the Western Hemisphere in 1976. The 1965 Amendments provided that, within country limits, Eastern Hemisphere visas subject to numerical limit were to be allocated on the basis of a preference system. For the Western Hemisphere a first-come, first-served system was used until the same preference system was extended to the Western Hemisphere in 1976.

The preference system developed in the 1965 Amendments consisted of several categories:

First
preference: Unmarried adult children of United States citizens (20 percent of visas).

Second
preference: Spouse and unmarried children of permanent resident aliens (20 percent of visas plus any not used in a higher preference).

Third
preference: Professionals and persons of exceptional ability
                       in the sciences and non-performing arts who will
                       benefit the economy, culture, and welfare of the
                       United States (10 percent of visas). Requires a
                       labor certification.

Fourth
preference: Married children of U.S. citizens (10 percent of
                       visas and any not used in a higher preference).

Fifth
preference: Siblings of adult U.S. citizens (24 percent of visas
                       and any not used in a higher preference).

Sixth
preference: Skilled workers "needed" in the United States
                       labor market (10 percent of visas). Requires a
                       labor certification.

Seventh
preference: Refugees from communist countries or commu-
                       nist-dominated countries or the general area of
                       the Middle East (6 percent of visas).

Non-
preference: A catch-all category for any visas remaining af-
                       ter satisfying claims for the first through sixth
                       preference categories. Primarily for persons who
                       can show their skills are "needed" by obtaining
                       the same labor certification required under the
                       third and sixth preferences, and for persons in-
                       vesting money in a United States business they
                       will operate.

The spouse and minor children of a visa recipient would generally
also receive visas in the same preference category. For example, if a sibling
of a U.S. citizen immigrated with his wife and four small children, six visas
would be charged to the fifth preference. Although 20 percent of the visas
subject to numerical limitation are to be distributed on the basis of skills,
two-thirds of the third- and sixth-preference visas were used by the spouses
and minor children of workers who received labor certification. Although

the nonpreference category was initially a source of additional skilled workers and investors, the extremely rapid growth in the number of visa applicants in the fifth preference (siblings of U.S. citizens) absorbed all available visas, virtually ending non-preference immigration.

Despite their apparent comprehensiveness, the 1965 Amendments neglected some problems and created others. The amendments effectively precluded the adjustment of status by Cuban refugees, and this had to be rectified by a subsequent special Act. It soon became apparent that no adequate provisions had been made for refugees. Perhaps the most pressing problem was that although immigration from the Western Hemisphere was about 120,000 persons a year in the years prior to 1965, the rapid growth in the supply of immigrants meant that the number of persons wanting a visa soon came to exceed the annual limit. Thus, the restrictions on residents of the Western Hemisphere resulted in a growing illegal migration from Mexico and other Latin American countries.

Additional legislation during the 1970s expanded the ranks of "temporary workers" by abolishing the requirement that they be of "distinguished merit." A 1974 law rid the books of antiquated coolie laws. When Vietnam fell in 1975, orphans were immediately paroled into the United States, and funds were appropriated to help resettle at least 200,000 Indochinese refugees. By 1981 over one-half million Southeast Asian refugees had been admitted to the United States.

However, restrictions were also enacted. In 1976, third-preference workers were required to have a sponsoring employer and the fifth category was limited to petitioners at least twenty-one years of age. The Health Professional Education Assistance Act tightened restrictions on foreign medical graduates, but these restrictions were later relaxed for doctors who would practice in areas with a "shortage" of doctors. Dissatisfaction with the complexity of immigration legislation was reflected in the 1978 Amendments, which created the Select Commission on Immigration and Refugee Policy to study current immigration policies and recommend future ones.

Judicial decisions during this period marked contradictory trends in the treatment of alienage. A 1966 Supreme Court decision offered guidelines favorable to aliens apprehended for fraudulent entry, but a subsequent decision upheld a 1913 ruling that denied the criminal procedure rights of the Fifth and Six Amendments to deportable aliens. Also, a Ninth Circuit Court held in 1967 that warrants were not necessary for border searches. Other decisions seemed to expand the rights of aliens by mandating that they be given the same access to state-administered resources that other state residents enjoyed. A 1973 ruling struck down a New York State statute that excluded aliens from competitive state civil service positions. In contrast, Espinoza *v.* Farah Mfg. Co. held that the Title VII prohibition of discrimination based on "national origin" did not bar discrimination based solely on alienage. That is, it is not against the law to discriminate against resident aliens as long as one does not discriminate against U.S. citizens, either native- or foreign-born, of the same national origin. At present, alienage is not considered a "suspect category" in civil rights legislation.

By the late 1970s it was obvious that there were two glaring problems in immigration policy that required solution: refugees and illegal aliens. The Refugee Act of 1980 was intended to resolve refugee issues, but within months after enactment the legislation was found wanting. The Refugee Act of 1980 removed refugees from the preference system and increased the number of visas for refugees from 17,400 a year to 50,000 a year. (The preference system ceiling was lowered from 290,000 to 270,000 a year, with the 6 percent share for the sixth preference given to the fifth preference.) More important, however, was the change in the definition of a refugee. In contrast to the 1965 Amendments, with their nearly exclusive focus on refugees from communist countries (a carryover from the early 1950s), the 1980 Act allowed any person with a well-founded fear of political, racial, ethnic, or religious persecution who was already in a country of first asylum to apply. The Act continued past policy by giving the President and Congress authority to admit additional refugees in emergency situations.

Shortly after passage, however, the Refugee Act of 1980 was found to be deficient. It was designed on the basis of the model of Vietnamese refugees; that is, refugees already in countries of first asylum far from U.S. shores. The Cuban "freedom flotilla" of 1980, however, resulted in 125,000 refugees who showed up on U.S. shores, making the United States the country of first asylum. Haitian refugees also came in small boats, claiming they were refugees from poverty, a category not included in the Refugee Act, and that once having left Haiti they would be subject to political persecution if they returned. It was alleged that the less favorable treatment of the Haitians was due to racial discrimination. Public policy toward the Cuban freedom flotilla and toward the Haitians is still ambiguous.

Most observers believe that during the past twenty years illegal immigration has increased sharply. Apprehensions have certainly increased, from about 60,000 a year in the early 1960s to over one million a year by the end of the 1970s. The Ford, Carter, and Reagan administrations all have had interagency task forces charged, with varying degrees of intensity, to study the issues and offer recommendations. The Select Commission on Immigration and Refugee Policy had a similar charge, and issued its recommendations in 1981. In 1982, the Reagan administration recommended and the Senate passed legislation to grant amnesty for illegal aliens already in the United States and to impose sanctions against employers who knowingly hire illegal aliens, but the legislation died in the House of Representatives.

Summary

Government action in the regulation of immigration has passed through three distinct phases. The first phase, the period before 1875, involved relatively little regulation and no numerical or national-origin quotas. What regulation existed at this time was designed principally to exclude undesirable individuals.

The second phase, from 1875 to 1965, was the era of both numerical and racial or ethnic restrictions. Most notable among these restrictions were efforts to sharply curtail or eliminate the immigration of Asians, an attempt to reduce the influx of Eastern and Southern Europeans as compared to Northern and Western Europeans, and a conscious effort to limit some forms of competition with American workers. But this second phase of American immigration regulation left immigration from independent countries in the Western Hemisphere unregulated. The special position of nationals from Mexico and Canada meant that there were few restrictions on their entry into the U.S.

The third phase of immigration regulation began in 1965 with the elimination of national-origins formulas and a new series of preferences based on family reunification, with a smaller role for personal skills. The 1965 Amendments were later modified to eliminate separate hemispheric quotas and establish a worldwide ceiling for visas subject to numerical limitation. No longer were Canadians and Latin Americans in a special exempt category. And the last vestige of nationality-based restrictions was the limit of 20,000 visas a year for any one country imposed in 1976. Immigration from Mexico has been more than double this limit since 1976 because the spouses and minor children of U.S. citizens are not subject to this ceiling.

Legislation eventually responded to public opinion, and public opinion shifted several times. A strong undercurrent of nativism has endured, but there have also been strong prevailing sentiments in favor of continued immigration. While contemporary public opinion would almost certainly oppose reinstitution of racial and national-origin quotas, questions of the absolute number of immigrants that can be absorbed and the criteria to be used for rationing the limited number of visas remain crucial in creating immigration policies acceptable to Americans. The price of eliminating the special treatment of the Western Hemisphere has been the definition of hundreds of thousands (if not millions) of Mexican and Central American nationals as illegal aliens. These problems are the contemporary expression of the immigration dilemma.

4

A Social Portrait of the "Old" Immigrants

In one sense there is no such thing as an "old" immigrant group. The Irish, the Germans, and even the English are still coming to America. The famine Irish were not the post–Civil War Irish; nor were they, in turn, like the post-1916 Irish immigrants. And all earlier groups were different from the college-educated Irish who swarm into San Francisco and from the current crop of illegal Irish housepainters. After all, Ireland in 1850 was very different from Ireland in 1950, and both are very different from the Ireland of 1980 that has become a country of positive net migration.

Nevertheless, most of the Irish came before 1900. Most of the Italians and the Poles and the Eastern European Jews came after 1880. Most of the Cubans have come since 1959, and most of the Southeast Asians since 1975. So there are degrees of "old" in the status of immigrant groups. These various groups were different in many respects—no one ever accused the Irish of being too frugal, no one ever accused the Jews of drinking too much—but they all had one thing in common. It was charitably predicted of them, even of the Germans, that they were not thrifty enough, not industrious enough, not independent enough, not free-thinking enough to be able to succeed in American life. There is a second thing they have in common. Including the racially despised Chinese and Japanese, the religiously despised Jews, and the ethnically despised Irish and Germans and Italians, all of them have become successful in American life, some of them spectacularly so (Chiswick, 1977, 1979, 1982a, 1983b; Greeley, 1982; Lieberson, 1980). There are exceptions. The older immigrant cohorts from Mexico and the Philippines have been far less successful economically. Still, if one is going to assume that new immigrant groups as a whole are not going to be economically and socially successful, then one has to show why this pattern will arise when it did not previously.

The story of the old immigrant groups is a story of initial traumas and trials in the passage and settlement, a story of tenuous networks strung across long distances to the home village, a story of encountering the new while clinging to the old, and above all, a story of risk-taking and hard work. It is, in the fullest sense of the word, an epic story. Even stay-at-homes can dream about the wanderings of Ulysses or Aeneas or Roland or Huckleberry Finn—but in American families, there is also, two or three or five generations ago, a family model of the epic hero. Even if the individual story is lost or shrouded in family myth, we know that some forebear is part of this larger story.

Who They Were

Official government sources never tell the full story of immigration. Nevertheless, the official record is an appropriate starting point. The number of immigrants swelled throughout the 1800s and early 1900s, from 152,000 in 1820-30 to 8.8 million between 1901 and 1910. Between 1820 and 1982, more than 50 million immigrants were recorded as having come to the United States. Numerically, the largest number came from Germany (7 million), followed by the Italians (5 million), Great Britons (5 million), Irish (5 million), Austrians or Hungarians (4 million), and Canadians (4 million). The numbers from Canada and Mexico in particular are underestimates because for many decades in the earlier period persons crossing these land borders were not included in the statistics.

After 1924, as would be expected, the immigration stream slowed down; during the Depression of the 1930s, it was a mere trickle, and in fact yearly quotas for many countries, particularly in Northern and Western Europe, were not filled between 1931 and 1948. Since 1950, the numbers in the official record have been quite stable, with modest, controlled growth. The absolute numbers are not large (460,000 in 1979, compared with 805,000 in 1921), especially considering that the United States population base has more than doubled since 1920.

Although there was an upward trend in the numbers of immigrants during the 1800s, the fluctuations in the trend were closely timed with the American business cycle. The speed and effectiveness with which immigrants notified relatives in the home country of conditions seem quite remarkable, especially considering the slowness and difficulty of trans-Atlantic communication until after World War II.

The early immigrant stream was overwhelmingly male. While the American population in 1850 had about 104 males for every 100 females, in the immigrant population the number was closer to 164 males. This disparity persisted until after 1930, when females began to dominate in the immigration stream, probably as a result of the family reunification provisions of the immigration regulations. Later, with the admission of war brides and fiancees, the female predominance was even more marked. By 1950, the sex ratio among immigrants was 92 males for every 100 females. By the late 1970s, the ratio was 88 males for every 100 females. The ratio of children to adults among the immigrants was well below the ratio in the general population until 1945. During the periods of peak immigration, this ratio was lowest because of the large numbers of single males dominating at those times. As with the sex ratio, the youth ratio began to rise during the era of controlled immigration.

Most national groups displayed similar patterns in their immigration histories. At first, there was only a trickle of immigration from a country. Few people came to the United States, so there was no one to broadcast the news back home about life in America. In the second stage (which lasted about fifteen years during the last century), there was a growing stream of immigration by a few adventuresome souls. Stage three was mass immigration, supported by information and often funds from those who had established themselves during stage two. There are, of course, variations in the patterns. The pattern of German immigration in the 1800s displays pronounced peaks and valleys, especially when compared to the pattern for the Irish. The German pattern appears more closely tied to economic conditions in America ("pull factors"), while the Irish pattern may be more closely tied to conditions at home ("push factors"). The Scandinavian immigrants—the one group among whom agricultural pursuits predominated in the new country—became fewer and fewer as farmland became less available and more costly. The period of Italian mass immigration is obviously interrupted by the legislation of the 1920s.

The popular image of the old immigrants is that they were largely unskilled peasants and laborers who brought little but their muscle power to their new land. While this does describe many of the early immigrants, it is not a complete picture (Easterlin, 1980). In 1820, roughly 79 percent of the American labor force and 9 percent of immigrants were farmers. By 1850, the American labor force was 55 percent agricultural, compared with 14 percent of the immigrants. By 1880, agricultural workers had declined to 51 percent of the labor force and 10 percent of the new immigrants. In 1920, when 26 percent of the labor force was in agriculture, only 6 percent of the immigrants reported themselves to be farmers or farm workers. Compared with the American labor force as a whole, the immigrants were less likely to think of themselves as agricultural workers.

The proportion of immigrants who were skilled workers was actually somewhat higher earlier in the 1800s than it was later. About 11 percent of the 1820 workers were skilled, compared with 8.5 percent in 1850. The proportion went back up to 11 percent in 1880 and 13 percent in 1920. Throughout this period, there were substantial numbers of professional and commercial workers in the immigration stream as well.

Another interesting trend is the decrease in the proportion of immigrants who reported "no occupation," a decrease no doubt partly influenced by legislation against persons likely to become public charges. About two-thirds of the 1820 immigrants reported no occupation; this proportion declined to 60 percent in 1850, 48 percent in 1880, and 40 percent in 1920.

One conclusion that can be drawn from this review is that the trend to better skilled immigrants began fairly early. Although as late as 1920 the immigrant stream probably did contain many persons who had few skills, immigration was always a source of workers with skills needed in a young country.

Where They Went

The geographic distribution of immigrants within the United States was influenced by four factors: their port of entry, their environment, chain migration, and avoidance of the South (Zelinsky, 1973). Particularly in the 1800s, immigrants tended to cluster near seaports, especially those on the East Coast, with New York City being of primary importance. To a lesser extent, they also clustered near the West Coast entry ports, and Mexicans clustered near the southwestern border.

The environmental factors were not only climatic, but also economic and social. Some immigrants surely sought geographic areas in the United States similar to those they had known at home; this was especially true for agricultural workers. But for most workers, the influence of environment was principally economic: where work was available for immigrants, immigrant communities sprang up. In some cases, this work was available inland, especially in the upper Midwest and the cities of the Great Lakes. It is interesting to note that for some groups there was a slight concentration near the entry port, and then virtually no concentration until their rail destination in the Midwest was reached. For example, there were very few Danes to be found in Ohio or Pennsylvania, and large numbers in Minnesota.

Chain migration was a result of the previous two influences. It was the rare immigrant who arrived in the New World knowing no one or having no conception about America. Most of them had a cognitive map formed through conversations and correspondence—they had some sense of where they could find jobs, where they could speak their own language, where they could find others from the homeland. In this way, the formation of an ethnic community within a city tended to encourage the migration of others to the same area.

The final phenomenon, avoidance of the South, should be seen in terms of the other three. Seaports, economic opportunities, and chain migration all tended to work to locate new immigrants in northern cities. The "cognitive map" the immigrant carried with him did not necessarily carry hostile information about the South; the region was merely terra incognita. However, the anti-Catholic and anti-Semitic attitudes of many Southerners, attitudes that found their most dangerous expression in the Ku Klux Klan, were an additional deterrent. With a few exceptions, such as New Orleans, immigrant communities were relatively rare in the South (Ward, 1980).

What They Did

The record of immigrant workers in the new land is well documented. Much of the transportation infrastructure of the North and Midwest was built with immigrant labor: immigrants dug the canals and built the railroads and even provided substantial numbers of American seamen. The industrial revolution in the United States proceeded with immigrant laborers building the factories, performing the factory work, and in many cases serving as foremen, supervisors, and recruiters. Immigrant conscripts fought for the Union during the Civil War. Immigrants broke the sod on the prairies, brought new crops to the Midwest, and vastly increased productivity with the old crops. In the mines and on the fishing boats, in the brass mills and in the flour mills, tending flocks or tending spindles, immigrants were found in nearly every branch of industry.

The part of the record that is less well known is how the immigrants built up their own immigrant communities. Although chain migration tended to operate through family channels, with family members providing money and lodging to the newcomers, many immigrant groups quickly developed a sense of community. Mutual aid groups were common, as were provisions for new immigrants or for relief in the homeland. Many of these groups provided benefits for their members that the larger society was unwilling to provide. For example, the work done by the Polish miners was considered too risky to allow them to be covered by ordinary insurance, so the National Alliance for Polish People provided insurance coverage. When Jewish migrant groups felt cheated by corrupt employment agencies, they often formed their own associations to help find employment. Jewish groups also opened vocational training services, and even day-care centers for the children of working parents. The Polish Printers Association kept listings of the unemployed and of job openings. The German Bakers Union opened an employment agency.

One of the most interesting aspects of immigrant self-help was the provision of thrift institutions and rotating credit mechanisms to assist ambitious newcomers. Eastern European immigrants were famed for their thrift; indeed, in 1911, one-sixth of the assets of savings institutions in

Chicago were in Polish savings and loans. Ethnic associations and banks lent money for starting new businesses and for college tuition. Nor were these types of economic assistance limited to European immigrants; there existed similar mechanisms among Asian and Caribbean immigrant groups (Light, 1972).

In addition to economic services, the immigrant (ethnic) societies provided social services of all types—literally from the cradle to the grave—ranging from orphanages to shelter for the elderly to burial societies. Associations of the Polish, the Lithuanians, the Greeks, and the Italians helped provide religious instruction for immigrants' children. Immigrant associations were politically active in seeking to influence both domestic policies (especially labor legislation) and foreign policies (especially those related to their home countries).

Reactions to the Immigrants

But the many constructive activities of the immigrants were not what was noted by the journalists of the day. Immigrant communities were described as hotbeds of crime, disease, filth, and family disintegration. The negative stereotypes varied from group to group, but every group had its stereotype: Scandinavians drank too much, Italians were clannish, Poles were miserly, Hungarians dumb. Micks, spics, polacks, hunkies—something was wrong with every group.

And indeed, there were social and individual pathologies in abundance to be chronicled. This is true in any uprooted community, whether the migrants are from within a country or from outside the country. Unfortunately, the concentrated scrutiny of pathologies caused many to overlook the quiet and growing success of the immigrant groups.

The pathological perspective was ultimately resolved into two major schools of explanation. The view taken by the Dillingham Commission and many scholars was that the immigrants, especially Eastern and Southern Europeans, were racially inferior and doomed to occupy the lower ranks of American society. The view taken by the "Chicago School" of sociology was that the immigrants brought with them an "inferior culture." Their plight was not inescapable, especially if the larger society made an effort to "Americanize" them.

Public opinion toward the immigrants was by no means entirely hostile. For one thing, by 1920, 50 percent of the urban population were either immigrants themselves or the children of immigrants, and so they were a substantial part of public opinion (Lieberson, 1980, p. 23). However, in an important sense the immigrants could not win. If they succeeded, their success was viewed with envy and a suspicious conviction that they had made their fortunes only by taking jobs or profits away from the native-born. If they failed, their failure was taken as proof of biological or cultural inferiority. All too often, both aspects of the negative stereotype were held simltaneously: successful immigrants succeeded because they were shrewd or pushy, and unsuccessful immigrants failed because they were not shrewd or pushy enough.

The Record of Immigrant Success

Contemporary data show that the immigrant groups of the late 1800s and the early 1900s have achieved remarkable success. Whether one examines data from the U.S. Bureau of the Census or other sources (such as the General Social Surveys conducted by the National Opinion Research Center), it is clear that the despised Jews, Poles, Italians, Slavs, and Greeks have "made it," much as the earlier Germans, English, Scandinavians, and Irish "made it." In terms of education, occupation, or income, and even when such confounding variables as region and urban location are controlled, the immigrants and their children have been successful. And success has by no means been limited to the European groups: Japanese, Chinese, Korean, Cuban and black West Indian immigrants have also achieved notable economic success. (See, for example, Chiswick, 1979, 1982a, 1983a, 1983b; Featherman and Hauser, 1978; Greeley, 1976, 1980, 1981; Lieberson, 1980; Light, 1972.)

Perhaps no one who read the report of the Dillingham Commission when it was issued (1911) or the articles it generated in the popular press could have expected the successful assimilation of the immigrants into American society. Given the data and statistical procedures available to the Dillingham Commission, a prediction of success for immigrants would have been unlikely. But a recent reanalysis of the commission's data showed that the apparently severe lags in economic achievement among some of the turn-of-century immigrant groups were quite temporary (Blau, 1980). With hindsight and with more sophisticated economic and statistical analysis than was available at the time, it is easy to dismiss the conclusions of biological inferiority that the Commission drew. But what about the conclusions of the "cultural inferiority" thinkers? One explanation for the immigrants' success could be that they had become "Americanized" and lost whatever distinctive cultures they brought to the United States.

A variety of recent studies reject this explanation and point to the continuation of ethnic subcultures among the children and grandchildren of the immigrants (Greeley, McCready, and Theisen, 1980; Greeley, 1974). In some cases, of course, this is part of a conscious ethnic identification. Ethnic food, the native language, native dress, and native music are preserved and cherished as part of a valuable heritage. But more subtle manifestations of ethnic background persist even among those who do not explicitly identify with a particular ethnic background.

Recent studies suggest that this persistence of ethnic diversity is transmitted and ensured through the socialization of children, and it can survive even ethnic exogamy and the move away from "the old neighborhood." This transmission tends to go on through more subtle behaviors that were not necessarily part of the "Americanization" movement—that is, it is more likely to be found in drinking behavior than in language diversity, more likely to show up in spending habits or occupational choice than in distinctive dress (Greeley, 1981).

What is especially interesting is that the characteristics that were most feared or ridiculed in the day of the immigrants may be the very characteristics that have aided the success of their children and grandchildren. There is no single path to "success" in the United States, and, among the many paths, some are disproportionately chosen by some ethnic groups. The propensity of the Polish peasants to save and to invest in real estate has been one route to success. The choice of higher education and professional credentials among Jews has been another. The Irish proclivity for political brokering is associated with their overrepresentation in politics, law, and related fields.

Thus, although the social scientists of the day were unable to predict it, the turn-of-the-century immigrant groups brought with them more than their muscle power and ambition. They brought subtle cultural resources of a type we are only beginning to understand.

Lessons for Contemporary Immigration

Today's social scientists are likely to explain the disorganization and pathology in immigrant communities as a temporary result of uprooting and relocation, not as a result of inferior individuals or cultures. Forewarned by the experience of social scientists of an earlier time, we are less likely to predict that certain groups are incapable of success. But we are also unable to determine in advance the particular cultural and social resources that will enable an immigrant group to become economically successful in the United States. How many paths there are to success—and what paths may be blocked by current economic conditions, or what new paths may soon be opened—is also unknown. But given the experience of old immigrants, it seems impossible to state in advance that the golden door is barred for any national group.

Summary

Each immigrant stream had a diversity of individuals from many nations. While each national group differed from the others, each also differed from previous migrant streams from the same nation. But the process of stereotyping was always the same: both native-born Americans and earlier foreign arrivals ignored the differences, blurred the details, and produced the typical immigrant caricatures.

Although the popular image of the old immigrants is that they were unskilled peasants and laborers who brought few skills to America, this was never true. From earliest times the new nation advertised for skilled artisans. Every immigrant stream brought skilled laborers as well as professional and commercial workers.

Immigration patterns were similar for each national stream. At first it was a trickle, but it soon swelled to large proportions, as friends and relatives were told of opportunities in America. Those who came settled together in immigrant communities, which were to be found in every American city by the middle of the nineteenth century (though less often in the South than elsewhere).

These communities of immigrants were viewed with hostile fear by many Americans who wished the immigrants were "more like us." Scholarly studies and articles in the popular journals decried the hordes of immigrants who had invaded American cities and threatened to corrupt American virtues and values. In spite of all this, the immigrants were successful in becoming an integral part of American society. The successful record of generations of immigrants cannot be ignored when one examines the characteristics of immigration in contemporary America.

5
The "New Immigration"— Discontinuities in the Debate

All those who addressed themselves to immigration policy questions in ages past would have insisted that their age had "special" problems. If we, too are about to make the same assertion, we must concede that past observations may well have been accurate in principle. If one can cut the continuum of immigration policies into certain "eras," it seems reasonable to say that each era had special problems. If we assert that there are special problems at present, it is with the uneasy awareness that future writers may not be willing to concede that our experience is quite as "special" as we think it is.

The claim that we are in a "new era" of immigration circumstances is based on one or more of three factors. The first has to do with the incoming population—the claim that the character of the immigration stream has changed. The other two have to do with the receiving country—the claim that the institutional apparatus into which the immigrants are received has changed, and the claim that the political climate has changed, mandating new elements in our immigration policy (see, for example, Tanten, 1979; Graham, 1980). We now examine each of these claims in turn.

The Character of the Current Migration Stream

Immigration continues, of course, from all over the globe. Nevertheless, most thoughtful Americans are especially aware of the movement of population across the largely unguarded and probably unsealable border between the United States and Mexico—a movement that might make Hispanic Americans the largest minority group in the country. What is not so obvious is that the northward flow across the border is only part of a larger stream of immigration that is also proceeding by air and water. Substantial numbers of immigrants, many illegal, are coming from Guatemala, El Salvador, and Nicaragua, as well as the other countries of Central and South America.

From the Caribbean, illegal entrants, often in the guise of Puerto Ricans, are entering from the Dominican Republic and Haiti. Except for

75

the Haitians, all of these illegal entrants speak Spanish. Furthermore, there are substantial numbers of illegal immigrants from Europe, from the countries whence came many of the immigrants who arrived on our shores betwen 1850 and 1920—particularly from Poland, Yugoslavia, Italy, and also the Republic of Ireland. Some are visa overstayers. Others, particularly those from the British Commonwealth countries, enter undetected across the Canadian border.

The argument that Hispanic immigration constitutes a "crisis" usually contains the following elements:

> The current invasion of large numbers of Hispanic immigrants, many of them illegal, constitutes a radically different crisis because the immigrants are, for the most part, so unskilled and uneducated that they cannot find employment in adequately paid jobs. Instead, they are segregated in dead-end, low-wage jobs, and threaten to enlarge the poverty class. They are likely to become a further burden on an already-overworked welfare system. Employers pay them a pittance and refuse to upgrade their productivity, knowing that their poverty-level wages will be supplemented from the public purse. In addition, these immigrants represent an increase in the "nonwhite" component of the population, thereby adding to the nation's chronic racial problems. They seem to be strongly wedded to their own Hispanic culture, and under the influence of the current bilingual militancy may become a permanent, rapidly growing "un-Americanized" segment of the population. Because of the proximity of these immigrants' lands of origin, the flow of immigration is out of control, there is a great increase in undocumented aliens, and the immigrants lack a permanent commitment to the United States. Finally, for reasons that have to do with their culture, their high fertility, their lack of commitment, the lack of economic opportunity, or American racism, they seem to be much less able to convert education and labor market experience into occupational attainment and higher earnings. It would appear, therefore, either that they cannot be assimilated or that they can be assimilated only at costs that are so high that the country cannot afford them.

The implicit claim here is that all, or a great number, of these supposed traits of the Hispanic migration are different from those of other migrations. If the present large immigration stream, with its noticeable Hispanic character, is not different in any fundamental fashion from past immigration, then it would seem to follow that the traditional response of the United States to immigration, as it has been shaped through the years, can with minor modifications deal with the current "crisis." But part of the difficulty in dealing with the illegal immigration "crisis" is that it has been all too readily assumed that the present "invasion" of immigrants is fundamentally different from previous "invasions." This assumption must be carefully analyzed to see if it is true, and, if so, in what respects. For only when the deviation from past immigration is clearly specified will it be obvious which aspects of the policies that have served us through the years need to be drastically changed.

In the argument that today's immigration crisis is truly different, the key elements seem to be the following:

Large

Illegal

Unskilled and uneducated

Labor market

Poverty class

Nonwhite

Hispanic culture

Bilingual militancy

Out of control

Lack of permanent commitment

High rates of fertility

From these points emerges the conclusion by some that the current immigrants are not assimilable. In raising questions about each of these terms of argument, we do not intend to suggest that they are necessarily erroneous or necessarily valid, but merely to indicate that each must be investigated carefully to determine precisely the difference between contemporary immigration and previous immigration. We discuss each of these in turn, and we add a discussion on the "brain drain," the migration of highly skilled workers, particularly from developing countries, to the United States.

Large. Current legal immigration is around 600,000 persons a year; this includes the nearly 300,000 admitted by quota, relatives who are admitted ouside the quota (about 125,000 a year in recent years), and refugees. For obvious reasons, the refugee component fluctuates the most from year to year. (As an addition to the population, immigration can be compared to the approximately 3 million live births that occur every year.) Current illegal immigration is no doubt substantial, but we do not know how large. A recent study by three statisticians at the U.S. Bureau of the Census estimated that in 1980 there were 3 million to 6 million illegal aliens in the United States, but the estimates of the annual net or gross increase are even less precise (Siegel, Passell, and Robinson, 1981). Nor do we know what the possible upper limit for such immigration might be. But however large the current immigration may be, it is being absorbed by a population base much larger than that which absorbed a million immigrants a year in the early years of this century. We do not know the answer to the question "how large?" and we have no theoretical answer to the question "how large is too large?" To answer these questions, we would need to know a great deal more about the country's ability to absorb immigrants and about the immigrants themselves.

Illegal. Illegal immigration is not new. There are persons who are now Americans who jumped ship, slipped over borders, or connived in other ways to enter the country without detection or in a fraudulent manner. The fact of illegality creates a host of subsidiary problems—crime, corruption, exploitation—that must not be ignored. But the critical questions have to do with other subjects—skills, jobs, assimilation. The legal immigration of poor Hispanics has been sharply limited, making some of them illegal entrants, precisely because it has been assumed that the cost of absorbing large numbers of poor and uneducated persons from other countries is greater than the U.S. is willing to pay.

Unskilled and uneducated. The Hispanic immigrants are certainly no less skilled or less educated than many earlier European immigrants. The critical issue is whether the structure of the American industrial economy has so changed that the ladder of occupational success is far more difficult to climb for the uneducated, and for their children as well. In fact, as we shall show in the next chapter, it is an error to assume that all illegal immigrants, Hispanic or otherwise, are unskilled. Many skilled workers are in the illegal immigration stream; this is particularly true of skilled workers in the building trades. Some illegal aliens are from the middle class in their country of origin. This was brought home to Americans most forcefully over the July 4th weekend in 1980, when thirteen illegal Salvadorean entrants—all from the middle class—died in the Arizona desert while trying to enter the country. Other illegal aliens are professionals who receive training in the U.S. and overstay their visas rather than return home.

Labor market. Most immigrants to the United States started in low-level, low-wage jobs in times past; so the critical question is not whether the Hispanic immigrants take low-level jobs, but whether there is a chance for them to leave those jobs. If they remain in low-paying jobs they may become part of a new "welfare" or "near-welfare" class, putting an even greater strain on the rest of the nation.

Poverty class. The pertinent question is not whether the new immigrants are poor. Many immigrants have been relatively poor. The question is whether there is any realistic possibility that they will emerge from poverty. Research with 1970 Census of Population data suggests that non-Hispanic immigrants have little trouble reaching earnings parity with native-born Americans after a decade, but the achievements of Mexican immigrants—for whatever reasons—are much less dramatic and even native-born persons of Mexican origin have lower levels of schooling and earnings than other native-born Americans (Chiswick, 1978a, 1979, 1982a).

Nonwhite. This word is so loaded that we hesitate to use it. Yet it does seem to be the case that Americans regard Hispanics as "nonwhite," regardless of their skin color. Some Hispanics describe themselves as a racially distinctive "brown race." In fact, Hispanics do not constitute a single racial group. Hispanic is an ethnic not a racial label, and many races are represented within this ethnic group, including white, black, native-American, and Asian.

Yet some of the fear and resentment of Hispanics probably is racial in origin, and we do not wish to minimize its importance. But this is hardly new. Asians were certainly the objects of racial prejudice. Chinese were excluded from admission beginning in 1882; the Japanese "gentlemen's agreement" in 1907 was intended to bar the immigration of Japanese. The "Asiatic barred zone" eliminated the immigration of most other Asian groups, especially Hindus and Malays. But the Dillingham Commission also spoke quite explicitly of Southern and Eastern European immigrants as "racially inferior stock." "Nonwhite," whatever the word connotes, may be a special problem only because it is combined with the other realities described by the words "large," "unskilled," "illegal," and "out of control."

It is interesting to consider the case of the Puerto Ricans in this regard. Puerto Ricans are not immigrants; they are American citizens. They are part of the constant internal migration in America that is characteristic of an ambitious, restless people. They are citizens of the United States traveling within its national boundaries. Yet, along with Mexicans and other Hispanics, they are seen as foreigners who take jobs and housing away from native-born Americans. The United States government has classified them as a minority, and both their detractors and their leaders describe them as members of a "brown" race.

In fact, the portion of the Puerto Rican population that classifies itself as nonwhite results from the mix of Spanish conquistador and African slave. But this group does not, by any standard, constitute a separate race.

The black populations of Washington, D.C., and of Atlanta are greater than the black population of San Juan. Puerto Ricans, less color-conscious than other U.S. citizens, classify themselves as white, negro, or trigueño and accept the variety of color and the mixture of race on the island. Once they migrate to northern cities, Puerto Ricans lose the sense of great variety of coloring intrinsic to a people who accept racial intermarriage freely, and blend into a nondescript "nonwhite." They are seen as darker than the Italians and Greeks who were feared sixty years ago. And, in turn, it is often immigrants from Southern Europe who resent the movement into their neighborhoods of the darker skinned Puerto Ricans.

Puerto Ricans are the first people to become part of American society who rather freely accept social mingling between blacks and whites. The problems this presents have been extensively documented by both mainland and Puerto Rican sociologists, but nowhere is it as poignantly expressed as it is by the Puerto Rican writer Piri Thomas (1967). In his autobiography, *Down These Mean Streets*, he is constantly torn by not knowing whether to identify with blacks or with Puerto Ricans. Another book, *Two Blocks Apart*, very effectively contrasts the lives of an Irish boy and a Puerto Rican boy who live in the same neighborhood. The complications of roles for Puerto Ricans in mainland cities is summed up by the Puerto Rican child: "Me, I'm Puerto Rican, colored, and I'm not going to turn my back on that, but, if you ask me, if I could say: 'Which would you rather be?' Well, I mean you've got to face it. I mean anybody would. If you ask me, which I'd rather be, well, man, I'd rather be white" (Mayerson, 1965, p.14). It is easier for the white immigrant to be accepted by American society than it is for the immigrant—or even the citizen—with dark skin.

Hispanic culture. Some observers have contended that there is an especially tenacious loyalty to Hispanic culture that would slow down, if it did not impede entirely, "Americanization." It may well be that Hispanic immigrants do have a special loyalty to their culture. However, the economic success of Cuban immigrants in Miami and of some Dominican immigrants in New York suggests that Hispanic culture, as such, is no obstacle to achievement. Indeed, one may do quite well economically and still preserve much of one's own culture. We are discovering two things. First, the durability of the ethnic cultures is quite amazing and subtle. To a greater extent than previously supposed, most Americans tenaciously cling to their ethnic cultures, and the Hispanics are therefore no different. It is true that the culture is transmitted in only dimly perceived ways through childrearing, patterns of family interaction, and other subtle social cues, but it is nonetheless transmitted. Second, it may well be that the very traits that critics have labeled as least "American" have provided the measure of success for some immigrant groups. The Polish habit of thrift, the Chinese habit of working long hours, and the Jewish habit of investing in the children's education have all aided the economic success of these groups. It is not at all clear that one must abandon one's heritage to be successful in America.

If this is true, then the fear of Hispanic cultural endurance must be a fear of a tenacity that is unusual and of a culture whose persisting characteristics retard Americanization or economic success. It may be, however, that it is the cultural difference per se that is feared. There is some historical evidence to suggest the latter. The close proximity of Mexico to the Southwest has led to some friction between Mexican and "anglo" (white anglophone) cultures, as happens when any two distinctive populations share overlapping land areas. The concern about Hispanic culture may be a concern about cultural dominance—not so much a fear that Hispanics will not assimilate as that they will seek cultural dominance, especially in those parts of the country where their numbers are significant.

This concern is not new, for it has been present to some extent with all large immigrant groups. From its beginnings as a state, Pennsylvania was concerned about the predominance of German language and culture versus English language and culture. Nor is the concern about Hispanic culture new. As the western and southern expansion of United States settlers continued through the early 1800s, more and more contact with the Spanish colonial empire became inevitable. This was true not only in what is today the Southwest, but also in California and along the Gulf Coast. The tension between the "anglos" and the "Hispanics" was perhaps inevitable, and it culminated in repeated skirmishes and war. Subsequently, the victorious "anglos" on many occasions so dominated and discriminated against the indigenous Hispanic population (not to mention the small Hispanic immigrant population) that some degree of hostility was bound to remain on both sides (McLemore, 1973). The Hispanics were encouraged to turn in upon their own community and reinforce already-strong familial ties, as well as their cultural heritage, and the "anglos" were affected by some fear and guilt over what had occurred. In two senses, then—the historical basis for hostility and the proximity of Mexico—Hispanic culture may prove to be a stumbling block: not necessarily a stumbling block to the economic success of the Hispanics, but rather a stumbling block to their acceptance by the surrounding society.

Bilingual militancy. Although other groups, most notably the Germans, tried to maintain separate cultural enclaves complete with their own language and fought this battle with resourcefulness and vigor, the Hispanics are currently doing it with much wider support in the elite nonimmigrant society because of the cultural values of the time. The civil rights militancy of the 1960s forcefully changed the passive acceptance of an inferior status by any group. Both a Supreme Court decision and Congressional initiatives made it politically possible to offer extensive bilingual training, although the views about what constitutes an appropriate bilingual education program are nearly as numerous as its advocates.

Hostility toward bilingualism is powerful among many Americans. The Quebec separatist crisis in Canada is often used as an example to demonstrate that language can be an enormously divisive force in a society. This argument ignores the historical reality of the political, social, and economic segregation of the French-speaking Quebecois, and the fact that, although officially bilingual, Canada in reality consists of two monolingual populations. An ever-increasing, geographically concentrated, and more militant and impoverished Hispanophone minority might well be the most serious threat to the country's unity since the Civil War. Still, it is not clear that the United States could not absorb more linguistic diversity, although a multilingual society or a monolingual society may be more stable than one in which a language dichotomy exists along regional, ethnic, or economic lines.

It is worth mentioning that there is also considerable opposition to bilingualism in the Hispanic community, and this opposition will grow among parents if they become convinced that it is an obstacle to the economic achievement of their children. Finally, there has been for a long time a Hispanophone cultural minority in the Southwest that has not greatly disturbed the tranquility of the republic. We do not wish to minimize the bilingual/bicultural difficulties, but we believe that the assumption that bilingualism is itself the problem should be replaced by a pragmatic investigation of this issue within the context of the broader issue of ethnic diversity.

Out of control. In the sense that our current policies cannot stop it, illegal immigration is out of control. But it is not beyond the control of the United States should the nation decide to mount a massive campaign to stop it, with the appropriate economic and political resources. In addition, most who argue that illegal immigration is not controllable, and hence that we should not try to control it, do not apply a similar test to other violations of the law. One would not argue that the existence of murder, robbery, and littering, in spite of attempts to enforce laws against such behavior, means that there is no public control over such acts. The question is the optimal level of enforcement of law, whether in regard to illegal migration, murder, robbery, or littering, and whether current enforcement efforts are at this optimal level. Indeed, the increase in illegal immigration in the last decade is not surprising. The growing disparity between employment opportunities in the U.S. and in Mexico has been accomplished by a decline in enforcement efforts. This decline is due in part to court-imposed restrictions on INS activities and in part to a decline in real resources devoted to interior enforcement. Periodic efforts to obtain amnesty for illegal aliens already in this country appear to spur additional illegal immigration, probably because of the possibility of later claims to amnesty.

In another sense, the current immigration stream, like those that preceded it, is being controlled by the market. When we reach the point at which earnings differentials no longer compensate for the costs of immigration—and there is no way of knowing the numerical size of the labor force that corresponds to that point—then immigration will stop. But most Americans seem to be unwilling to let the market serve as the sole control on immigration.

Between the market solution and mobilization of the Armed Forces, then, lies the solution to the question of "control." The political clout and the economic muscle to exercise the control have not yet been ensured. And one should not expect perfect enforcement of immigration laws as long as there are substantial wage differences between the U.S. and its neighbors.

Lack of permanent commitment. There was much reverse migration (or reemigration) among earlier groups of immigrants. Today, however, circular migration between Mexico and the United States is considered a major problem. But just as the flow northward from Mexico to the United States cannot be easily stopped, neither can the return flow of illegal immigrants be easily stopped. When immigrants leave, the United States is not necessarily poorer. The nation benefits from their production and their consumption while they are here and benefits through exports from the dollars they take back home. But the cultural and social instability from such "wandering of the tribes" back and forth across the border seems to be unacceptable. Although this circular flow may account for a substantial proportion of border crossings, there is reason to believe it directly affects only a very small proportion of Mexican and other Hispanic immigrants in the U.S. either legally or illegally. Census data on geographic mobility and surveys of "settled" illegal alien populations suggest that the reality of the circular flow is much less than the mythology would have one believe. (See, for example, Chiswick, 1980a, ch.4; Cornelius, 1976.) Ascertaining the precise magnitude of the circular flow warrants further study.

High rates of fertility. With immigration itself constituting 20 percent of American population growth, the rate of the immigrants has become a topic of considerable concern. Most recent immigrant groups have fertility rates that are somewhat higher than the American norm. In the case of Hispanics, the rate is dramatically higher: 97 births per 1,000 women per year, compared with 61 births per 1,000 non-Hispanic women (aged 14 to

44) living in the same states. But all the evidence shows that immigrant group fertility rapidly moves toward the American norm when the immigrants begin to move upward economically (Guest, 1982; Rindfuss and Sweet, 1977). Once again we are faced with the underlying issue of the potential for upward mobility among immigrants—and of the potential of the economy for supporting the mobility. It is worth noting, however, that recent research shows a movement toward the norm in fertility among several generations of Hispanic women. The convergence is most pronounced, as might be expected, among better educated women (Bean and Swicegood, 1982).

The brain drain. The political fears discussed above have mostly dealt with the internal politics of the United States. More recently, there has been a rising concern with the impact that U.S. immigration has on other nations, and on our relationships with them. Perhaps the most sensitive issue has been the "brain drain." But here the argument is that the immigration of skilled workers is contrary to U.S. interests because it complicates foreign policy and retards the economic development of the country of origin. (For an exchange of views on this issue see Chiswick, 1982c, Part One.)

The United States has many good reasons to encourage the immigration of skilled, productive workers to its shores. Every other country has a similar interest in retaining its skilled native workers. When native workers leave, the home country loses its investments in their childhood maintenance, their schooling, and whatever job experience they have gained. However, the loss might be offset in part or in full by immigrant remittances and by the increased skills and capital acquired in the U.S. by returning emigrants. Nothing stops immigrants from making voluntary contributions to their countries of origin. In addition, if one views the economic welfare of the population of the country of origin as including the well-being of the emigrants, a stronger case can be made for the benefits of emigration from low-income countries.

In the case of highly skilled professionals, the net loss or net gain may be much greater. Some have suggested that the United States should indemnify foreign countries for each immigrant admitted. A problem arises in part because many foreign professionals have been trained in American universities. Most universities make a good-faith effort to encourage their students to return to their home countries, but it is always tempting to encourage the best students to stay for a few more years. The additional stay is usually devoted to further training, and perhaps to research or to job experience. In some cases the university itself will offer a permanent position to the former student; in other cases, the "job experience" convinces a potential employer that the foreigner would be an excellent permanent employee. And even if neither of these events occurs, the former student may find that returning home has lost its charm, and remaining in the United States is more attractive. For other skilled immigrants, political instability or repression, or racial, ethnic, or religious discrimination, may have encouraged them to leave their home countries, and they may be loath to contribute funds to a regime that engages in such behavior.

There are, of course, other ways in which the brain drain may operate. American firms working abroad employ local counterparts, and then wish to keep them in employment. Foreign professionals seek a job change in a new setting. Political instability, which is most likely to alarm people with higher socioeconomic status, may encourage some professionals to leave for the United States.

In none of these cases is the "brain drain" planned or actively encouraged by American officials. Rather it is the result of America's higher salary structures, better working conditions, more modern technology, and often greater political stability and lesser discrimination. Receiving skilled workers seems to be, on balance, good for the United States. But its effects on our international relations and on the development of the Third World deserve concern as well.

The Character of the Receiving Country

Current immigration is different from previous immigration, according to some claims, because the United States of the 1980s is not the United States of the 1880s. The differences in the social, political, and economic environment affect the ability of the United States to absorb new immigrants. From this point of view, any group of immigrants, not just low-skilled immigrants, will have difficulty adjusting to the United States: if recent Hispanic immigrants have difficulties, it is partly the times and not just their personal characteristics.

This argument is predicated on the assumption that vast, far-reaching structural transformations in the United States have particularly serious consequences for those who come here from other countries. These changes may be summarized under three categories: legal-definitional changes, transformations of the economy, and institutional changes in the sending countries.

Legal-Definitional Changes

As chapter 3 explains, the 1965 Immigration Amendments had the effect of intensifying the problem of illegal migration from the Western Hemisphere because no numerical restrictions had previously been placed on this migration. Thus, this legislative action defined much of the increased migration across the southern border during the 1960s and 1970s as illegal. We have good reason for regarding the problem of illegal immigration as recent.

A second issue, dealt with at length in subsequent chapters, is the extent to which legal entitlements to income transfer benefits were extended in the United States between 1924 and 1965, when immigration from the Eastern Hemisphere was strictly regulated. Not only was the prosperity of the United States being limited more strictly to those within the nation's borders, but also the distribution of that prosperity was being altered. The groundwork for current transfer payment programs was laid during the 1930s, when more people were leaving the U.S. than were entering and immigration was not regarded as a problem. The issue of entitlements for the foreign-born arose with a vengeance in the late 1960s and the 1970s, not just because of changes in the number and characteristics of immigrants, but also because of the political concerns embodied in the "War on Poverty" and "Great Society" programs. Large waves of Asian and Hispanic immigrants arrived just as affirmative action guidelines were being drafted to include Asian-Americans and Hispanic-Americans. Alarm about the need to provide welfare benefits for Americans who did not work was quickly associated with alarm about foreigners. Immigrants seemed to aggravate the welfare burden, whether they worked themselves, allegedly taking jobs away from native workers, or whether they received welfare and refused to work. And roughly the same arguments made to explain the internal migration of U.S. minorities were applied to the immigration of foreigners: they were coming here because welfare benefits were higher and life was better. But because the same cities were often the destinations of both the native minority groups and the immigrants, greater racial tensions and greater welfare burdens were feared.

At the same time, the growing emphasis on civil rights made us uneasy about excluding immigrants from the programs once they were here. It seemed easier for a variety of reasons to exclude them at the border. While it is true to say that restrictionism is an old theme in U.S. immigration thought, the current restrictionism takes shape against this somewhat different background.

A different issue is the redefinition of the United States from a country with vast resources and one that needed immigrant labor, to a country with limited resources and growing demands on those resources. A new emphasis on air quality, water quality, the depletion of minerals, and the loss of farmland has taken shape through the environmental movement. Many of the environmentalists oppose continued immigration for fear that it will merely increase the numbers dependent upon the natural resources without in any way increasing the resources. It is easy to caricature this position as one that states, "immigrants are pollutants"—a comment surely worthy of the Dillingham Commission. But this concern is more serious than that caricature recognizes.

It is true that the U.S. population is much larger now than it was during the height of the European immigration. And certainly there is no longer any sense that we require further immigrants merely to exploit resources already here. But because economic development is to some degree a continuation of the development of natural and human resources, the economic absorption of immigrants has been able to continue. Indeed, the foreign-born are now a much smaller portion of the American population than they were in 1900. It seems difficult to muster data to support an argument that immigrants are less frugal, less productive, or less concerned with natural-resource and environmental issues than the native-born.

But the argument can be made that immigrants increase the burden on the environment because they increase the rate of population growth, both by entering the population themselves and by having children. Fertility is frequently higher among immigrants than among native-born Americans, but that generalization does not hold for all groups, and a rapid movement toward the American fertility norm usually takes place. Although it is true that immigrants increase the rate of population growth, it is difficult to discern a significant increment of environmental degradation due to their presence. Experts are divided about the "optimal" rate of population increase for promoting economic growth. Some believe that in the U.S. context economic growth and population growth are largely independent of each other. At any rate, the U.S. population growth rate could certainly be considered moderate.

Economic Transformations

The most important single transformation has been in the types of skills demanded in the labor force. The relative demand for unskilled labor has shrunk, as has the relative demand for semi-skilled workers. Demand for white-collar and professional workers, in contrast, has remained strong. The reality of the change in demand from blue-collar to white-collar, and from industrial work to the service and professional sectors, is unquestioned. But one may question the conclusions about immigration that have been drawn from this fact.

First, not all of the immigrant stream is untrained. There were always skilled and unskilled workers in the immigration stream to the United States. The Hispanic migration stream contains substantial numbers of skilled workers, especially craftsmen, and other workers who have come from urban rather than rural settings. This is true even of illegal immigrants.

Second, there are still jobs available for the untrained and unskilled, and they are known on the immigrant grapevine. Even skilled workers often take these jobs on a temporary basis while they "get their bearings" in the United States. Many of these jobs are not found in manufacturing, although some are; our image of unskilled work in the industrial sector is partly out of date. Many of the unskilled jobs are found in the service industries, especially in personal services. Domestic work continues to attract large numbers of immigrants. And farm labor is perhaps the best-known of the occupations for Latin American immigrants.

If the jobs are available—and the immigrants would not come if they were not—why are they not filled by Americans? It is too facile to say simply that these are jobs that Americans won't take. Americans do demand higher wages than many immigrants, partly because Americans have alternative sources of income, both public and private, if they do not work. The immigrant usually has no alternatives and has come here because a low-wage job in the U.S. may still provide a higher standard of living than the immigrant's best opportunity in the home country. The geographic distribution of labor demand is different from the distribution of unemployment, and the wages offered for the jobs Americans won't "fill" may be too low to induce relocation of American workers. This may explain why farm labor jobs in the Southwest have not drawn workers from the distressed industrial cities and black ghettos of the Northeast. In some jobs, the employer may prefer foreign workers. Some employers hire illegal aliens as part of a plan to avoid complying with government regulations, knowing that their work force will be unable to complain about wages or working conditions to the regulatory authorities.

There is another answer to the question of why Americans won't take the jobs immigrants take, and that is that many Americans do take them. Many of these jobs are entry level and offer a low wage and work experience, but little else. They are often temporary or seasonal and offer little in the way of fringe benefits. Many Americans, particularly youths or adult women newly returned to the labor market, have held such jobs and then moved on to better paid, more secure work. Immigrants are often willing to take the same entry-level jobs and for the same reasons: they offer a chance to learn skills relevant to the labor market and to earn money at the same time. It is fairly typical to find that there is some downward occupational mobility among new immigrants when comparing their last occupations in their home countries with their first occupations in the U.S. If immigrants are permitted to change jobs, they are likely to move to better paid and higher status occupations after they have become familiar with the American setting (Chiswick, 1978; North, 1978).

No matter how well-enforced government regulations are, and no matter how computerized, automated, or efficient American industry becomes, it is inevitable in any complex economy that there will be nooks and crannies of labor demand, odd jobs and temporary work, seasonal jobs and tide-me-over paydays. And so it is inevitable that unskilled immigrant workers will find places where they can fit in and earn a wage, even if it is a small wage by the standards of American workers. Viewing these possibilities as holes to be plugged, so that the demand for foreign labor will be quenched, is futile and counterproductive for a smoothly running economy. Moreover, as long as America is a country in which entrepreneurship is rewarded, some immigrants will seek to open one more ethnic restaurant, or offer one more gardening service, or provide better or more reliable goods or services of some other variety. Some immigrants will create their own labor demand.

The fact that there are many job opportunities that pay very little or are insecure is a public policy issue only if it becomes impossible for anyone—native- or foreign-born—to leave the insecure job and compete for a better-paying and more secure job. This is the issue that so-called "dual labor market theorists" have raised. They have argued that for a variety of psychological, structural, and economic reasons, workers in the lower-paid "secondary" jobs become locked into a "secondary" labor market from which they can never escape. There is considerable debate about the extent to which such a dual market exists, but the debate itself would seem to be evidence against a limitation on the labor mobility of immigrants. And there is no support in the empirical literature on the earnings or occupational mobility of immigrants for the view that they are locked into the low-wage jobs they may accept upon arrival. Indeed, what is impressive is the rise in both their earnings and their occupational status with exposure to the U.S. labor market. Although the earnings and occupational statuses of Mexican immigrants are lower than those of European immigrants, Mexican immigrants (including illegal aliens) also experience a rise in earnings, employment, and occupational status with a longer period of residence in the U.S. (For studies of the earnings and occupational mobility of legal and illegal immigrants, see Chiswick, 1978a, 1978b, 1979, 1982b; Featherman and Hauser, 1978; North, 1978; North and Houstoun, 1976.)

The American economy has undergone vast transformations since 1924. The question that must be asked is, What is the impact of these changes on immigration? Does this transformation mean that immigration today is necessarily different from that at the turn of the century? Or is our capacity to absorb immigrants drastically diminished? We are not convinced that it is. There are times when our absorptive capacity has been strained—the depression of the 1930s being the foremost example—and in those years emigration from the United States exceeded immigration. To the extent that immigration to the United States is economically motivated, it is at least partly self-correcting.

However, a complete reliance on market mechanisms is not possible because of the relatively large number of immigrants who do not migrate solely for labor market reasons. Low-skilled immigrants are aware of the availability of income transfers that may well exceed what they could earn only by hard work in their home countries. To the extent that noneconomic factors are important determinants of the migrations of persons called refugees, these persons too may come to the U.S. in spite of what may seen to be adverse labor market opportunities. Others may be willing to sacrifice income to accompany or to be reunited with family members. To the extent that immigration policy emphasizes family reunion, political migration, and other noneconomic motivations, a concern with the absorptive capacity of the economy will be necessary.

Changes in the Sending Countries

Europe experienced a population explosion of sorts during the 1800s. That, combined with enclosure procedures and the displacement of peasants, encouraged the great outmigration to the New World. Immigration to the United States as a response to population pressures is thus nothing new. But the magnitude of those pressures has grown dramatically, putting American immigration in a new context.

World population growth has accelerated rapidly since World War II. An estimated 2 billion people inhabited the globe in 1950; that number had doubled by the mid-1970s to over 4 billion. Even the most optimistic observers concede that world population is likely to exceed 6 billion people by the year 2000, and some expect an even higher figure. Although fertility rates have declined in many parts of the world, mortality rates, particularly for children, have also fallen. The large number of children born after World War II and now becoming parents themselves will provide considerable momentum for population growth in the next twenty years.

This population growth has little affected Europe, the traditional source of U.S. immigrants. Birth rates have fallen to record low levels throughout all parts of Europe, with several countries now reporting reproduction rates that, if sustained, would lead to smaller populations. Even in Eastern and Southern Europe, whose explosive population growth at the turn of the century so alarmed some Americans, birth rates have been low. Indeed, in some cases, these rates have remained low despite considerable, even desperate efforts by Eastern European governments to raise them. Where population growth rates have zoomed is in developing countries. In Asia, an area largely barred from U.S. immigration until 1965, the population growth rate, if sustained, would lead to a doubling of the population within thirty-five to forty years. In Africa, never yet the source of large voluntary streams of immigrants to the United States, fertility rates are often even higher than in Asia, although higher mortality rates have produced some dampening effects on population growth (Hauser, 1979). But both of these continents are separated by oceans from the United States, and the lack of a tradition of immigrating to the United States and the difficulty of transportation may retard immigration.

In Latin America and the Caribbean, population growth rates continue to be high and there is a well-established pattern of northward migration, though some of it is circular. In contrast to Asia and Africa, whose people were all but barred from entering the United States until 1965, there had been only minor regulation of immigration from the independent countries of the Western Hemisphere. Although changes in all sending countries are of interest to us, those in Latin America and the Caribbean must be of particular interest.

Latin American and Caribbean mortality rates fell rapidly with the introduction of modern medicine; this reduction, combined with sustained high fertility rates, led to rapid rates of population growth during the 1950s, 1960s, and early 1970s (United Nations, 1973, pp.27-28). More recently, there has been a leveling off or decline of fertility rates in many of these countries. The decline has been quite remarkable in some countries, such as Colombia; in other countries, such as Mexico, the decline appears to be more modest but is a decline nonetheless (Lightbourne and Singh, 1982). However, in every country of Latin America there are large numbers of young persons born during the high fertility years and now looking for employment (for example, see U.S. Department of Labor, 1979). In Mexico, about one-half the population is age 15 or younger. This is typical of most other Latin American and Caribbean countries, with the exception of Argentina and Chile.

Besides entering their prime working years, these young people are also entering the prime migration years. Most migration streams (except for refugees) are dominated by young adults. Unemployment rates are high in many of these countries. Migration, either to cities or to other countries, presents itself as an attractive alternative to remaining in increasingly crowded agricultural areas. But even in the cities, unemployment is likely to be high, and international migration appears to be a better alternative. The data on international migration in Latin America and the Caribbean are sparse, but one has the impression of an entire continent potentially on the move. Illegal immigration streams flow from Paraguay to Argentina, from Colombia to Venezuela, from Guatemala and El Salvador to Mexico, and from Haiti to many Caribbean countries. And of course, illegal immigration into the United States is attractive and feasible.

For Mexicans, the U.S. alternative is especially attractive because of its proximity, the relative ease of entry (land border rather than water border, and relatively little guarded), and because many Mexicans have relatives with experience in the United States. Indeed, many have relatives with whom they may stay, or friends from their villages who may give them help. As with any other migration stream, those who have gone before can provide a helping hand to those who come later. That is why a history of migration is an important key to future migration.

Illegal immigration, as we implied above, is not limited to the United States. There is a continuing illegal migration stream among the Latin American countries, as well as to and within Europe and within Africa and the Middle East. Wherever there are jobs and legal barriers to mobility, there is likely to be illegal immigration to take advantage of the jobs. In early 1983, in response to falling oil prices, Nigeria was expelling one to two million illegal aliens from Ghana and other west African countries. And although national boundaries are much more closely watched than they once were, they are by no means sealed.

This situation has suggested to many Americans that one key to reducing the migration stream to the United States is to encourage further economic development in Latin America and the Caribbean. The idea is to provide jobs within the economy of these countries to employ those who would otherwise migrate to the U.S. While this idea has merit, it will take far longer than today's young people are likely to wait. Furthermore, some studies have indicated that initial efforts have backfired. The "border industrialization" program was designed to reduce illegal Mexican immigration by providing job opportunities in cities on the Mexican side of the border. Some believe that these programs, rather than keeping Mexican workers in Mexico, have attracted Mexican farm workers from the interior to the border towns, with illegal entry into the U.S. as the next step. In addition, the industrial jobs created have primarily employed young women, whereas most Mexican illegal alien workers have been men (Cross and Sandos, 1981).

Industrialization programs away from the border attracted young people to the cities, and from here they could also begin to see the advantages of moving north. The industrialization of agriculture means not only increased productivity, but also often a smaller number of workers producing the increased output. To draw an analogy, it was the economic development of Europe that in part displaced the peasants who later became immigrants. The economic development of Latin America, which is likely to produce many jobs in the long run, may displace many workers in the process.

For those who argue that today's immigration is dramatically different from that of previous eras, there is both contradictory and confirmatory evidence here. The "push" factors for immigration today are indeed very similar to those of the nineteenth and early twentieth centuries, but they occur on different continents and they occur at quite different degrees of magnitude. Most important, they occur at a time when receiving countries are far more cautious about immigration than they were in the nineteenth century. In the end, this may prove to be the greatest difference between today's immigration and that of a century ago.

Summary

Many of the same immigration issues we face today have been faced by policy makers of the past. There are important continuities in both the issues raised and the answers made to them. But there are also legitimate grounds for arguing that today's immigration problem is set in different circumstances. Despite the similarities to earlier immigration streams, it is true that today's immigration stream, including illegal aliens, is disproportionately Spanish-speaking, that it is lower skilled relative to the U.S. labor force, and that for reasons of both history and geography there are new push factors encouraging immigration across the southern border. It is easier to be an alien (legal or otherwise) when one need only cross a contiguous border. It may also be true that today's economy is less well able to "absorb" large numbers of unskilled workers, although we are uncertain what the absorptive capacities are. It is our judgment that, overall, the continuities outweigh the discontinuities, and the similarities between past and present periods of immigration outweigh the dissimilarities. Certainly in terms of economic success today's immigrants are for the most part repeating the history of earlier migrants. This story is presented in the next chapter.

6

A Portrait of the New Immigrants

The "new immigration" now refers to that initiated by the 1965 Amendments to the 1952 Immigration and Nationality Act. This statute, whose provisions were implemented between 1965 and 1968, changed the character of American immigration in several ways (Keely, 1971). First, the abolition of the old national-origins quota system and of the severe restrictions on Asians led to changes in the ethnic composition of the immigrant population (Bouvier, 1977). One of the first effects of this change was a notable increase in the number of Asian immigrants (Hirschman and Wong, 1981). India, Pakistan, and Thailand became important sources of immigrants, along with Asian countries from which small numbers of immigrants had come in the previous two decades—the Philippines, Hong Kong, China, and Korea. In addition, with the fall of Saigon in 1975, a substantial Indochinese immigration started, and since 1975 over one-half million Indochinese refugees have entered the U.S.

Theoretically, the broadening of country-of-origin limitations should also make it possible for large numbers of Africans to immigrate to the United States. This has not as yet happened because of the lack of immediate relatives in the U.S. and the much lower average level of labor market skills. In addition, there has been little pressure to admit refugees from such African trouble spots as Somalia, Uganda, and Zimbabwe. Considering the unstable economies and political turmoil in Africa it would seem only prudent for policy makers to consider Africa as a source of increased immigration, both of economic immigrants and of refugees, in coming decades.

The new immigration also includes, to a far greater extent than previous eras, Latin American and Caribbean immigrants. Residents of the Western Hemisphere were not subject to numerical restrictions (except for the small subquotas for the dependents of European nations), but they migrated in relatively small numbers in the first half of the twentieth century. However, by 1965 there was a growing immigration from Latin America. This was one reason that the limitation of 120,000 visas a year was introduced in the 1965 Amendments. Since then, however, the supply of immigrants from the Western Hemisphere has risen sharply.

A second shift in the new immigration is the increased emphasis on family reunification. Although the principle of family reunification existed in previous legislation, it received new prominence in the 1965 Amendments. The legislation made kinship ties the primary rationing device for the Eastern Hemisphere, both through the exemption of immediate relatives of U.S. citizens and through the preference system. Immediate relations of U.S. citizens living in the Western Hemisphere were also exempt from limitations, but for those subject to numerical limits a first-come, first-served rationing system was used until 1977 legislation that extended the kinship-based preference system to the Western Hemisphere. One practical result of this shift is the increased number of women, children, and older persons in the immigrant stream. Although this represents an increase in the dependent population, in many cases these family members are joining earlier immigrants who are already working in the U.S. labor market.

A third shift in the new immigration is the decline in the relative emphasis on skills as a rationing criterion. Under the 1952 Immigration and Nationality Act half of the national-origins-quota visas were to be based on some measure of skill. While one may question the effectiveness of the skill criteria adopted at the time, the 1965 Amendments and subsequent revisions represented a downplaying of the role of skill. Only 20 percent of the visas in the preference system are to be allocated on the basis of skill, but about 60 percent of these visas are used by the spouses and minor children of workers who receive the required labor market certification. Because of adjustments for the relatives of occupational-preference beneficiaries and the admission of immediate relatives of U.S. citizens, only about 6 percent of the nonrefugee immigrants in recent years have had to obtain labor certification. Of these, about two-thirds were in the United States when they received their immigrant visas. (For a more detailed analysis, see Goldfarb, 1982.)

The abolition of the national-origins quota system resulted in increased immigration from Asian countries. Because few potential immigrants from Asia had close relatives in the United States in the late 1960s, owing to earlier restrictions, other categories were the major avenues of entry. Many used the occupational preferences, and others used the nonpreference category, both investors and those with labor certifications, when visas were available. As of February 1983, for example, the third preference (professionals and persons of exceptional ability in the arts and sciences) had queues for only five areas in Asia: China, India, Korea, the Philippines, and Hong Kong. (As a dependency Hong Kong is subject to a ceiling of 600 visas a year instead of the 20,000 for an independent country.) The "backlog" of third-preference visas for the Philippines extended to August 1970, that is, applications approved 13 years ago were finally at the head of the queue to receive visas. The other occupational-preference category (sixth preference, for workers with skills in "short supply") had visa backlogs for the same areas.

As skilled Asian workers immigrate, and become citizens, the immigration of their relatives from Asia, under the exempt category and the kinship preference, is increased. In recent years backlogs have been forming, and growing, for the kinship preferences from the five Asian countries, in particular the second preference (spouses and children of resident aliens) and the fifth preference (siblings of U.S. citizens). The "longest" backlogs in these two preference categories are for the Philippines, stretching back to 1970 and 1979, and Hong Kong, stretching back to 1971 and 1978 (U.S. Department of State, 1983). As noted above, many Asian immigrants also entered the United States as refugees.

Immigration opportunities from African countries were also restricted by the national-origins system and the small subquotas within the mother country quota for dependencies. These limitations were not binding, however, because of the small supply of immigrants. Under the 1965 Amendments, immigration from Africa could not rapidly expand because of the absence of kinsmen already in the U.S., a consequence of immigration patterns over the past fifty years. In addition, the limited educational system in Africa has not generated a large number of persons who could obtain an additional preference as professionals or other skilled workers. Moreover, there is a tendency for African refugees to remain in Africa. What emigration has occurred among nonwhites from Africa has primarily been to the former European colonial powers.

Geographic Distribution of the New Immigrants within the United States

The new immigrants have more choices than did the immigrants of the 1800s in terms of entry ports. Many more immigrants arrive today by air than by sea, and so the port of entry may be inland. The growth of new international airports away from the traditional eastern seaboard sites makes it possible for the initial entry to be in almost any part of the country. Nevertheless, in 1970 the state of New York was still disproportionately preferred by immigrants. The remarkable persistence in the geographic dispersion of immigrants is due in part to the durability and vitality of ethnic communities that are still able to provide a welcome to the immigrant from the old country.

However, some important new sites have emerged. Traditionally, the South received few immigrants. A new exception is Miami, with its large concentration of Cubans who fled Fidel Castro's communist revolution. Since then other Hispanics have been attracted to the Cuban-dominated Spanish-speaking enclave in Miami. Miami has become an important center for Latin Americans of all nationalities, and this in turn has helped to strengthen Miami's role as a center of banking, trade, and transportation with Latin America.

Mexican immigrants are more widely dispersed than conventional wisdom might suggest. Although, according to the 1970 Census of Population, 85 percent live in southwestern states, and in particular the large metropolitan areas of California, Texas, and Arizona, Mexican immigrants are also found in large numbers in midwestern industrial cities and New York City. Nor are Mexican immigrants predominantly rural; as with the general labor force, agricultural occupations account for smaller and smaller percentages of the Mexican labor force.

The immigrant population in the West Coast states, particularly California, increased with the growth in Asian immigration. In an effort to share the burden nationwide, Indochinese refugees were originally dispersed across the country, although it now appears that through secondary migrations many are gravitating to California (Gordon, 1980).

The Success of the New Immigrants

Perhaps the most remarkable story about immigrants in general, and apparently about many new immigrants as well, is their economic success—a success that can be found in their earnings, employment, and occupational status in comparison with the native-born (Chiswick, 1978a, 1978b, 1979, 1982b; Featherman and Hauser, 1978; Martin, Poston, and Goodman, 1980). As we have already noted, immigrant men initially have lower earnings, but they reach earnings parity with equally situated native-born men within ten to fifteen years after immigration, and thereafter they have higher earnings. The native-born sons of immigrants earn 5 to 10 percent more than equally situated native-born men with native-born parents (Chiswick, 1977b, 1979). By equally situated we mean a comparison of men of the same age, schooling, area of residence, and race and ethnicity.

The dynamics of this situation appear to be related to two phenomena—the self-selection of immigrants and the transferability of skills (see Chiswick, 1978a, 1878b, 1979). Immigrants tend to be different from their friends, neighbors, and kinsmen who choose not to leave their familiar surroundings. Immigrants tend to be more highly motivated, more aggressive, more entrepreneurial, and more ambitious, and some of these characteristics are passed on to their native-born children. As is the case for both inherited and environmental characteristics, there is a "regression toward the mean" between successive generations—the children of the most highly motivated parents would tend to be less highly motivated than their parents but more so than average children. By itself the self-selection factor would result in immigrants and their children having higher earnings than the native population, with the advantage dissipating as the number of generations a family has lived in the U.S increases. Indeed, data for the U.S. show that immigrants in this country for more than fifteen years and their children have higher earnings than natives, but the effect virtually disappears by the third or fourth generation.

The issue of the transferability of skills is particularly relevant for immigrants from non-English-speaking countries during their first fifteen years in the United States. On arrival their earnings tend to be low, but they rise sharply with duration of residence as English is learned, skills acquired in the country of origin are modified, and the immigrant obtains information about where and how his skills can be most highly rewarded. As a result of the increasing productivity in the labor market with duration of residence, earnings rise and, as indicated, reach parity with those of the native-born at about ten to fifteen years.

One notable exception to this pattern is the refugees. Selection is different for refugees; by definition, it includes political, religious, or ethnic factors far more often than is the case for economic migrants. Refugees may, therefore, be less favorably self-selected for labor market success. In addition, refugees tend to have skills that are less readily transferable than those of economic migrants. Were it not for the noneconomic motives many of them would not be migrants. Among professionals, for example, physicians are found in both economic migrant and refugee streams because their skills are readily transferable; lawyers and judges, whose skills are country-specific, appear in refugee streams, but seldom as economic migrants. As a consequence, refugees have lower earnings than economic migrants on arrival, and although their earnings rise more sharply with duration of residence, and the gap narrows, the earnings of refugees approach, but apparently do not equal or exceed, the earnings of the native-born.

The pattern just described for earnings also appears in studies of the occupational attainment of immigrants (Chiswick, 1978b). When comparing the occupation in the home country with the occupation held within the first five years in the U.S., immigrants experience downward occupational mobility, but with increased residence in the U.S. their occupational level rises. This U-shaped pattern of occupational status is deeper for economic migrants with less transferable skills (e.g., from Germany, France) than for economic migrants with more transferable skills (e.g., from Canada and England). However, the U is deeper for refugees (e.g., Cubans), whose skills are even less readily transferable. That is, refugees experience the steepest downward occupational mobility when they first come to the U.S., but they also have steeper upward occupational mobility with duration of residence (see Chiswick, 1978b).

The patterns described in the preceding paragraphs appear to be relevant for the new immigrants as well as for older immigrant groups. Although the countries of origin have changed, and for some countries there has been a change in whether the immigrants are primarily economic migrants or refugees, there is reason to believe that within these categories there have been no fundamental changes in the degree of economic success.

There is, however, one important exception to the generally optimistic picture of economic adjustment for immigrants, and what is particularly disquieting is that this is a rapidly increasing portion of the immigrant stream. Mexican immigrants earn substantially less than other white immigrants, even after one adjusts for their lower level of schooling, their lower average age, and their geographic concentration in the Southwest. Nor does the effect dissipate by immigrant generation (Chiswick, 1979, 1980a; Featherman and Hauser, 1978). Other things being equal, adult men of Mexican origin earn 15 to 25 percent less than other white men of the same immigrant generation.

Hispanics and the New Immigration

Major public concerns with the "new immigrants" have been centered almost exclusively on Hispanics, by which we mean Spanish-speaking immigrants from Latin America and the Caribbean. And, for many purposes, Haitians are included among Hispanics. Puerto Ricans are excluded from this discussion because they are U.S. citizens and therefore free to travel between the mainland and Puerto Rico at will. We assume that these circumstances may make their situation substantially different from that of other Caribbean immigrants.

Hispanic immigration to the United States is by no means new. Hispanic settlements in the Southwest and Florida predated the immigration of most groups to the English-speaking colonies. For several hundred years, and despite hostilities between the United States and Mexico, Spanish-speaking persons moved freely back and forth across the southern border.

To speak of "Hispanics" is almost inherently misleading. Although nearly all Latin American immigrants share a common language and there are similarities in their colonial history, the Hispanic countries differ greatly among themselves in economic, political, and ethnic characteristics. They are much more heterogeneous than is often recognized. The Hispanic immigrant streams include physicians who are themselves the sons of recent European immigrants to Argentina, unskilled dirt farmers from the Dominican Republic, Chilean professors, Colombian factory workers, Peruvian restauranteurs, Salvadorean merchants, and Mexican nurses. Among them are political refugees from the Cuban right, from the Chilean and Argentinian left, and from the Salvadorean left, right, and middle. Any discussion of "Hispanic immigrants" should not be construed as overlooking these differences. It is true, however, that most of the adverse reaction to Hispanics centers on those with few or no skills, particularly from Mexico, or on sudden large influxes of refugees.

At least since the time of the Monroe Doctrine, the United States has recognized a special relationship with the other independent countries of the Americas. "Good neighbor" policies were considered to be economically, politically, and socially sound. In this climate, relatively free movement across borders was commonplace and rarely challenged or obstructed, except of course for surveillance of smugglers and contraband. The extension of restrictionist sentiment to the Western Hemisphere is relatively recent.

The Closest Case: Mexican Immigration

The southern border with Mexico, because of the tradition of free movement, is a political border that does not accurately reflect the boundaries of language and culture. It is a long border that runs much of its course through desolate and unpopulated areas. For geographic, historic, and political reasons, some observers consider this border to be virtually unsealable. The passage of the 1965 Amendments and the imposition of numerical limits on Western Hemispheric migration has not been sufficient to obliterate these facts.

Illegal Immigration and Mexican Immigration

Illegal immigation is not new, although there may be greater concern about it today than there was previously (Select Commission on Immigration and Refugee Policy, 1981, p. 35). There have always been a certain number of ship-jumpers, a certain number of visa overstayers, and the occasional person who for one reason or another enters the country clandestinely. There are basically two types of illegal immigrants: the first group, properly called the "undocumented," have entered surreptitiously; the second group, whose documents are improper, include visa overstayers and abusers, as well as those who entered with fraudulent documents. It is probably easier for residents of the Western Hemisphere to enter the United States surreptitiously because of the long borders we share with Mexico and Canada and the relatively unguarded shoreline. But there are also large numbers of illegal aliens who are visa overstayers or abusers, and many of them are from the Eastern Hemisphere.

It is generally believed that eight to ten nations are the major source of the 3 to 6 million illegal aliens believed to be living in the United States (Siegel, Passel, and Robinson, 1981). It is believed that about half of the illegal aliens are Mexican nationals and that another 25 percent come from Mexico, Jamaica, Haiti, Taiwan, Korea, and the Philippines. The stock of Mexican illegal aliens would be much greater if it were not for the sustantial return flow. Most of the Mexican illegal aliens are from the five central Mexican states and the border state of Chihuahua (Cross and Sandos, 1981).

Illegal immigration and Mexican immigration are separate issues. The popular identification of Mexican immigration with illegal immigration confuses the two issues and overlooks the half of the illegal aliens who are not Mexican, as well as the many legal Mexican residents. One reason for this perception is the emphasis placed on the apprehension of Mexican illegal aliens by the Immigration and Naturalization Service (INS). In recent years nearly 90 percent of apprehensions have been of Mexican nationals who entered without inspection, that is, who entered surreptitiously. Apprehensions per dollar of budget expenditures are greater if resources are concentrated at the border, even if the net deterrent effect of the revolving-door border policy is minimal. In addition, recent policy decisions by the Department of Justice and budget appropriations, including a decline in real resources devoted to interior enforcement, have limited the interior enforcement capabilities of the INS. Thus, because of enforcement policies, apprehensions are not representative of the illegal population as a whole, and inferences made from such data should be interpreted with caution.

Nevertheless, the issue of Mexican immigration cannot be addressed without considering the issue of illegal immigration. Native-born Americans of Mexican descent as well as legally admitted Mexican immigrants are fearful that restrictions on illegal aliens and punitive measures against their employers will subject them to indiscriminate and arbitrary action. There is a basis for such fears in the wholesale deportations of the Mexican-origin population in the 1930s. Although comparable actions would almost certainly be considered unconstitutional today, Hispanics may well wonder if the political will to enforce the Constitution may once again be as weak as it was then. Failure to address the issue of illegal immigration, however, may have an adverse effect on the economic opportunities of Mexicans and other Hispanics legally admitted.

Trends in Mexican Illegal Immigration

In an important sense, the illegal alien "problem" along the southern border was created by the 1965 Amendments. Frequent border crossing to visit family, take temporary jobs, or shop was an established practice well before 1965. Efforts to trace the illegal alien problem to the previous existence of a Bracero Program, or to an inefficient and understaffed border patrol, or to demographic and economic changes on either side of the border offer only part of the story.

There was a substantial increase in the net influx across the Mexican border during the 1970s. Population and economic factors in Mexico were the "push" factors (Cross and Sandos, 1981). The Mexican population has been growing at an annual average rate of more than 2.5 percent; as a result, about 50 percent of the Mexican population is below the age of 15. Ever-larger numbers of teenagers and young adults look for work every year. Mexican government policies for the rural sector during the Green Revolution favored large capital-intensive farming, and the low fixed prices for maize in the 1960s and 1970s had the effect of subsidizing the urban population at the expense of the rural population. The impoverishment of the rural sector, particularly in the central region, encouraged migration to Mexico City, the border cities, and the United States. During the early 1970s, it was thought that the "Mexican miracle" of rapidly increasing productivity would be capable of absorbing much of the new labor. Later in the decade, for a variety of reasons, the creation of new jobs did not seem able to keep up with the increased numbers of job seekers. Some Mexican writers see U.S. investment as the source of the labor problem: capital-intensive industries that export their profits, they reason, created few jobs in Mexico, and this movement of profits to the U.S. was not counterbalanced by the immigration of "runaway shops" in search of cheap labor. Yet, in the absence of these U.S. investments, job opportunities in Mexico would be even more scarce. The Mexican government's own development policies also favored capital-intensive and skill-intensive activities. The euphoria of the "oil bonanza" soon passed without a major impact on employment opportunities.

Whatever the reason that Mexico's economic miracle faltered, the attractions of the U.S. labor market to the north were intensified, and the rapidly growing population of young adults has swollen the supply of immigrants to the United States. Whether the U.S. labor market constituted a "pull" factor that was stronger than the "push" factors is not clear, but there is no doubt that the United States offers abundance in comparison to the Mexican opportunity structure. And economic positions are always relative: Mexico now considers itself to have an illegal alien problem, with larger numbers of Central Americans seeking jobs in Mexico because of its greater prosperity and political stability.

Studies of illegal aliens from Mexico indicate that they are likely to have relatively more education than the average Mexican, to be young male workers, and to have some previous experience in an urban labor market (Cornelius, 1976; North and Houstoun, 1976). Data on the origins of Mexican illegal aliens in the U.S. suggest that about 70 percent are from the rural areas in the Central Plateau and that this proportion has not changed since the 1920s (Cross and Sandos, 1981). Many illegal aliens have worked for several periods in the United States, and their stays in the United States are often short. However, one study comparing legal with illegal entrants found that the stays of illegals were slightly longer. Some believe that circular migration among some subgroups of Mexican immigrants may be quite common along the southern border, and not only for agricultural workers, but the myth may exceed the reality. Using data from the 1970 Census of Population, an index of circular migration shows no difference between Mexican and other immigrants. (The index is the extent to which immigrants in the U.S. in 1970 who first came to the U.S. before 1965 were living outside the U.S. in 1965). The index is quite low—1.5 to 2.2 percent—for all immigrants (Chiswick, 1980a, ch. 4).

Illegal aliens have been located in all types of jobs, including relatively well-paid industrial jobs. No longer are they found only near the border, although most have probably spent at least some time near the border while learning about the U.S. labor market. Illegal entrants are less likely to bring dependents with them. Several studies have shown that illegals tend to be concentrated in manual occupations in urban areas (North and Houstoun, 1976). Illegal aliens appear to be overrepresented in low-paying industries, including household work, personal services, and the manufacture of nondurable goods in nonunionized shops. Comparisons of occupation distributions indicate little difference between legal and illegal aliens from Mexico who have been in the United States for the same length of time (Chiswick, in press).

The exact number of illegal aliens in the United States has been an issue of considerable speculation. Fragmentary data indicate that there has been a dramatic increase (Heer, 1979; Robinson, 1980; Bean, King, and Passel, 1983). Examples of these data include increased INS apprehension, otherwise inexplicable fluctuations in Texas mortality rates, and anthropological studies of Hispanic neighborhoods. With current demographic techniques, it is virtually impossible to pinpoint the number of Mexican-Americans or Hispanics in the country. The size of the Census undercount of Hispanics is difficult to determine with precision because vital statistics (birth and death rates) and immigration and emigration data are too inexact.

The Question of Mexican Mobility

Perhaps the most puzzling and disturbing research finding about Mexican immigrants has been their relative lack of success in the U.S. labor market. They are not the first group to have entered the country with relatively few educated members; previous racially identifiable groups, including the Chinese and Japanese, also started with mostly low-paid, low-skill employment. But the Mexicans are the only recent large immigrant group to have such low levels of education, occupation, and income, not just in the first generation in the U.S., but even in the second and third generations.

If it is the case that Mexicans are permanently different in some way from other groups, then the critics of the "new immigration" may be partially right. They have claimed that (1) new groups of immigrants are unassimilable, or (2) conditions have changed so much that previously assimilable groups can no longer be assimilated. As we have seen, such charges have not previously proven to be correct. Perhaps the Mexicans are the exception. It seems appropriate here to review the major explanations for the "Mexican exception."

The difference in composition of the Mexican immigrant group. It is true that there are differences in the composition of this group in comparison to other immigrant groups, but these do not account for the lack of success among Mexican immigrants. In the studies alluded to above, such factors as years of schooling, labor market experience, and age were held constant. Even when one holds constant these variables, those of Mexican origin have lower levels of occupational status and lower earnings. The differentials are greater when these variables are not held constant (Chiswick, 1980; Poston, Martin, and Goodman, 1982).

Spanish language as a drawback. Native language retention has been greater among Mexicans than among any other immigrant group. The retention of Spanish is aided by the existence of old and well-established barrios in some cities, where it is possible to shop, to worship, and to learn about jobs with little or no knowledge of English.

Critics of the view that the Spanish language is a barrier argue that Cubans are Spanish-speaking, and have nevertheless been successful. There are, however, differences between the Cuban and Mexican experiences. First, in the early 1960s Cuban political refugees were the recipients of a comprehensive program that provided, among other services, English-language lessons (Sullivan and Pedraza-Bailey, 1979; Pedraza-Bailey and

Sullivan, 1979). Similar educational and other social service programs have not been provided to other immigrants on such a massive scale. In time the Cubans did develop their own Spanish-language neighborhoods (Wilson and Portes, 1980; Wilson and Martin, 1982). But this may have been a different phenomenon from that of settling into a well-established barrio in San Antonio or Los Angeles. Finally, many of the earliest Cuban refugees were middle-class persons with professional backgrounds, and the success of the group may reflect these characteristics.

There is no evidence that native-language retention impedes economic success; however, there is evidence that lack of proficiency in English, the language of the marketplace, is a barrier to economic achievement (Tienda and Neidert, 1981). Other low-skilled immigrant groups from non-English-speaking countries established ethnic enclaves and had more success than the Mexicans in upward social and economic mobility.

Proximity to the homeland. Because Mexico is so close, this argument runs, the Mexican enclaves in American cities are continually being replenished with recent arrivals who know relatively little of American culture. In addition, many who reside in the United States frequently return home to visit friends and relatives. For these reasons, it is argued, Mexican culture is kept more vibrant and active than were the cultures of other immigrant groups. It is not the case that this vibrant Mexican culture itself retards economic success, only that it provides an attractive alternative to the usual acculturation patterns followed by previous immigrant groups. It is this lack of acculturation, in turn, that retards success in the labor market.

It is noteworthy that other immigrant groups also experienced waves of immigration up to the early 1920s, and it has been argued that the earlier waves facilitated the economic adjustment of the later waves. It is not obvious why the argument is reversed for Mexican immigrants. In addition, on average, the extent of to-and-fro migration does not seem to be much greater for Mexican immigrants or for native-born Mexican-Americans than for other immigrant and native-born non-Hispanics. Census data for 1970 indicate that for immigrants admitted to the U.S. five or more years previously, 2.2 percent of Mexicans and 1.5 percent of non-Hispanic white immigrants were outside the U.S. in 1965 (Chiswick, 1980a, ch. 4). For the native-born the proportions were 1.0 percent for those of Mexican origin and 0.6 percent for non-Hispanic white men. Circular migration for those immigrants in the U.S. less than five years would be expected to be greater for Mexican nationals because of the lower costs of this movement. However, there are insufficient data to allow us to draw firm conclusions. Thus, while some segments of the Mexican immigrant population may experience considerable to-and-fro movement because of the proximity to the homeland, this does not seem to be a general characteristic of Mexican immigrants or native-born Mexican-Americans who appear in Census data, the same data that show the substantial income disadvantage of first, second, and higher generation Americans of Mexican origin.

If the causal element in the lack of success among Mexican immigrants is the proximity of the U.S. to their homeland, then the French Canadian immigrants, particularly those in New England, should be in a similar position. A group with a distinctive language and culture, the French Canadians have usually settled close enough to the border for frequent visits to Canada, and their numbers are often replenished by visitors or permanent additions from Canada. Second-generation Americans of French Canadian origin can be compared with other second-generation Americans using 1970 U.S. Census data. Such a comparison shows a slight earnings disadvantage for French Canadians, controlling for other variables, but nothing of the magnitude found among Mexican-Americans.

One variation on the proximity explanation stresses that it is the location of the ethnic enclaves, and not merely their existence, that matters. Thus, the French Canadian enclaves in New England and the industrial cities of the Northeast face a different economic climate from the Mexican enclaves in the Southwest. If recent economic trends continue, however, this would seem to work to the relative disadvantage of the French Canadians and to the relative advantage of the Mexicans. A further problem with the comparison is that the French Canadians are a minority group within their country (although not in their home province), and may thus be expected to have a somewhat different attitude toward being a linguistic minority in the United States than do persons of Mexican origin.

Location and occupation in the United States. Does the geographical location of Mexicans in the United States, in particular their concentration in the Southwest, offer an explanation for the "Mexican exception"? The research typically holds constant region of residence and whether it is an urban or rural area. It therefore can compare people living in the same place, and has found a lower level of success among Mexicans. And, in California, for example, the Japanese and the Chinese have been more successful than the Mexicans. Indeed, native-born Japanese and Chinese men have higher levels of schooling and earnings than native-born white men, although the earnings difference disappears when schooling level is the same (Chiswick, 1983a). Nor is the occupational distribution, in particular the greater proportion of farm workers, the explanation. Occupational level is itself an outcome of the socioeconomic adjustment process. But even when comparisons of earnings are made within occupation groups, the Mexican-origin group is less successful.

Racial discrimination. Another argument that is advanced, often by Mexican-Americans themselves, is that of discrimination by the host society. Certainly there is a long history of discrimination against racial minorities in the United States. Many Mexicans are dark-skinned, and many are the product of a racial heritage that includes years of intermingling of the blood of the Spanish conquistadors with the native Indians. Among some other Hispanic people, even darker skins come from the intermingling of these populations with African slaves. As a result, many Hispanics do not view themselves as racially white, black, or Indian, but rather as Mexican or Puerto Rican or Dominican. And because this mestizo race often exhibits nonwhite racial characteristics, its members are easily identifiable targets for racial prejudice by whites (Bryce-Laporte, 1977).

This country has a long history of discrimination against Mexicans and other Hispanics, just as there has been a long history of discrimination against blacks, native-Americans, Catholics, Jews, Chinese, and Japanese. Some of these groups have been successful, others have not (Chiswick, 1982a, 1983a, 1983b). The variations in the nature and intensity of the discrimination may in part explain group differences. The reactions of these groups to the discrimination may also be relevant. Thus, while we know that there has been discrimination against Mexicans, we do not know the extent to which this is responsible for their lower earnings and occupational status.

Differences in fertility. We have already noted that the Mexican-origin population has a substantially higher fertility rate than other Americans of the same immigrant generation. The higher fertility rate among Mexican-Americans may be due in part to perceptions of lower cost for additional children (coming, for example, from the population's rural residence, lower level of education, and very low rate of labor force participation among women) and higher cost for controlling fertility. A higher fertility rate, combined with lower wealth, implies a larger number of children competing for the smaller bundle of parental resources for investment in the children's human capital. As a result, the children would have fewer years of schooling and less of other forms of human capital that are more difficult to measure. The consequences of this would be lower earnings and occupational attainment, even when other variables were held constant.

This approach is consistent with a wider range of outcomes than those for Mexican-Americans. It may explain the otherwise puzzling pattern of intergroup differences in success in the U.S. labor market. Among persons born in the United States and subject to discrimination in access to schooling and in the labor market, the highly successful minorities (the Chinese, Japanese, and Jews) appear to have low fertility rates, even in previous decades, compared with the population as a whole, while the groups that are much less successful than average (Mexican-Americans, Filipinos, blacks, and native-Americans) have higher than average fertility rates. While the hypothesis that intergroup differences in labor market outcomes can be related to parental decisions regarding the "quantity/ quality tradeoff" for children (number of children and investment per child) is still in its formative stage, it offers an explanation that appears consistent with the pattern for a range of racial and ethnic groups in the United States (Chiswick, 1982a).

All of the above and something else. The reason for the relative lack of success among the Mexican-origin population in the United States may be an interaction among the factors discussed above, or it may be something that has eluded the research community. The puzzle has not been fully explained, and continued research on this issue is important.

Implications for Contemporary Policy

The implications of the foregoing for current policy on Mexican migration are not yet clear. The current data suggest that most immigrants have done well. The astounding success story of American immigrants does not suggest the need for any special legislation, economic "floor," or social entitlements for immigrants. Indeed, it would not be clear that we should welcome them if they required such special protection. While the unexpected nature of the migration of refugees results in their requiring some assistance upon arrival, they apparently adjust rapidly. Any special assistance that is other than temporary may be counterproductive. Conferees at the U.N. World Population Conference in 1974 called for resettlement assistance to immigrants in their "World Population Plan of Action" (1975). But except perhaps for refugees, the provisions for relocating and maintaining immigrants that are called for in the "Plan of Action" do not appear to be necessary.

The data suggest that there are differences in economic success by country of origin, even if demographic and training variables are held constant. In particular, Mexican immigrants earn less and have lower occupational levels than others. It would be wrong to adopt the approach of the 1911 Dillingham Commission and assume that this dooms them and future Mexican immigrants to a lower economic status. It would be equally wrong to ignore these findings and assume that the current and future Mexican immigrants will be as successful as the European and East Asian immigrants. The past and current data offer no conclusive statement about the future. They do raise important policy questions, but thus far the explanation for the pattern of economic success eludes us.

The finding that, in general, migrants do well suggests that legal immigration, at any rate, is not in a crisis situation. But it does not mean that policy makers may sit back and leave immigration matters to take care of themselves for another decade. The appropriate question for a rethinking of immigration policy is not solely whether the consequences are acceptable, or even good, but also how immigration policy can be modified to better serve the legitimate interests of American society.

Summary

The "new immigrants" of the last two decades differ from earlier immigrants in their national origins, their skill levels, their geographic distribution, and their success rates. A variety of studies have indicated that some of the "new" immigrants, and in particular those from Mexico, do not appear to be doing as well as the recent immigrants from the "old" sending countries of Europe, although others seem to be doing quite well. Even when duration of residence in the United States has been controlled, there are systematic differences in the success of some of the new immigrants in converting their skills into earnings and occupational attainment. Several possible explanations have been offered for this finding, but none is as yet compelling. This issue will remain an important research topic for social scientists in the next decade.

Part II
CONSEQUENCES OF
IMMIGRATION POLICIES

7
Immigration Policy and Foreign Policy

Immigration policy became permanently linked to foreign policy with the emergence of the modern nation-state and the need to guard well-defined national boundaries. Treaties and bilateral agreements are the most important formal mechanisms linking immigration policy with foreign policy, but the receiving country must also decide whose passports it will recognize in the absence of formal agreements. All governments retain a strong interest in protecting their nationals in foreign lands. In cases of dual citizenship, the definition of citizenship by the sending country may become an important consideration for the host government as well. As a result, any review of U.S. immigration policy must consider foreign policy implications as well.

It is helpful at the outset to distinguish several kinds of links between foreign policy and immigration policy. The first might be called "sphere-of-influence" policies. These policies involve the movement of persons among areas that are geographically distinct but within a common allegiance or citizenship. Examples of this include the migration of black Surinamese, who are Dutch citizens, to the Netherlands, and the movement of British Commonwealth nationals into Great Britain. Such movements are usually, although not necessarily, the legacy of a colonial relationship. What is common to all such cases is the existence of a politically dominant central authority. Depending on the political definition of the situation, such movements might be considered internal migration rather than international migration.

Typically, sphere-of-influence policies offer as a rationale the putative unity of the persons affected. This unity may be cultural, religious, linguistic, or economic, or it may derive from a common political base—for example, adherence to a common ideology, such as communism among the Soviet Republics. Entry into the receiving country is usually facilitated by being from a country that is part of the sphere of influence. There may be a multitiered admission system, with preference given to those in the sphere of influence. Sending countries are likely to claim privileges for their nationals on the basis of an existing common allegiance, or of alleged oppression or fear of a common enemy in the past. In the receiving country, such policies may be justified on similar grounds or simply as "noblesse oblige."

In the case of contemporary U.S. immigration policy, entry from Puerto Rico, the Virgin Islands, and Guam, all of which are United States territory, must be considered within this sphere-of-influence context. The movement of residents of these areas to and from the mainland is officially defined as internal migration. Similarly, "mainlanders" are free to move to these outlying areas.

Until 1965, entry of all persons from Latin America could also be considered within a U.S. sphere-of-influence policy. All potential immigrants from independent nations in the Western Hemisphere were admitted regardless of quotas that applied to immigrants from other countries, assuming that they were not barred by the qualitative restriction and that they paid the relevant annual head tax (visa fee). This was, to be sure, a controversial policy. Congress repeatedly debated the exclusion of Mexicans and Central and South Americans from the quotas legislated during the 1920s. The same arguments, based on racial and cultural inferiority, that had been made against Eastern and Southern Europeans were made against Mexicans and other Latin Americans. On the other side, proponents claimed the common heritage of the New World as justification for unrestricted entry. More pragmatically, business interests in the sparsely settled Southwest depended upon continued immigration to provide low-skill and low-wage labor. The compromise that was reached in the 1920s endured until 1965: Latin American immigrants as a class were not restricted, but individual immigrants were required to pay the head tax and to meet other qualifying requirements. With the passage of the 1965 Amendments to the Immigration and Nationality Act, the entire Western Hemisphere was given a quota of 120,000 visas a year, although the immediate relatives of U.S. citizens were not subject to the quota restrictions. Subsequent legislation imposed a country ceiling of 20,000 visas a year for those subject to numerical limitation, a limitation that was imposed on the Eastern Hemisphere countries in the 1965 Amendments. (The separate hemispheric quotas were combined in 1979 into a unified worldwide ceiling.) Because of the immigration from Mexico by immediate relatives of U.S. citizens, and for other reasons, legal immigration has been about 52,000 immigrants a year in the last few years.

With the passage of the 1965 Amendments, formal recognition of a sphere of influence in U.S. immigration policy with regard to the independent countries of the Western Hemisphere came to an end. The most important formal recognition of such policies today exists in the former colonial powers of Europe: the Ugandans, Pakistanis, Indians, and West Indians in Britain; the pieds-noirs and Vietnamese in France; the Indonesians and Surinamese in the Netherlands; and the Angolans and Goans in Portugal. Complicating these migration streams is the differentiation of the "returning colonials," often civil service retirees returning to the mother country, from the "natives," racially distinct but acculturated sons and daughters of the former colony.

Although the United States no longer recognizes a sphere of influence with regard to other independent nations in its laws and immigration policies, the underlying notion that we must protect those who are "like us" in some fundamental way has become an important rallying cry for many who advocate changes in the current policy. The ramifications of this notion for refugee policy are discussed below.

A second class of policies recognizes a formal, political relationship among countries as the basis for immigration, but does not necessarily imply that these relationships are permanent. Instead, the relationships are based on treaties or bilateral agreements—more rarely, memoranda of understanding—and are regarded as constructed, political realities. To be sure, pragmatic considerations of location and economy are involved in both sphere-of-influence and treaty-based immigration provisions, but the legal basis of the latter is a sufficient justification. A recent example of treaty-based immigration provisions is the movement of guestworkers among the members of the European Economic Community (EEC). Full members of the EEC are permitted greater freedom of movement among member countries than are the associate members of the EEC. Some European industrialized nations also have bilateral agreements with countries that are not part of the EEC. Similarly, Canada has had a bilateral agreement with Mexico, under which Mexican workers are admitted to Canada on a temporary basis, since 1973. Not all such agreements facilitate immigration, however; the "gentlemen's agreement" with Japan in 1907 restricted the entry of Japanese workers into the United States.

Despite the case of the gentlemen's agreement, however, treaties and bilateral agreements in the United States have historically been used principally for purposes of admitting short-term workers. Under present U.S. immigration laws, permanent residents are admitted on the basis of their individual attributes, although nationality does play two roles. First, every independent nation has a ceiling of 20,000 visas to be issued each year for immigrants subject to numerical limitations. Second, past immigration policies and trends influence the likelihood that a potential applicant for an immigration visa will have a kinsman in this country, and thus influence his likelihood of obtaining a visa. But bilateral agreements are a significant foreign policy tool because they recognize the interests of the sending country. In the case of a permanent migration, the views of the sending country might not be relevant. But in the case of temporary workers, sending countries do have a vital interest in the health and safety of their nationals abroad, the conditions of their employment, and the terms under which they can be repatriated or deported. Sending countries would also be expected to have a continuing interest in other nonimmigrants, such as students, tourists, and traveling businessmen.

Refugee Policies: A Special Case

Both sphere of influence and treaty-type immigration policies recognize shared interests with the sending countries. A third type of policy, the "political refugee" policies, denies that the sending country's interests in the immigrant are legitimate. In this sense, the decision to admit political refugees is a foreign policy option that has the effect of criticizing the foreign government—or at the least, of saying that the refugee is "more like us" and "less like them" (the sending country).

In the days when the United States had virtually unlimited immigration, many political refugees came to our shores without any foreign policy conclusions being drawn. The era of restricted immigration brought with it the necessity to choose the cases of political, racial, ethnic, religious, and other persecution we would recognize as legitimate, or, alternatively, the option to ignore politics and to let political refugees join the queue on the same basis as nonrefugees. Even after we had limited the immigration of Europeans, the immigration of Latin Americans remained essentially unrestricted, and so political refugees from Latin America continued to enter the United States. The failure to acknowledge exceptions to the policy for refugees led to troubling incidents prior to U.S. entry into World War II, when the U.S. refusal to admit Jewish refugees from Hitler's Germany almost surely resulted in many of them being put to death.

The failure to admit refugees bothered many Americans; it seemed to fundamentally ignore the American creed. A small start was made toward a refugee policy by the executive decision of President Truman to admit about 400,000 displaced persons after World War II. In the succeeding decade, as the cold war intensified, Congress saw the need to admit those refugees who were "like us" politically in the sense that they were opposed to communism. Provisions were made in the 1952 Immigration and Nationality Act to admit refugees from communism. With the passage of time a few other special groups were also included: those fleeing from violence and property expropriation in the Middle East, and a limited number of persons displaced by natural calamities. Those in the latter group were not political refugees, however, and so were of little concern to foreign policy makers.

From 1952 to 1980, most refugees admitted to the United States were fleeing communism. At first, refugees were treated more or less like economic immigrants—they were expected to manage without explicit governmental assistance. Private welfare agencies and ethnic associations did, of course, provide aid. Whatever governmental assistance was available usually came from the states. After World War II, several states had "displaced persons commissions" to help settle these populations. Beginning with the refugees from the 1956 Hungarian uprising, the federal government made some provisions for the reception and acculturation of refugees. The Hungarians were provided with shelter at Camp Kilmer, New Jersey, and a limited program of acculturation to the United States was offered, including English lessons and a brief American history course (Smith, 1966). But this special treatment for refugees did not include attention to all of the practical matters that the refugees would face after orientation, specifically migration within the country and the varying degrees of transferability of their skills in the United States.

The first major governmental effort to aid the adjustment of refugees came with the Cuban refugees after Castro entered Havana in 1959. The federal government initiated a coordinated effort to aid Cuban refugees that involved state and local agencies, private welfare associations, and foundation aid. The refugees were provided with subsistence, English lessons, help in finding jobs, and education for themselves and their children. The government program even included college courses to help Cuban professionals "transfer" their skills into American credentials. Physicians were trained in the English language and in American medical practices, lawyers were retrained as librarians, and teachers were assisted in obtaining American teaching certificates (Pedraza-Bailey and Sullivan, 1979).

The Cuban refugee program provided a model for the later reception of Vietnamese, Laotian, and Cambodian refugees, and for later waves of Cuban refugees. That nearly all refugees who entered the country were from communist regimes was in part a consequence of the provisions of the 1952 legislation; refugees from noncommunist regimes could not ordinarily be admitted under the regular refugee provisions. Some refugees from noncommunist countries were admitted, however. For example, a small number of Chilean refugees entered after the overthrow of the Salvador Allende regime.

With the waning of the cold war and the emergence of the era of detente, many observers expressed dissatisfaction with the refugee policies. In addition to the problem of refugees from rightist regimes, there were the additional groups persecuted for their race, religion, or ethnic origin. Before the quota system was introduced, these persons could have found a refuge in the United States; under the immigration legislation of the 1920s and the 1952 Immigration and Nationality Act, they could be admitted only as regular immigrants, and that often involved a long, frustrating wait. Critics of this policy noted its resemblance to the quota system that kept some persecuted Jews from entering the United States on the eve of World War II. The preference system in the 1965 Amendments provided only a small quota for refugees (6 percent of the 190,000 visas allocated to the Eastern Hemisphere), although the Attorney General was given the authority to parole additional refugees into the U.S. in emergency situations. In March 1980, President Jimmy Carter signed the Refugee Act of 1980, which made it possible for refugees to be admitted on account of racial, religious, or ethnic persecution, as well as political persecution more broadly defined, regardless of the political ideology of the persecuting regime. The act also increased the annual quota for refugees from 17,400 (6 percent of the 50,000 worldwide ceiling of 290,000 visas) to 50,000, and provided for the Attorney General to admit refugees under a special parole power.

Almost immediately, the new law was challenged, and many observers felt that it failed its first test. The "freedom flotilla" from Cuba presented the Administration with a fait accompli: it was politically unthinkable to turn back all of the tiny boats putting into Florida ports, especially because most of them had at least one American citizen aboard. But it was also a serious threat to the new Refugee Act to have American citizens defining refugee status for themselves. The administration wavered from day to day, and the Castro regime took advantage of the vacillation by effectively expelling many more Cubans, some because they were politically undesirable and others because they were social misfits and criminals. New issues cropped up almost immediately. Small boats filled with Haitians were washing up on the same shores where the Cubans were disembarking. Were they not "boat people" too? They argued that they were refugees from a poverty so hard that it was as deadly to them as political repression. Moreover, they argued, if they were returned to Haiti they would then be politically oppressed as well. The Haitian case forced the United States back to first principles in its immigration policy once again. The Refugee Act of 1980 was not the final word in defining who is a refugee. In spite of the inconsistencies inherent in implementing the Refugee Act of 1980, however, the Select Committee on Immigration and Refugee Policy endorsed the Act and otherwise ignored refugee policy.

Who Is a Refugee?

The Refugee Act of 1980 tried to define a refugee in terms of political, racial, religious, or ethnic persecution. This "definition" raises more questions than it answers; certainly, it does not eliminate many cases. For example, by Amnesty International's definitions, practically every country in the world has political prisoners. (Within the United States, for example, Amnesty International faults the treatment of apprehended illegal aliens, although few illegal aliens are imprisoned for violating immigration law.) The United Nations High Commissioner on Refugees estimates that there is a worldwide total of 16 million refugees—these are persons literally displaced from their homes.

By the Refugee Act's more liberal criterion of "persecution," entire minority groups in many countries could be admitted. Consider just a few cases that might possibly be thought of as "religious persecution": Catholics in Northern Ireland, Philippine Moslems, Bangladesh Hindus, and Lebanese Christians, Druse, and Moslems, depending on which faction has the upper hand at the moment. This is not to say that all of these groups necessarily are persecuted, or that claiming refugee status is the only way they could enter the United States. For example, many Catholics from Northern Ireland might well be able to enter the United States under the regular preference system, particularly if they have relatives already in this country. The point is that "persecution" is a broad and ill-defined concept that could describe the situation in any country that does not enforce principles of religious freedom with the zeal Americans have for the First Amendment. The claim of religious persecution can easily be made by millions of the world's people—but should we accept the claim? In the case of the countries mentioned above, to accept religious refugees could well alienate the governments of Great Britain, the Philippines, Bangladesh, and Lebanon. Accepting Jewish or Orthodox dissidents from the Soviet Union raises fewer foreign policy complications, although even in this case there is a complex interaction between the "warmth" of U.S.-Soviet relations and the Soviets' issue of emigration visas. This was apparently one reason for President Gerald Ford's refusal to meet with Soviet exile Alexander Solzhenitsyn.

Plainly, the Refugee Act of 1980, if short on definitions, had to provide for some system of limiting the admission of refugees. There were two provisions for this: the first was the annual numerical limit of 50,000 refugees; the second was the requirement that the refugees come to the United States from a country of first asylum. The Cuban and Haitian "refugees" were not in a country of first asylum; they sought direct entry into the U.S. However, the Refugee Act also gave the President authority to admit refugees above the numerical limit and waive the country-of-first-asylum provision. In the case of the 1980 Cuban exodus, Castro was initially willing to let the emigrants go to any country whose embassies would accept them, and many fled to the embassies of Peru and Costa Rica. However, Castro soon realized the negative propaganda implications of thousands of disaffected Cubans in Latin America and the positive benefits to be achieved by putting the U.S. in an awkward position. He then requested that the refugees go directly to the U.S., and announced that the Cuban government would determine who could leave. In the case of the Haitians, those who deliberately or accidentally landed in other Caribbean nations were deported to Haiti—where, they claimed, they would face prison or worse. In short, the Refugee Act of 1980 requires the acquiescence of at least one other government in our refugee policy—a foreign policy consideration that seems to have been overlooked in the planning. What is said of the generals planning for the next war is equally true of the planners of immigration policy: decisions are made on the basis of the last battle. The 1980 Refugee Act was modeled on the U.S. experience with Southeast Asian refugees.

The Haitian challenge to the definition of refugees is an ingenious and troubling one. It is ingenious because it pushes our definition of what it means to be a refugee back to first principles: to be a refugee is to face the direst possible consequences if one remains in a place. To starve is certainly a dire consequence. Yet, a poverty-level standard of living is not the exception but the norm for the bulk of the population in Africa, Asia, the Caribbean, and some parts of Latin America. Furthermore, to acknowledge poverty as grounds for refugee status is to undercut the entire separation of refugees from other immigrants. Under such a definition, most potential immigrants would have two chances to enter the United States: once under the regular quota sysem and once as a sort of economic refugee. Refugee status then becomes the "wild card" of the immigration system. But refugee status becomes a particularly difficult wild card to play—every group, and every individual within a group, must be admitted on the basis of deliberate administrative decision, and always with the knowledge that millions of others are being left to dire consequences.

The economic definition of refugee status has other serious consequences as well. Ever since the Cuban refugee program of the 1960s, there has been at least some expectation that the federal government would provide some assistance to refugees. This makes sense for many reasons. Political refugees often must leave in great haste with few possessions; economic migrants are more likely to have been able to plan for the move and generally can take some if not all of their assets with them. Economic migrants are generally self-selected for their employment opportunities in the U.S., whereas political refugees are rarely self-selected on this basis. But economic refugees are a different case, and the provision of extensive government services for the economic refugee would not be as appropriate as it is for the person fleeing genocide or war. What then? A differentiation of refugees according to the reason for immigration?

Economic refugee status brings us back to the general problem of rationing slots in the immigration system. The potential number of economic refugees, if we use the Haitians' construction of the term, is in the hundreds of millions. Do we have a responsibility to so many of the world's poor? And if so, does that responsibility require admitting them to the U.S.?

Guilt and Immigration Policy

Indeed, we do have a responsibility to the world's poor according to some. The argument made for our responsibility to all of the world's poor is a derivative of the sphere-of-influence argument made for immigration policies. The argument runs something like this: The United States has made itself rich and powerful by profit taking in the developing nations of the world. By exporting those profits to itself, the United States has contributed to the worldwide poverty problem, and has incurred a responsibility to redress the damage. The sphere of influence for which the United States must accept responsibility is thus not only its former possessions and protectorates, but the entire world. And the more "dependent" a nation has become on the United States' economy—for example, for the purchase of its raw materials—the greater the responsibility of the United States for its poverty.

One way of meeting this responsibility is to admit many more immigrants. The critics are not entirely happy with this solution, correctly guessing that many potential immigrants will be the most energetic of the unskilled, looking for opportunities; the most skilled, raising the "brain drain" charge; or the children of the local "elites." To admit these people would make the United States even more culpable in impoverishing other countries—added to the depletion of natural resources would be the depletion of human resources. The usual solution proposed is to return the profits and redress the imbalance in technical skills through foreign aid. It is in this way that an additional major aspect of U.S. foreign policy becomes closely tied to immigration.

But foreign aid is also condemned by some as a partial and unsatisfactory way of compensating developing countries. Some critics have suggested a large indemnification of the sending country for each immigrant admitted. This indemnification would be larger for more skilled workers. The argument for this program is that the sending country has invested in the human capital of the immigrant by providing basic necessities and schooling throughout the immigrant's childhood and early adult years. In addition, the sending country will lose the potential tax payments and other contributions the immigrant could have made to his native country. Rather than foreign aid, given with at least the hint that it is international charity, the receiving country should send immigrant indemnities to the home countries as a matter of justice. Under this view, voluntary emigrant remittances are deemed inadequate to recompense the home country.

Two further comments on this approach are warranted. First, compensation would further intensify the efforts of some regimes to pressure people to leave—not only would they get rid of the "troublemakers," the U.S. would pay for receiving them. Given the behavior over the past few years of governments in Uganda, Cambodia, Vietnam, and Cuba, one can imagine other regimes adopting an "expulsion for profit" scheme. Second, implicit in the indemnification approach is the idea that people are the property of the state. The approach ignores the sources of the resources used to provide publicly supplied goods and services to children—the adult generation that includes their parents. If such public goods and services are viewed as an aspect of the intergenerational transfer of resources, it is not obvious that the state has a claim on the children's future earnings.

Finally, the evidence does not support the view that the U.S. has a moral responsibility to aid other countries because U.S. investments caused their poverty. It is the developing countries that have had the greatest contact with U.S. and West European investment that have had the most rapid advances in their development. Korea, Taiwan, and Hong Kong have progressed because of such interactions and are now classified as in the intermediate stage of developoment, while Bolivia, Chad, and Burma have had little progress because of the absence of investment and trading opportunities, either because of economic circumstances or, in the case of Burma, conscious government policy.

This discussion is not intended to suggest that the U.S. has no interest in assisting developing countries, but rather that such assistance should be based on U.S. self-interest and a genuine desire to help those less fortunate and not on misguided feelings of guilt. In addition, immigration and development assistance are two separate issues, and attempts to link them may be counterproductive.

The Creation of Refugees

From the point of view of foreign governments our treatment of refugees is probably the soft underbelly in our immigration policies. It is the place where the greatest pressure can be brought to bear on us, partly because we are known as a humanitarian people and partly because of the American creed. We value our political, economic, and religious freedom, and we sympathize with those who yearn for it. We are a place of refuge, we are proud to be so, and we are ashamed of those times in our history when we let our own prejudices bar the entry of those fleeing for their lives. The United States points to "voting with your feet" as a justification and confirmation of the American system. After all, how many immigrants are trying to enter the Soviet Union or Cuba? We have used the Voice of America and U.S. magazines, books, movies, and television programs to broadcast the wonders of our system and its advantages. Unfortunately, these policy weapons can be used against us. Not only did we awaken and increase the desire to come here, we also offered a statement of our principles that could provide the rhetorical basis for forcing us to accept immigrants. A new foreign policy option has become available to governments everywhere: creating refugees.

For nations within the recognized sphere of influence of a receiving nation, expelling a group can be tantamount to forcing that receiving country to take them in. When Idi Amin expelled the South Asians in Uganda, it was with the knowledge that Great Britain would feel a strong moral responsibility for them. The creation of refugees becomes an alternative to genocide or concentration camps, and an appeal to the humanitarian instincts of the receiving countries to save the intended victims from death. At one time Hitler offered to let European Jews emigrate, but the potential receiving countries would not cooperate. The Asians in Uganda and the ethnic Chinese in Vietnam were offered the choice of emigration or extermination. Cambodian refugees in Thailand may not have been offered an explicit choice, but they felt themselves safer as refugees than in their native land. The 1980 Cuban refugees were probably not facing the prospect of death, but their case was similar to the extent that the regime deliberately engineered their status as refugees.

The creation of refugees is an attractive foreign policy for "cleansing" one's country without being forced to use violence. It offers a regime the opportunity to appear to be "humane" by letting unwanted groups leave rather than suffer more serious consequences. However, the threat of violence must be at least implicit if the tactic is to be credible. Such a policy neatly catches the United States and some other receiving countries in their own rhetoric. Finally, the tactic appears to be absolutely safe for the sending country. There have been few sanctions, even of a symbolic nature, against regimes that create refugees or use them for political purposes, and it is unlikely that serious sanctions will ever be imposed. It is, therefore, necessary for the United States to consider what its unilateral policy on refugees should include.

Policy Issues for the United States

The first issue to be considered is, Who shall define refugee status? In past crises we have allowed the U.N. High Commissioner, the ideology of foreign governments, and the families or ethnic groups of the persons involved to define who is a refugee. The congressional effort to define refugees in the Refugee Act of 1980 does not appear to be sufficient. The second issue, related to the first, is: Under what circumstances shall we consider ourselves to have a special obligation to receive refugees? When we have made their plight worse, as in the case of the Vietnamese who had worked closely with the U.S. Army abroad? When we have a common enemy, as in the case of refugees from left-wing governments? When we have been selected by the home government as the destination and must receive them "or else"?

The third issue is how we shall allocate refugee "slots" or visas among the available applicants. If we consider the United Nations refugee camps alone, without making allowances for the sudden massive refugee flows that accompany wars and insurrections, we realize that every U.S. refugee "slot" could be filled by five or six potential immigrants.

The fourth issue is how we shall keep the refugee policy sufficiently flexible to allow for sudden "bursts" of refugees as international crises quickly develop. We have done relatively little by way of planning for large refugee flows, although it is foreseeable that a number of new Cubas or Vietnams could develop. Throughout Africa, for example, the potential for political violence is growing. There are refugee camps in the Ogaden in the horn of Africa, in Angola in the southwestern part of the continent, and in Algeria in the northwestern part. And it seems likely that racial violence in Zimbabwe and South Africa could also produce a refugee stream.

The fifth issue is more directly related to foreign policy concerns: To what extent should the United States involve third-party nations in its refugee policy? The cooperation of other nations is sought today in several ways. Through the United Nations High Commission on Refugees, the United States participates in a permanent international organization concerned with refugees. More common are ad hoc consortia to handle refugee problems as new international situations arise. An example of this is the group of allies who assisted in the resettlement of Vietnamese refugees. This consortium consisted of receiving countries, such as the United States, France, and Canada; countries of first asylum that provided refugee settlements, such as Thailand, Malaysia, and Hong Kong; and countries that provided indirect assistance (e.g., financial aid or medical supplies), such as Japan. The Refugee Act of 1980 assumes the continuing existence of countries willing to serve as places of first asylum, for it permits the entry of refugees only if they are using the United States as their country of second asylum.

Alternatives to admitting large numbers of refugees to the United States include offering financial incentives to countries of first asylum, or even to other countries, to provide for the permanent settlement of the refugees. The United States already provides support for some refugee camps—for example, those in Thailand and Malaysia—but has devoted few resources to permanent settlement in countries other than the U.S. The United States has acted in such situations on what appears to be an ad hoc basis, and usually from humanitarian motives. For example, when forty-one Haitian refugees were stranded on Cayo Lobos, an uninhabited island in Bahamian waters, the United States provided them with food and water until the Bahamian government was willing to act (in this case, to deport them to Haiti). Offers of technical or financial assistance to countries of second asylum are more rare, but there are precedents for it. The Netherlands provided material assistance for the resettlement in the United States of Indonesians displaced by the revolution there. Japan has accepted only a few refugees for permanent settlement, but has provided financial assistance for the settlement of refugees in other countries.

The reasons that refugees need financial assistance for resettlement have been alluded to above: Unlike economic immigrants, political immigrants are likely to leave in haste, with few belongings, and with little capital other than their skills. Unlike economic immigrants, refugees are not necessarily self-selected on the basis of their energy, youthfulness, or the transferability of their skills. In addition, when entire ethnic groups are displaced, as they sometimes are in the case of refugees, the burden of dependents is likely to be greater than it is among economic immigrants.

These considerations bring up a sixth policy consideration. Assuming that refugees are admitted to the United States, to what extent should the government provide resettlement assistance? If this assistance is provided by the government, what level of government should provide and fund the aid? If it is to be provided by the private sector (including voluntary organizations, which currently provide most of the aid), what kinds of guarantees should the government demand before admitting the refugees?

Although some world leaders do have the power to "create" refugees, most situations that displace people arise in unpredictable and uncontrollable ways. A policy on refugees must above all preserve the flexibility to handle these extraordinary situations. But, while we cannot predict where the next wave of refugees will originate, we can be sure that it will come, and our immigration policy should recognize that refugee crises have become routine. Recommendations regarding U.S. refugee policy are developed in Part III.

Summary

America's role as a refuge from political, religious, or other forms of persecution is an important part of the American creed. But a number of issues confront American refugee policy. Worldwide, there is an enormous number of refugees; thus, some sort of rationing procedure seems to be important. But our rationing rules are frequently manipulated by world leaders and world events, creating new refugee streams that claim special rights to admission.

Unlike economic immigrants, refugees are now given substantial assistance from both the public and private sectors. Also unlike economic immigrants, the refugees are selected on some basis other than their economic ambitions and abilities or the transferability of their skills. As a result, refugees pose potential economic problems different from those that might be posed by economic immigrants. Our handling of these problems has been complicated by our piecemeal, crisis-by-crisis approach to refugee policy. The recent refugee legislation, while a step in the right direction, does not represent a fundamental shift in refugee policy.

8
Immigration Policy and Domestic Policy

The admission of immigrants, even in small numbers, is bound to affect the workings of domestic policies. Some analysts have argued against this idea on the grounds that the number of immigrants admitted to the United States every year is so small as to be negligible, especially when compared with the size of the population as a whole. But we believe that a study of U.S. immigration policy is incomplete if it neglects the ramifications of the policy as it affects every aspect of American society. Even if the impact of an individual policy seems small, the cumulative impact of one policy over the years or of several policies together can be very large. If we are concerned with the state of the national economy, we cannot ignore the economic consequences of making thousands of small decisions to admit or reject immigrants. And while economic consequences often tend to dominate the discussion, it is also important to review the political, social, and cultural consequences of immigration.

The Geography of the Immigrants

There has been a great deal of interest in the countries of origin of immigrants, but much less study of where they go once admitted to the United States. Some receiving countries, notably Canada, offer incentives to immigrants to settle in the less-developed portions of the country. Others, such as Germany with its temporary workers, limit the geographic mobility of immigrants through restrictive visas. In the United States, where freedom of travel among the states is constitutionally protected, states once competed vigorously to be selected by immigrants as their new homes. Indeed, until the third decade of this century, some states allowed resident aliens to vote, apparently a vestige of the efforts once made to encourage immigrants to settle in particular localities.

Today there is much less active competition for immigrants, although occasionally states will try to attract certain kinds of skilled immigrants. For example, in the early days of the Cuban refugee program, several states were eager to receive Cuban professionals to serve as teachers of Spanish. Some of these states offered retraining programs and facilitated the acquisition of teaching credentials (Sullivan and Pedraza-Bailey, 1979).

For the most part, however, states are not competing for the immigrants, and indeed many states seem rather apprehensive about the effects of having "too many" immigrants within their borders.

But the states are not able to restrict the entry of immigrants. Under this condition, it seems likely that the same states and metropolitan areas that attract native-born migrants will also attract immigrants. Historically, with the exception of the nineteenth century Scandinavians, nearly every immigrant group to the United States has settled in urban areas. Immigrants flocked to the eastern seacoast cities because these cities had jobs available and were close to the ports of entry. Chicago in 1920 was described as a "foreign city" because of its concentration of foreign stock (32 percent in the 1920 census; in New York City the proportion was 44 percent—Lieberson, 1980, p. 24). Although Mexican-Americans settled in the Southwest, they too tended to choose urban areas.

Two competing forces seem to be at work today in determining the settlement patterns of immigrants. The first is social inertia: today's immigrants are likely to go to the same destinations as yesterday's immigrants, either because they have kin there or because jobs are still available or believed to be available there. For this reason, major northern metropolitan areas such as New York, Philadelphia, Boston, and Chicago have substantial immigrant populations. The second force is the lure of the sunbelt. Just as native-born Americans are migrating to the southern and western states, so are the foreign-born. While most Mexican and many Asian immigrant groups have always been concentrated in the Southwest, there is now reason to believe that other groups are following them. Moreover, the immigrant in the Southwest, once confined primarily to agricultural jobs or menial urban labor, is now just as likely to be working in industrial or service jobs in urban areas. The growth of jobs in the Southwest has encouraged the settlement of more immigrants there. And now that this settlement pattern has become well-established, a new social inertia will come into play. With the expansion of "international" airports and the growth of air travel, as well as increased Asian migration, the potential ports of entry have moved inland or to the Pacific Coast. This means that today's immigrants, like those of the last century, can remain near the port of entry and still settle near kin who have immigrated previously.

The federal government is cognizant of the local area impacts of sudden large influxes of immigrants, especially refugees. While local governments incur much of the short-term financial burden of refugees and other immigrants, because of the constitutional guarantee of freedom of movement within the country they have no direct control over internal migration. Some state and local governments, most notably in California and Florida, fear severe adverse impacts from a sudden influx of Indochinese refugees and the more recent Cuban refugees. They have relied on moral suasion to encourage federal relocation programs that would provide a wide geographical dispersion. The federal government has been responsive and worked toward a geographically dispersed pattern of initial settlement. A study by the Immigration and Naturalization Service of the subsequent internal migrations of refugees revealed a strong tendency for the Indochinese to gravitate to urban California, the area that was, for reasons of climate, kinship, and jobs, their first preference (Gordon, 1980). Although the dispersal policy was only partially successful and created the additional costs of secondary migration, it did cushion the impact of the sudden influx on the areas where the refugees wanted to live.

To the extent that politics in the United States are based on geography, these settlement patterns can be significant. When a substantial number of an area's voters are naturalized citizens, elected officials are more likely to be sensitive to immigrant issues. Pressure from foreign-born voters was believed to be instrumental in delaying the adoption of restrictive quotas, in amending those quotas, and, in some cases, even in the structuring of U.S. foreign policy toward their native countries. And, whether naturalized or not, immigrants are included in the population figures used to determine apportionment of seats in the U.S. House of Representatives (and hence the Electoral College), as well as in state legislatures, and in the allocation of federal funds among state and local areas.

There is another political issue that is also important today: the political impact of illegal aliens, and its relationship to the political power of immigrants, at both the local and national levels. The key phrase here is "political impact." In what ways can illegal aliens have political impact? Obviously they cannot vote or hold public office, and may be too frightened of civil authorities to apply for government programs. But they can be counted in the U.S. Census and form the basis for reapportioning the Congress and the state legislatures. Because it is likely that some illegal aliens were counted and others were not, adjusting the Census figures for illegal aliens may be impossible.

Thus, illegal aliens can have political impact, and this impact has the effect of magnifying the *apparent* impact of legal immigrants at the local level for the following reason: no one knows the precise relationship between the number of legal immigrants in an area and the number of illegal ones, but there are many good reasons for assuming it to be strongly positive. Like legal aliens, illegal aliens will migrate to areas where there are jobs and where friends and relatives have already settled. Existing legal alien communities provide a supportive cultural network for the illegal aliens—they are made up of persons who speak the same language, eat the same food, and perhaps even come from the same village or family. This both provides a familiar environment and reduces the possibility of apprehension by allowing the illegal alien to mingle with sympathetic fellow countrymen and blend into a larger ethnic population.

As the settlement pattern of immigrants shifts from the Northeast to the Southwest, and as illegal aliens also settle disproportionately in the Southwest, the geographic composition of Congress could be altered. Although immigration contributed to the increase in congressional seats for the Northeast and Midwest during the century prior to 1920, in coming decades the West Coast and the Southwest are likely to be the beneficiaries. For this to happen, it is not necessary that there be large numbers of aliens—all that is necessary is that there be enough aliens to provide the margin of difference. Studies done by the U.S. Bureau of the Census indicate that the shift in the population of a state required to produce a change in the state's representation may be merely a few hundred persons or a few hundred thousand persons, depending on the populations of all the states (Siegel, et al., 1977, p. 106). And in recent reapportionment cases, that margin has often been small. After the 1970 Census Oklahoma received an extra congressional seat at the expense of Connecticut, following a small adjustment for servicemen abroad (Garcia, 1980), and after the 1980 Census New York gained a seat at the expense of Indiana by a small margin (Gilford and Causey, 1981).

Political Activism among Immigrants

During the last century, one common complaint against immigrants was that they could not adjust to the American political process. Coming as most did from monarchical governments, many of which were repressive, they were not expected to understand and value political freedom as native-born Americans did. With little knowledge of English, they could easily be led astray. The nativists argued, for example, that the Catholic immigrants could not swear allegiance to any power because of their lasting fidelity to the Pope.

Within only a few years, the opposite fear was being voiced. The immigrants had indeed learned American ways, and they were about to subvert the system from within. Many had been exposed in Europe to dangerous doctrines such as communism and socialism, and these beliefs were often linked in the nativists' minds with the immigrants' labor activism. The growth of machine politics in major cities, which increased simultaneously with public-sector employment, and agitation for welfare measures were blamed on the immigrants. Far from being unable to understand American politics, the immigrants seemed only too capable of governing.

The fears of the nineteenth century were based on the immigrants' use of ballots and city treasuries, the principal political tools of the era. Current fears seem to be based on immigrants' use of today's political instruments, the lobbyist and the court decision. Especially in the Southwest, where in some quarters there is a barely concealed fear of an irredentist movement, immigrant politics is again an important issue. This may be as localized an issue as the treatment of illegal alien children in the schools, or it may be a broader concern. The civil rights movement of the 1960s provided an obvious model for immigrant activist groups. A number of these groups, which often began as ethnic mutual-benefit societies, testified before the Select Commission on Immigration and Refugee Policy and before congressional committees; and many of them lobby on legislation of interest. The American Committee on Italian Migration, among other immigrant ethnic groups, followed the work of the Select Commission and Congress very closely and lobbied hard and successfully for the retention of the preference for the brothers and sisters of U.S. citizens in the Commission's recommendations. The Mexican-American Legal Defense and Education Fund lobbies on behalf of perceived Mexican-American interests, including more generous treatment of illegal aliens and a larger ceiling on immigration for Mexico. Indeed, it would appear that nearly every recent immigrant group has one or more lobbying organizations.

Various immigrant lobbying groups have instituted court suits on such issues as the civil rights of immigrants, their entitlements to various social programs, and the conditions of their admission to the United States. The most straightforward political action of all—direct political action if ever there were any—was the freedom flotilla that set off from Florida to bring back the relatives and friends of Cuban refugees already in the United States. The number of immigrants involved in the freedom flotilla may have been small, but the political effect of the immigrants' activities is not determined entirely by the number of persons involved. Even a small number of political activists may influence the making of immigration policies.

Social Welfare and the Immigrants

Probably the most volatile issue affecting immigrants is their access to and use of social welfare programs and their corresponding responsibilities to the society. During the last century, very little was available in the U.S. in the way of relief or welfare other than that provided by family members, private individuals, or organized philanthropies. Immigrant groups often banded together in voluntary associations to provide succor to their members in trouble. The Knights of Columbus is one of the most successful of these organizations. For some ethnic groups, including the Asian immigrants on the West Coast, voluntary associations, often kin-based, provided venture capital for new businesses and loaned the money to bring additional relatives to the United States.

The income transfer or welfare programs were born in the middle 1930s and grew rapidly in the 1960s (AFDC, Medicaid) and the 1970s (Food Stamps, Supplemental Security Income). Immigration increased sharply after the 1965 Amendments. Hence, immigrants have been arriving in a country that has a substantial amount of state welfare, but feels profoundly ambivalent about the welfare system. While almost everyone admits that some welfare programs are necessary, most wish that they were not available to those groups in society with whom they feel no kinship. And as resentful as citizens are about the native-born receiving "something for nothing," they are even more exercised about the foreign-born receiving benefits without ever having contributed to this society. No benefits are explicitly provided for immigrants, except for special assistance from the federal government for some refugee groups, but they are generally entitled to benefits on the same basis as the native-born. The question comes up repeatedly whether specific transfer payments or services can or should be denied to immigrants. One policy in this direction is a recent amendment to the Social Security Act, which prohibits the use of Supplemental Security Income (a cash welfare program for the aged, blind, and disabled) by immigrants in the U.S. less than three years unless the disability arose after immigration.

Here again a problem of federalism is involved. The federal government admits immigrants. Although for over a century paupers have been theoretically excluded, many immigrants would have income levels deemed inadequate by U.S. standards if they were not given financial assistance. Even with the increased federalization of the welfare system in the past fifteen years, it is not the federal government that bears the exclusive welfare burden for the immigrant. It is state and local governments that fund much of the welfare system.

Language and Culture: The Issues of Bilingualism

Although it is not a new issue, the question of language diversity has received increased attention, at least partly because of the tenacity with which Mexican immigrants have maintained their Spanish language. Language and culture are closely linked in defining national identity. Indeed, we often use the same word to signify both language and national identity: Spanish, German, English, French. It is natural to do so since the process of defining national boundaries is closely linked to that of establishing a national language. For example, when the various kingdoms of the Iberian Peninsula were united under one flag, it was the language of the powerful kingdom of Castile that became the language of the new country.

In America, national identity and establishing a national language are just as closely identified. However, the process is different because it is not a case of various "kingdoms" uniting politically, although this was relevant in the nineteenth century for the former Spanish and French territories, including Florida, the Louisiana Purchase, Texas, and the Mexican cession. Rather, it is a case of immigrants of various nations coming together as individuals to create a new nation.

The process of becoming an American has been experienced by millions of immigrants for over two centuries. Each immigrant defines the process anew as each succeeding wave of immigrants causes the society to examine and again define the American experience. The fact that the process has been repeated millions of times over three hundred years does not lessen the uniqueness for the individual immigrant, nor does it lessen the complexity of assimilation for a nation of immigrants. While one does not easily become a German or a Swiss citizen, one can easily become an American, de facto or de jure.

The process of naturalization is deceptively simple. Since 1790, several basic qualifications have been prescribed for naturalization. The applicant for naturalization must have been lawfully admitted to the United States and must have resided here for five years (this period of residence has been substantially changed only once: between 1798 and 1802 the period was lengthened to fourteen years). This term of residence, plus proof of good character and knowledge of the American language and American history, were the sole requirements established by Congress in 1790 when it introduced a uniform rule of naturalization. Thus, the fact that to be an American one had to speak English was established by the first naturalization laws.

But although naturalization may be a simple process, assimilation is not. The United States did not become a homogeneous nation of assimilated immigrants who lost the birthright of their native cultures. Ethnic diversity was the reality that defined America from its earliest national period. When Hector St. John de Crevecoeur wrote his *Letters from an American Farmer* to attract new immigrants to the growing nation, he defined an American as a "new man":

> He is neither a European nor the descendant of a European; hence that strange mixture of blood, which you will find in no other country . . . he is an American, who leaving behind all his ancient prejudices and manners, receives new ones from the mode of life he has embraced, the new government he obeys, the new rank he holds. He becomes an American by being

received in the great lap of our alma mater. Here individuals of all nations are melted into a new race of men, whose labors and posterity will one day cause great changes in the world (1963, pp. 63-64).

Crevecoeur also describes a typical American village scene:

There, on a Sunday, is a congregation of respectable farmers and their wives, all clad in neat homespun, well mounted or riding in their own humble wagon . . . the next wish of this traveler will be to know from whence came all these people. They are a mixture of English, Scotch, Irish, French, Dutch, Germans, and Swedes (1963, pp. 61-62).

The highlight of Crevecoeur's narrative was that this race of new men had an amazing facility to speak to one another. In his idyllic pastoral setting all good Americans spoke a common language.

It had not been many years since English had become the language of the country. In 1786, Congress had debated the possibility of having both French and English as the official languages of America, and adopted only English. Only four years later, in the myth that preceded the reality of America, spoken English had become necessary for naturalization.

The fact that a nation that has acknowledged and extolled the richness of its diversity should also be formally monolingual is one of the more fascinating riddles of the complexity that is America. Language and culture are so intertwined that to ignore the one is to eradicate the other. Yet America, which established public schools as early as colonial times to teach English to the children of immigrants, did not nationally acknowledge the benefits of bilingual education until 1968, and then only as a medium for the children of immigrants to learn English. Although references to special courses for immigrants began appearing in the annual reports of school districts in the 1890s, the development of distinctive and massive programs of Americanization for the foreign-born did not occur until shortly before World War I. The programs and their scope were further increased with the passage of legislation in 1917, adding the requirement of English literacy for naturalization. This caused the education of the foreign-born to become the dominant activity of the public evening school by the end of World War I (Knowles, 1962).

This is not to say that bilingualism has not been a factor in American education, for indeed it has. Immigration communities established and maintained their own language schools from the earliest days of the nation. In the mid-nineteenth century, the Germans even persuaded the city of Cincinnati to teach both German and English in its public schools. Nevertheless, the speaking of English has long been associated with the opportunity for social and economic advancement, so that fluency in English, rather than bilingualism, is highly prized by the society.

Affirmative Action and Discrimination Against Aliens

Workers already fear the impact of immigration on their jobs; the current affirmative action guidelines make the perceived, if not also the real, impact on native-born minority groups even more severe. A majority of today's immigrants are Asian, African, or Hispanic in origin; as soon as they enter the United States, they can be identified as members of a minority group and can be used to satisfy affirmative action requirements imposed on employers and schools. Many businesses have been able to delay or avoid hiring members of native-born disadvantaged minority groups by hiring immigrants. However, employers are not required to hire immigrants at all. Employers are permitted to discriminate on the basis of citizenship as long as they do not discriminate on the basis of the national origin of U.S. citizens. The Supreme Court held that the Farah Manufacturing Co. did not violate the 1964 Civil Rights Act by refusing to hire Mexican-origin resident aliens because the firm did not discriminate against citizens of Mexican origin, whether naturalized or native-born.

Whatever the merits of affirmative action policies, such policies do not constitute a rationale for hiring the foreign-born, whose ancestors were not subjected to discrimination in the U.S., to be used by employers and others to satisfy affirmative action goals. Such an interpretation of affirmative action amounts to discrimination in favor of immigrants. But neither should public policy sanction discrimination against immigrants. A statute barring employment discrimination against aliens legally entitled to work, except where issues of national security are involved, would be consistent with other aspects of civil rights legislation. However, the addition of "alienage" to the protected categories in the 1964 Civil Rights Act should not be interpreted as requiring that employers establish goals and timetables for this category in addition to the others. At this writing, the federal civil service is closed to aliens, and several states have tried to limit a number of occupations to citizens. So far the courts have struck down most of the state actions.

Citizenship, the American Creed, and Immigration

Relatively little thought has been given in recent years to the significance of citizenship for Americans, whether they be native-born or immigrants. Such a disregard of the meaning of citizenship, and the devaluation of the highly elusive value of being an American citizen, has led to part of the confusion in the U.S. about immigration. In its most elementary form, fear of immigration is the fear of the stranger. The "otherness" of the stranger makes us uneasy and fearful that our values, our possessions, and even our lives may be endangered. These fears have run throughout immigration history, and have been counterbalanced only by a sense that the "otherness" can be overcome—that the stranger can become that "new man," an American.

In earlier years, "Americanization"—the process of adopting not only American values, but also American ways—was the process by which a nation responded to the immigrants' otherness. But "Americanization" implied a homogenization that confused fundamental political and social concerns with ephemeral superficial mores. It was more concerned with eating hot dogs than appreciating the First Amendment. "Americanization" implied a substantial if not complete break with the past and its traditions.

One could become an American only by casting off the past; one pledged allegiance to the new land in a brief and seldom-witnessed ceremony, and renounced allegiance to the old; one spoke the new language (no matter how imperfectly) and refused to speak the old (even with one's aged parents). Those who would not completely cast off "the old man of Europe," no matter how successful they became economically, were not accepted politically and communally. They remained suspect, often rejected by their sons and daughters as hopelessly old-fashioned embarrassments and always separated from their kin in the old country by distance and recent events. Ironically, they were even suspect in the eyes of patriotic Americans for having rejected their native lands.

More recently, the argument has been heard that American citizenship is not really that important. Like any other ascriptive characteristic— race, sex, age, national origin—it is something that is irrelevant in defining a person and his beliefs. Indeed, many consider it irrelevant both to the individual and to society. In the United States, we have seen the continuing erosion of the meaning of "citizenship," once an almost mythic term and now nothing more than a legal definition of entitlements and privileges.

To understand this phenomenon, it may be helpful to distinguish among civil, political, and social rights in the English-speaking world. Civil rights were historically granted before political rights; while many Americans—women, non-landholding males, and children—could not vote in the early republic, they were guaranteed fundamental civil rights. The next entitlement was a progressive expansion of political rights, especially the right to vote and to hold office. In the United States, this was a slow process that involved the progressive inclusion of slaves, women, native-Americans, and 18-to-21 year-olds in voting. In more recent times, social rights, including a claim on the state for basic subsistence, became widespread among those who came to the United States as immigrants. Most civil rights are guaranteed once one has entered the country. Some social rights, such as schooling for children, are apparently guaranteed once one has entered the country; one can become qualified for others, such as certain income transfer programs, after a period of time. In America, citizenship is not necessary for entitlement to civil and social rights.

Citizens do have political rights that are denied aliens. However, unless an individual values these political rights very highly—and the fact that large numbers of citizens do not exercise their right to vote suggests that many do not—there is little incentive to seek citizenship. Citizenship is required for working in the federal civil service, and citizenship or the start of the naturalization process is required for some state and local employment and some occupational licensing, although these state and local government regulations have largely been dismantled by the courts (Ueda, 1980). Citizenship is required for voting and for holding public office. Thus, there are few benefits of citizenship and there may be disincentives to acquiring citizenship, the most important of which may be greater difficulty in returning to one's home country either permanently or temporarily.

What reasons can we offer the immigrant to become an American citizen? In these days, when as a nation we put little value on patriotism, we are left with few compelling arguments. Many believe it is somehow unfair to benefit, year after year, from American prosperity and freedom without contributing to the nation's political strength by the act of affirming allegiance to American values—if not American ways—by becoming a citizen. We are weaker to the extent that the stranger in our midst chooses to remain a stranger, the argument goes. Others believe that the adoption of American values, rather than the affirming of allegiance, is the key.

Contemporary Americans find it difficult to tell foreigners why it is that they should want to be one of us. And yet some suspect that if this generation of immigrants does not become Americans we will have reason to fear a weakening of the American nation, since their sons and daughters will be born American citizens without being taught to prize being American.

Summary

American immigration policy must be considered in light of its effects on domestic policies. Because immigrants do not distribute themselves uniformly across the landscape, and because federal funding and electoral representation are based on population distribution, the concentration of immigrants in certain states and cities has been a matter of historical and contemporary concern. The potential for political activism and political apathy on the part of immigrants has been viewed with alarm by some and with approval by others. The impact of immigrants on social welfare services remains an important issue, perhaps more important now than it was in the days of mass immigration because of the greater entitlements to welfare in recent years.

Language policies, in schools and in government services, are affected by the size and composition of the immigrant population. Many of today's immigrants from racial or ethnic minority groups could qualify under affirmative action programs for preferential job placements, although this would appear to be a misapplication of these programs. Finally, naturalization and the effects of citizenship among the foreign-born are areas of concern.

In the concluding part of this book, we turn to recommendations for new immigration policies. We will return to the areas of concern mentioned in this chapter and in the preceeding chapters, and we will discuss how the proposed policies would meet these concerns more effectively than do the current policies.

Part III
A NEW IMMIGRATION POLICY

9

Rethinking Our Attitudes toward Immigrants: The Resident Alien

Unrestricted immigration is no longer a realistic policy alternative. Contemporary world conditions make it necessary for every receiving country, including the United States, to limit the number of admissions in the context of its national interests. Most of the debate about immigration has centered on the number of visas: How many is too many, how many is not enough? While this is an important point, its centrality in the debate has obscured another point: How is it to be decided which of multiple applicants will receive visas? This problem arises whenever the numerical limit on the number of visas issued is less than the number of persons wishing to immigrate. The central task for every discussion of immigration policy, then, has become the basis on which new immigrants are to be admitted.

Rationing Immigrant Visas: Past and Current Systems

Historically, the United States has used several methods to regulate immigration. Although it often appears to be a convenient taxonomy, it is somewhat misleading to label these methods as either "qualitative" or "quantitative," for even the so-called qualitative techniques reduce the numbers of immigrants admitted. But several distinctions can be made among the exclusionary criteria. The first group of criteria might be considered "personal disqualifiers." These are attributes of individuals that completely disqualify them from further consideration as immigrants, but they are criteria that do not distinguish among immigrants on the basis of racial or national origin. The second groups of criteria may frankly be called "racial or national disqualifiers." When used as disqualifiers, these criteria mean that no matter how meritorious an individual immigrant might be, his group membership disqualifies or handicaps him in consideration for a visa. The third group we might call "personal limitations." They do not disqualify a person so much as they indicate his relative attractiveness as an immigrant. The fourth group we might call "national limitations." They do not disqualify an individual who is otherwise qualified, but they limit the number of such individuals who can be admitted from any one country. We discuss below the previous use of such criteria and suggest a replacement for them based entirely upon personal disqualifiers or limiters.

Personal Disqualifiers

Even in the days before numerical immigration quotas, there were categories of undesirable persons excluded from immigration. Although the categories included on this list may vary from time to time—the most recent argument has been over the exclusion of homosexuals—it seems unlikely that all personal disqualifiers will ever be removed from the regulations. Among the many exclusionary criteria have been disease, pauperism, criminality, sexual deviance, illiteracy, and mental deficiency. We suggest a revision of this list to ban, on a priori grounds, only two categories of persons: those with infectious diseases, and those who have been convicted of a felony. In the latter case, the crime must be one that would have been a felony in the United States as well. Persons convicted of political crimes, or of minor offenses punishable by jail in other countries but not here, should not be excluded on that ground alone.

National Disqualifiers

In the past the United States explicitly barred entire racial or national groups from entry. The first occasion was the Chinese Exclusion Act of 1882; the second was the Gentlemen's Agreement of 1907, which was intended to virtually eliminate Japanese immigration. More generally, the definition of an "Asiatic barred zone" in 1917 legislation had the effect of eliminating immigration from most parts of Asia.

The national quotas of the 1920s, although they did not bar any European groups, had the effect of sharply limiting immigration from countries that did not already have substantial emigre groups here. The idea of these national quotas was to ensure that the future composition of the immigration stream would be similar to the composition of the United States.

We do not advocate any such disqualifiers based on race, national origin, or ethnic origin.

Personal Limitations

The current preference system has the effect of selecting certain immigrants from the available pool. The selection characteristics are primarily a relationship to a U.S. citizen or resident alien; skills play a minor role. An immediate family relationship to an American citizen counts as a "wild card"—such persons are eligible without regard to numerical limitations.

We advocate a substantial restructuring of the preference system, resulting in a focus on skills and use of a point system to combine the multidimensional aspects of skills. These recommendations are discussed below.

National Limitations

Under the 1924 legislation, the maximum number of visas from a particular country in any year was based on the size of the American population derived from that country. The 1965 Amendments to the Immigration and Nationality Act and subsequent amendments have resulted in a ceiling for independent countries of 20,000 visas issued each year to immigrants subject to numerical limitation, and a worldwide ceiling of 270,000. Thus, for persons who were otherwise qualified, the queue within one's nation could be sufficiently long to prevent immigration. For example, in February 1983, the queue for the third- and sixth-preference immigrants (the occupational preferences) from the Philippines extended back to visas approved in 1970 and 1979, respectively, the queue for second-preference immigrants (spouses and children of resident aliens) from Mexico extended back to 1974, and the queue for fourth-preference immigrants (married children of U.S. citizens) from the Philippines back to 1977. There were backlogs of various lengths in the various preferences (with the exception of the first-preference unmarried adult children of U.S. citizens) for five independent countries and two dependencies (U.S. Department of State, 1983).

The system introduced in the 1965 Amendments was touted as "fair," in comparison with the previous system, because it did not discriminate against any region or country. Not only were no countries excluded, but also the privileged position of the Western Hemisphere was eliminated.

Although the worldwide ceiling is consistently reached, most national ceilings are not reached, while American embassies in some countries are besieged with applicants. Moreover, potential immigrants from countries with large populations are in effect penalized compared with smaller countries. Immigrants from India and Iceland both face the same country ceiling, a ceiling that is in fact binding on India but not on Iceland. We propose a system in which there is an annual quota limit with no national or regional restrictions at all. Only the personal qualifications of individual immigrants would be considered in the decision to admit immigrants.

A New Basis For Rationing

It is appropriate to be straightforward in any revision to the rationing system for visas. There is a kind of fuzzy humanitarianism about immigration that suggests we admit immigrants only for their own good—as if the United States had a duty to provide upward mobility for some tiny fraction of the world's ambitious people. Since restrictions are a necessary evil, the most important aspect of the system becomes a difficult-to-define standard of "fairness." Such "fairness" seems to mean both that every country has an equal chance to send immigrants and that every potential immmigrant from that country has an equal chance to be selected. Current law, in which every country has an equal ceiling of 20,000 visas subject to the preference system, is a move in the direction of "fairness" in that it gives every country equal access to immigration. This doctrine of "fairness" is an extension of the American ideal that a social system is "fair" to the extent that everyone can begin the race at the same starting line. Unequal results may be inevitable later in the race, but everyone should have an equal chance at the beginning.

However, the current preference system for admitting permanent residents is confusing and occasionally arbitrary. It provides no relief for potential applicants who might be qualified under several preferences but live in a country that has a large immigration to the United States. In contrast, potential immigrants from some smaller countries, or countries from which few can obtain a U.S. visa, need only apply, because annual ceilings are not reached. For example, the ceiling of visas per million population in the country of origin is drastically different for, say, India as compared with Iceland, as noted, or for Indonesia as compared with Ireland. Because the immediate relatives of U.S. citizens are not counted against the quota, immigration from some countries far exceeds the 20,000 limit.

There are competing views about what policy would constitute a "fair" one. One view of the "best" way to administer immigration policy is through a lottery—or failing that, through a first-come, first-admitted policy. This would not be a new phenomenon in American immigration policy. In fact, during the 1920s the steamships that raced the Atlantic to be the first in New York Harbor at the first of the month did so in response to a first-come, first-admitted policy.

Another approach holds that immigrants should be good for the country. The best potential immigrants are those who work hard and bring useful human and capital resources, so that they will enrich the country socially and culturally as well as economically. From this point of view, the best way to admit a limited number of immigrants is to select them for the most desirable characteristics. Under this selection criterion immigration policy does not pretend that immigrants are admitted principally for the immigrants' own good, but rather for the good of American society.

A third criterion for admitting immigrants is the benefit to individual Americans rather than the benefit to American society in general. The policies that grant preference for family members are a result of this view. Under current legislation, this preference is exercised in two ways: immediate family members of citizens are admitted without regard to numerical quotas, and the preference system is oriented toward the immigration of immediate relatives of resident aliens, as well as other kin of citizens.

We propose a new system that we discuss below in terms of four elements: the number of visas issued annually, the point system, the exempt category, and the immigration tax. Although this system will not be viewed as entirely "fair," it combines aspects of the three preceding definitions of "fairness."

The Number of Visas Issued Annually

We know of no way to set the optimum number of visas to be issued every year. This is a political as well as a technical problem, but a feasible working number would be to admit 0.2 percent of the current U.S. population annually, on the basis that this number is well within the proven capacity of the United States to absorb new immigrants. This would result in approximately 500,000 immigrant visas based on the present population. This number would apply only to permanent resident alien visas subject to numerical limitation. This represents an increase from the current level of 270,000 visas a year subject to numerical limitation. The immediate relatives of U.S. citizens, refugees, and temporary workers would not be included in this ceiling, as in current policy.

Some have proposed that this number be adjusted annually in line with the performance of the economy. We do not endorse this suggestion, for two reasons. During the periods of relative economic slack in the U.S. the demand for immigration visas slackens, and it expands during periods of economic growth. This provides for self-correction mechanisms. Post–World War II business cycles have been too short and unpredictable to serve as a basis for finetuning the number of immigrant visas. The proposed 0.2 percent of the population is a goal—not a quota—which is based on the history of successful assimilation of immigrants into American society.

The Point System

It is likely that in most years far more persons will wish to immigrate to the United States than there are visas allowable under the proposed system. The point system provides a way for distinguishing among the applicants for visas. The advantage of the point system is that it permits the comparison of potential immigrants who are qualified on several criteria rather than merely one; that is, it combines the multidimensional aspects of qualifications into single numbers that can be ordered. A person qualifying for a visa under the point system would be granted a visa for his or her spouse and for minor, unmarried children, but applicants would not be allowed to combine the characteristics of two or more family members to gain additional points.

The largest number of points would be awarded for work skills. This should be measured in several ways, including completed years of school, type of school or other training, and years of relevant work experience. In some cases it may be desirable to validate the skills with an appropriate test. For potential immigrants who had the promise of a job already waiting for them, additional points might be added. This could occur, for example, in the case of a transfer by a multinational corporation.

Smaller numbers of points would be awarded for other relevant characteristics, including knowledge of English, kinship relations to U.S. resident aliens, distant relationships to U.S. citizens, and ability to bring capital investments to the United States. The points would be granted to the incoming relative only if the adult U.S. citizen or resident alien agreed to serve as a sponsor and guarantee that the immigrant would not become a public charge for a specified period of time.

The "investment capital" criterion deserves some discussion. Under current immigration law the non-preference category has theoretically been available to an immigrant who could demonstrate that he has the equivalent of $20,000 to invest in the United States, presumably in a small business. The provision is subject to abuse. The most common abuse arises in the admission of a person with $20,000 who opens a small business and then sends this $20,000 to a distant cousin; the cousin enters with the same $20,000 and then sends the money to another relative; and so on. In this way, the same $20,000 can serve no investment purpose other than financing chain migration. In practice, however, the sharp increases in fifth-preference migration—siblings of citizens—in recent years has closed opportunities for non-preference immigration and hence for the investor category.

In spite of the potential for abuse, not to provide some points for acquisition of working capital may penalize potential immigrants whose talents lie in entrepreneurial or mercantile areas. A small businessman may have very little in the way of measured human capital to offer, but may have much in the way of shrewd business sense that is valuable. So, although we believe that the general purpose of the skilled-worker preference is to increase the supply of human capital, we also recognize the value of bringing in other forms of capital.

Both Canada and Australia have successfully used point systems as the basis for their admissions policies, and there is evidence that after Canada instituted the point system there was a marked increase in the number of skilled immigrants entering that country (Parai, 1975).

The Exempt Category: Immediate Relatives of U.S. Citizens

Under current immigration policy, close relatives of U.S. citizens may be admitted without counting against the annual quota. We would also permit spouses, dependent children, parents, and grandparents of adult U.S. citizens to enter the country without counting against the annual quota. However, we would require guarantees of financial support and medical insurance.

Because of the declining birth rate and the increased use of abortion, many prospective adoptive parents in the United States must wait long years to receive a child to adopt, and many are never successful. Meanwhile, in many countries the orphanages are overcrowded. Many Americans have sought to adopt orphans from abroad, only to confront mountains of red tape from both governments. We would permit the admission of unlimited numbers of orphans under the following conditions: (1) adoption proceedings had already been instituted in any jurisdiction of the United States; (2) arrangements were being handled by an accredited social service agency; (3) the country of birth relinquished all legal rights to the child, and the parents, if living, relinquished all rights; (4) at least one prospective parent was an American citizen; (5) the child was to become an American citizen. Orphans admitted under this program would be treated as the children of U.S. citizens and could not serve as sponsors of their natural parents or siblings.

The Immigration Tax

The current immigration system offers the prospect of a windfall to a few selected immigrants from a much larger pool. An "immigration tax" would be a way for the native-born population of the United States to capture some of this economic rent and to provide reimbursement for the "social overhead capital" that benefits the immigrant—that is, the Immigration Service itself, the provision of public safety and national defense, and other public services.

The immigration tax would be a substantial sum of money, and requiring that it be paid in a lump sum at the time of admission would essentially bar immigration to all but the few who have good access to capital resources. Most would select the option that it be a surcharge on the federal income tax. For example, it could be a 5 percent tax on earned income to be paid until the immigrant ceases to be a resident alien by leaving the U.S. or by becoming a U.S. citizen. Resident aliens who earned no income would have to file an annual statement demonstrating no earnings. This requirement would replace the current requirement that aliens report any change of address. Resident aliens who entered the U.S. after enactment of the immigration tax would be required to file and to pay the appropriate tax on earned income annually. Violations of these tax policies—even if not felonies—would be grounds for deportation. This payment would help mitigate the concern that immigrants are a drain on publicly provided goods and services. Of course, immigrants would also pay state and federal income taxes, Social Security taxes, and other taxes.

The immigration tax could be used as the financing mechanism for the new national immigration commission (to be discussed in chapter 11). In addition, a portion of the tax could be earmarked to be allocated proportionally to revenue-sharing units based on the number of immigrant taxpayers residing within the locality. A portion of the tax might also be used to indemnify developing countries for the loss of their emigrants.

The immigration tax would have the effect of dampening the applicant flow. It would reduce at least some of the incentive to immigrate, and would require consideration of how good one's chances for success in the United States were. Permanent residents who wished to return to their home countries would need to make no further payments, although the tax they had already paid would not be refundable. So as to provide an equitable treatment among immigrants, the immigration tax or surcharge would be applicable to all entrants, including refugees and immigrants not subject to numerical limitation.

Categories of Entrants

Throughout American history, immigration legislation has been plagued by the assumption that all immigrants are similar. In particular, the assumption has been made that all immigrants are coming to the United States for economic reasons, that they will remain in the United States indefinitely, and that they will eventually become citizens. This formulation does not take into account refugees for political or other reasons, although we know that asylum has been an important function for American immigration. Nor does it take into account those who wish to work in the United States for a period of time rather than their entire working lives. In addition, our policies toward immigrants also affect the millions of persons who enter the United States each year as visitors. The erroneous assumptions about the homogeneity of immigrants have made necessary a kind of patchwork quilt of legislation and regulations. Attempts at reform have often not been sufficiently sweeping because the perspective of each agency administering immigration policy is limited and influenced by a number of narrow issue constituencies. Although immigration policies ultimately deal with all foreign nationals who enter the United States, each policy has been designed to deal with a specific category of immigrants, often ignoring their interrelated roles in the complexity of American immigration.

Any revisions of immigration policy, then, should consider several types of foreign entrants: the resident alien—a person who plans to enter the country for a more or less lengthy period of time, the refugee, the temporary worker, the student, and the tourist. Rethinking immigration policy means considering the role each of these types of immigrants will play in American society. In this chapter we discuss the permanent resident aliens and their role in American society, as well as existing policies on permanent resident aliens. In the next chapter, we discuss all other entrants. In each chapter we recommend the formulation of new criteria and legislative institutions to deal with each class of aliens.

The Resident Alien

The number of visas that is of greatest importance in any regulatory scheme is that regulating the number of permanent resident aliens. Other types of foreign entrants are more likely to be present in the country for short periods of time. The expectation of the permanent resident alien is that he or she will remain in the United States for an indefinite period of time. Only resident aliens can become citizens; of course, not all choose to do so.

Family Members of United States Citizens

Our proposal would shift the emphasis in the permanent resident alien program from family reunification to work skills, but it would still be possible for the immediate families of adult U.S. citizens (that is, their children, spouses, parents, and grandparents) to be issued permanent resident visas. We recognize that these people would have some labor market impact, but we believe family reunification values outweigh these factors. These visas would not be counted in the annual quotas. Resident aliens so admitted would require sponsorship by the American citizen. The sponsoring U.S. citizen would be required to certify and guarantee that the prospective permanent resident would be provided for financially, and that the immigrant would not be a drain on the income transfer or subsidized health care systems. An advantage of limiting the right to sponsorship under this category to adult U.S. citizens (as is the case under current law) is that it would reduce the incentive for illegal aliens and persons here on temporary visas to have a child while in the United States on the theory that the child, as an American citizen, would be the source of admission for the rest of the family.

The provision for the entry of immediate relatives of U.S. citizens does not include siblings, in-laws, or collateral relatives, nor does it include the relatives of permanent residents. Such persons could gain extra points through the point system in the application for permanent residence, but their applications would still be counted in the annual quota.

Work Skills as the Privileged Admission Criteria

While some humanitarianism will always be embodied in immigration legislation—particularly that applied to refugees—we believe that it is quite reasonable for the United States to adopt a consciously self-interested view of the economic immigrants we admit. Under the 1965 Amendments the admission of skilled and productive workers took a back seat to family reunification. Without eliminating the family reunification policy, we suggest a system of admitting permanent residents primarily on the basis of their skills and likely productivity in the U.S. as skilled workers.

While this represents some shift from the current emphasis, it is one that can be justified by the economic conditions that are likely to prevail in the coming decades. Several criticisms may be leveled at such a focus for immigration policy. At the risk of demolishing strawmen, we have collected them and present appropriate responses.

It is an elitist policy. As it is usually phrased, this criticism sounds important; when examined further, it is devoid of substance. Presumably, a policy can be elitist in several ways: it can be initiated for and by the elite of the United States; it can improve the relative life chances of the elite in the United States; it can harm the non-elite in the United States. The first argument is true, but not compelling: even in a democratic republic, no public policy is initiated without the support of at least some segment of the elite; other "elite" groups are just as likely to oppose the policy. If support of an exclusive group qualifies a policy for the label "elite," then many immigration policies deserve that title. A policy to admit skilled workers may be seen as elitist just as surely as the "open door" of the 1800s was believed to help the industrial elite of that time.

The second argument has little merit except perhaps for the hereditary elite of the United States, and that group is relatively small because influential persons in the United States tend to gain their influence through their achieved occupational status. With the decline of family capitalism, birth alone is usually not sufficient to ensure occupational prominence. That prominence is more often achieved through success in business or the professions. A policy to admit skilled workers, especially professionals, is more likely to increase competition among professionals and thereby reduce the relative incomes of native-born professionals, one elite group. In this sense, a skilled-worker policy is more likely to diminish the life chances of the indigenous elite.

As for the third argument, harming the relative position of the non-elite, the immigration of skilled workers is more likely to improve their economic conditions. First, as discussed in chapter 2, the principle of complementarity in production means that skilled immigrants would raise the productivity and hence wages of low-skilled native workers. Second, unlike low-skilled immigrants, high-skilled immigrants would not compete with native-born low-skilled workers for scarce income transfer (welfare) funds, but rather would tend to be net contributors to the treasury in the tax-transfer system.

It encourages a "brain drain." A second set of arguments against a skilled worker policy emphasizes the damage to the sending countries. The damage is summarized in the phrase "brain drain"; however, the characterization of skilled emigration as brain drain deserves further consideration. In some ways, this argument reverses the previous argument in assuming that the indigenous elites should not be allowed to emigrate from developing countries.

In the perjorative sense in which it is usually used, the "brain drain" refers to the loss of skilled workers—usually in the scientific specialties—to the industrialized countries. It is seen as evidence of the economic dominance of the mature capitalist societies. What is less often recognized is that much of the brain drain takes place among the industralized countries; for example, of the 35 naturalized citizens of the United States who have won the Nobel Prize, all were born in European countries that could not by any definition of the term be considered developing countries. Nobel laureates are obviously an exclusive sample from which to generalize, but it is true that skilled professionals, especially in scientific fields, tend to be highly mobile. In part because of the nature of the research enterprise, national boundaries have become relatively less important. But even if we consider the broader areas of skill upon which the current third and sixth preferences are focused, about one-third of those admitted in recent years are from developed countries, that is, from Europe, Canada, and Japan.

The attraction of the United States for these skilled workers is not merely a higher salary, as is often claimed; but a larger after-tax income is one component of the attraction. Many of the European welfare societies have significantly higher tax burdens than does the United States. Furthermore, the United States provides a research environment and the technological apparatus for research at the cutting edges for many scientific disciplines. From the point of view of the general progress of science, international migration is probably desirable. Without governmental intervention, it is also probably inevitable.

But the major thrust of the brain drain controversy has been the emigration of technicians and professionals, especially physicians, from the Third World to the United States. The harm of this, according to the critics, is that the countries that have nurtured these bright and ambitious people during unproductive childhood years lose their contributions during the productive adult period. The United States, which contributed little to their upbringing, will reap the benefits of their adult work lives. The indigenous elites of the developing countries are correspondingly weakened, and the progress of development is hindered by the loss of valuable human resources.

The brain drain from developing countries is not a trivial matter; it was recently reported that there were more Iranian physicians in the United States than in Iran (*New York Times*, 1983). Foreign students are a large proportion of the student body in U.S. engineering schools and in several fields of physical science. Many of these students will seek to remain in the United States after they have finished their studies.

The traditional answer to the brain drain is an insistence that all students return to their homelands after studying abroad. Studies have shown that indeed the vast majority of students do return to their homelands, although some foreign students in the United States who ultimately return extend their stays by one year or more to gain job experience in their fields of study (Glaser, 1978).

But this is an insufficient answer for the professionals who seek to emigrate after several years in their own countries. In analyzing the sources of the brain drain, it is helpful to consider the "push" factors as well as the lure of high salaries in the United States. In many developing countries, skilled professionals cannot use their highest skills. For example, doctors trained in technology-rich American hospitals may find that their diagnostic abilities depend in large part on machine read-outs, and their therapies depend on equipment that is not available. Under these conditions, their skills, while they could be of some assistance in development, would depreciate more rapidly than they would in a country where the skills could be further developed. Here again, immigration could improve the rapidity with which science advances.

Much of the brain drain problem arises from the educational and income distribution policies adopted by many developing countries. The heavy subsidization of higher education, including the earnings forgone while receiving the schooling, is combined with a policy of narrowing wage differentials by skill among those working. The result is a relatively large number of graduates, many of whom cannot find the kind of employment for which they were trained, and a larger differential between their earnings in the home country and in the West. Such an approach, well exemplified by India, encourages emigration. Indeed, 25 percent of the 4,822 Eastern Hemisphere workers who immigrated to the U.S. in 1978 under third-preference (professional) visas were Indian nationals.

Another factor is the political instability that characterizes many developing countries. Even in relatively well-off countries such as Argentina, a substantial exodus of professionals began after episodes of political violence. Highly skilled workers, especially those trained in the West, make attractive targets for terrorists—yet another way to waste the human capital of skilled workers. The alternative to the brain drain may not be the investment of human resources in development; instead, it may be the waste of human capital.

Probably the most effective way of reducing the brain drain is for developing countries to permit wider wage differentals between high-skilled and low-skilled workers, and to invest in the equipment and complementary skilled workers that would make work environments more attractive to their professionals. Ensuring the safety of professionals from terrorists would be useful as well. But neither of these is an easy solution. Investing in CAT-scanners may not make much sense if additional well-baby clinics are a more effective method of raising the country's health status, and there are too many other demands on the investment dollar. The control of insurgency and terrorism is a laudable goal not easily achieved. Development goals should include these considerations, but for the short run there are probably some skills that are simply too specialized for some countries to support.

When this is the case, then the developing country can consider how some return can be made on the export of skilled workers. Several unilateral possibilities come to mind. The Philippines levies income tax on its nationals who are working abroad; thus it can receive a return on their higher salaries without providing further services. Mexico has a series of graduated repayment schedules, with varying rates of interest, for the money it has loaned students to study abroad. Graduates who return to Mexico, and especially those who work for the Mexican government or for Mexican-owned companies, receive the most favorable terms. These are policies that can be enacted and administered successfully by the developing countries. Apparently as a punitive measure, the Soviet Union for a time charged large exit fees proportional to the amount and level of training the person received. This approach, unlike that of the Philippines or Mexico, suffers because of a capital market constraint—it is difficult for persons in Russia to borrow money on the basis of future earnings in the West.

It is worth noting that more than half of the recipients of occupational-preference visas are already in the U.S. on student, tourist, or other visas, and that many are already working, some in violation of their visas. In fiscal year 1979, for example, 53 percent of the third-preference visa beneficiaries (professionals) and 59 percent of the sixth-preference visa beneficiaries (other skilled workers) received an adjustment of status. Under current procedures, it is in practice much easier for persons already in the U.S. to obtain the labor certification required for an occupational-preference visa than it is for a worker outside the country.

The immigration policy we propose for the United States includes two provisions for dealing with the potential brain drain issue. First, students on visas would be required to return to their home countries and to remain there for at least twelve months before applying for other visas. A student visa could not be adjusted to resident status while the student resided in the United States; it could only be adjusted at the American embassy in the home country.

For humanitarian purposes, two modifications would be made to the requirement that students return home for at least one year. Students applying for political asylum—that is, for admission as refugees—could adjust their visas while in the United States. And those who have married American citizens would be able to convert their student visas into permanent residence visas after a shorter period, such as three months, in the home country.

The second provision relates to the proposed immigration tax. The United States might well consider the possibility of rebating a portion of the immigration tax to the country of origin as a form of foreign aid tied directly to the emigration of that country's nationals who have studied in the U.S. on student visas. Though the rebate might not fully compensate for the costs of schooling, it would be a direct government-to-government subsidy, paid in addition to whatever remittances the emigrants send home. To discourage repressive regimes from encouraging emigration either to rid themselves of undesirables or to obtain the subsidy, the rebate would not apply to persons admitted as refugees or for other immigrants who sign a rebate waiver. The U.S. should encourage countries receiving this compensation to use it for upgrading their own work facilities and job opportunities for skilled workers.

It violates American tradition. There is another way in which the admission of skilled workers is seen as elitist. The admission of skilled workers means that unskilled workers, the traditional immigrant groups, would have much more difficulty in entering the United States. For those who believe that the essence of the American tradition is the admission of the poor, the outcasts, and the wretched refuse, a policy that favors physicians and scientists is an aberration. In fact, however, the search for skilled immigrants was begun in the very early days of the republic. Coopers, smiths, carpenters, and other skilled workers were avidly sought by the states and territories. Special inducements were offered to attract them to the more sparsely settled areas of the country, and broadsides describing the United States as the land of opportunity were distributed to them in Europe.

It is true that the unskilled workers who arrived in such quantities were the great majority of earlier immigrants, but we believe that a shift in emphasis to skilled workers is justified by the shift in the circumstances within which immigration policy operates.

Summary

Rethinking our attitudes toward immigration requires distinguishing the categories of persons we desire to admit and setting minimal criteria for their admission. This chapter has set forth the outline for admission procedures for resident aliens. The point system for admission avoids many of the problems of previous admission systems. It is based solely on personal characteristics with a primary focus on the person's skills and without consideration of national or ethnic origin. The provisions for the immigration of the immediate relatives of U.S. citizens, as well as the allowance of a small number of points for other kinship relations with a U.S. citizen or resident alien, retain the humanitarian aspects of the present program without unduly stressing kinship as a criterion for admission. This approach could substantially increase the skill level of immigrants to the United States.

The immigration tax we propose would provide a way to capture some of the economic rent accorded those who are permitted to immigrate. It would provide a way to finance the immigration system and to provide some indemnification for the governmental agencies, here and abroad, that might be hurt by immigration.

10
Rethinking Our Attitudes toward Immigrants: Standards for Other Entrants

While most individuals who come to America come to stay, many others do not. America has attracted many who came to work or study for a time, or just to visit the new land. History records the migration of ironworkers from Lancashire as well as apple pickers from Mexico. Both groups joined the circular migration stream from many lands to the United States, returning home after earning American wages and learning American skills. Others came seeking only those skills. They came to study at American colleges and universities to take newfound knowledge back to their native lands. Still others came only as observers. Visitors, few as eloquent as de Tocqueville, come every year to see democracy in America—as well as Disneyland, and friends and relatives. In addition, there are those, relatively few in number, who come seeking freedom from political persecution, the refugees who continue to seek the promise of America.

The Temporary Worker

The United States has had several temporary worker programs. The largest and best known was the Bracero Program (1942 to 1964), which in peak years resulted in several hundred thousand Mexican farm workers being employed on a temporary basis in U.S. agriculture, primarily during the harvest season. Current regulations allow for the admission of temporary workers of "distinguished merit and ability" (H-1 visa, largely professionals); temporary workers to perform services for which "qualified labor cannot be found in this country" (H-2, largely unskilled farm workers); trainees (H-3); they also allow temporary intracompany transfers of employees with specialized managerial, executive, or other skills (I-1). Among the 42,979 entries (including multiple entries) of temporary workers and trainees (H-1, H-2, and H-3 visas) in 1978, the skill levels and countries of origin varied widely. Those from the United Kingdom (3,813), Japan (1,072), the Philippines (3,214), and Canada (8,215), as well as from other parts of Europe and Asia, were predominantly professionals and managers, whereas those from Mexico (2,271) and the West Indies (13,114) were predominantly farm laborers employed during the harvest.

Clearly, the stereotype that temporary workers are all unskilled Mexican farm workers is without foundation. But we know little about what other temporary workers do and why they are admitted.

Because the current immigration restrictions do not permit any aliens except permanent residents to work, special visas are needed in a variety of cases:

The manager who comes to run a foreign-owned plant or to serve as a troubleshooter for a brief period of time

The professor who comes to an American university to teach for a semester or two

The repairman who comes to work on a piece of imported machinery or to learn how to operate American machinery that is to be exported to his country

Besides these cases, there are many others in which it is desirable to permit the entry of workers, skilled or otherwise, for limited periods of time. But these temporary worker visas are far more easily obtained by the Japanese manager, the Israeli professor, or the German repairman—or even the Jamaican apple-picker—than by the Mexican farm worker. It has been claimed, and with some justification, that current American policy discriminates against Mexican farm workers.

To be sure, many undocumented Mexican workers have come to work without temporary worker permits. But under these circumstances, they are easily preyed upon by unscrupulous employers, rapacious "coyotes" (smugglers of immigrants), and criminals both native- and foreign-born. Because the demands of the American economy make it unlikely that this flow can be stopped entirely, a temporary worker program offers several advantages: legalizing the flow, ensuring the return of the workers when their jobs have ended, and protecting them while they are here. It was for these reasons that the Mexican government for years sought United States government cooperation in the regulation and protection of Mexican nationals temporarily in the United States.

Although few complaints have been raised about the Japanese manager, the Israeli professor, or the German repairman, a myriad of complaints are heard about a temporary worker program for the unskilled worker. The principal arguments against an unskilled-worker program are considered below.

Temporary worker programs exploit the worker. Such charges are rarely made from the point of view of the individual worker, who has freely contracted to perform a specific job for a specific wage. Instead, they are made from the point of view of groups of individuals: native workers, whose solidarity as workers might be undermined; the temporary workers as a group, whose very temporary nature precludes effective organization or assimilation; the families of the temporary workers, whether they are left lonely in the home country or isolated in the new country; the village neighbors of the temporary workers, who lose the production of their most ambitious countrymen. The term "exploitation" means different things to different commentators. To some it may mean lower relative wages or lower seniority in the U.S.; to others it means forgone production in the home country. As long as labor markets are formally free, however, these criticisms have little weight compared to the desires of the individual worker.

The worker is forever estranged from the receiving country. This claim is commonly made against the guestworker programs in Europe. It is based on two facts: most European countries do not permit the temporary workers to become citizens, no matter how long they remain in the country; and even in those countries that do permit guestworkers to become citizens, the effect of the homogeneous European societies is to keep them socially and culturally isolated. Neither of these problems need exist in the United States if temporary workers can adjust their statuses and if our pluralistic society retains its current vigor. Indeed, experience as a temporary worker—with its guarantee of a job—is far more likely to ensure that an unskilled immigrant will be able to fit into an industrial economy.

The worker is placed in a powerless situation in the work context. It is true that there are employers who will seek temporary workers because they are less likely to be unionized, because they speak a strange language and so cannot easily be hired by competitors, and because their expectations of wages are lower than those of native workers. Many European countries underscore the powerlessness of the workers by imposing strict regulations: workers may not be able to change employers or jobs; they may not be able to move from city to city within the country; they may not be able to join unions; they may even be forbidden to join clubs or ethnic associations for fear that these may become unions. But none of these restrictions is essential to a temporary worker program. There is no reason whatever to forbid temporary workers in the United States the freedom to travel, the freedom of association, or the freedom to change jobs and seek a better wage or a more congenial workplace. Indeed, all of these freedoms flow from the original assumption of a formally free labor market.

It is because the European countries have felt it necessary to sharply limit the labor market activities of their temporary workers that they have encountered many of these criticisms. We propose a program to admit temporary workers that includes restrictions primarily on the employer. Moreover, we believe that such a program, far from exploiting workers, could protect them.

We suggest a program in which the employer must request from a new immigration commission (see chapter 11) a specific number of employees for a specific period of time, with an acceptable justification for hiring temporary workers. The number of temporary workers to be admitted would not be fixed by legislation at an annual quota, but would be determined by the immigration authorities in response to demonstrated demand by the labor market. Because such a program would be a new experience in American immigration, the program should be evaluated yearly in a report to Congress for the first five years. After five years, the program would be evaluated and reconstituted as appropriate for another ten years, with reports to the Congress after each five-year cycle.

In order to justify employing temporary workers rather than native-born labor, the prospective employer would have to demonstrate that he had exhausted all reasonable means of recruiting native workers, including public and private employment agencies and appropriate advertising, or that the temporary workers had specialized talents or skills that would benefit the U.S. Further, the employer would have to provide the following: advance funding for the return ticket, to be placed in an escrow account; evidence of the purchase of medical insurance plans for the workers and their families (if the families accompany them); and a specific salary either at or above the federal minimum wage for that type of work or equal to the prevailing wage for that work, whichever is higher. (In the event that a teenage subminimum wage is established, the wage offered would have to be at least the adult minimum.) The employer would agree to pay Social Security taxes for the workers; federal income taxes would be withheld and a portion placed in a special insurance fund to provide disability insurance and supplementary revenue-sharing to the local area. Temporary workers would also be subject to the immigration tax that is levied on resident aliens. Workers would be free to leave the original employer and to work for a new one, as long as the new employer agreed to the same minimum conditions and had a certificate to hire temporary workers. The new employer would place the money for the return ticket in the escrow fund, and the money of the original employer would be returned.

We suggest that the families of temporary workers also be admitted, on the condition that the employer-purchased medical insurance cover dependents as well as workers. Wives and children of the temporary workers would be able to work only if they became temporary workers themselves, after which they would work on the same basis as other temporary workers.

These provisions would apply to any worker admitted to the United States for temporary work. It is important that this program be not merely for the bracero or the agricultural worker; it should also apply to other foreigners who would be working in the United States for a short period of time but not seeking permanent residence. The Japanese manager, the Israeli professor, and the German repairman would be bound by the same restrictions.

Temporary workers would be admitted on one-year visas (renewable for three one-year periods). After living in the U.S. on a temporary worker visa, workers would have to live outside the U.S. for a period equal to half the duration of the preceding stay in the U.S. before being readmitted. Temporary workers could not convert their visas to resident visas without going back to their home countries. However, they would receive a number of points toward resident alien status for being temporary workers and thus proving their ability to contribute to the U.S. economy. Such a program would not end illegal immigration, but it would slow it down by regularizing the status of some illegal aliens engaged in temporary work.

A note on employer sanctions. We do not advocate explicit sanctions against employers who hire illegal aliens. However, we do advocate that the records of a company found to be employing illegal aliens be checked to ensure that all regulations are being observed, including federal and state tax withholding, payment of unemployment insurance and worker's compensation, payment of the minimum wage, and observance of health and safety regulations.

Our opposition to sanctions against the employers of illegal aliens has several foundations. For employer sanctions to be effective some form of workcard or national identity card issued by a federal authority would be required. We discuss this issue further in chapter 11. To anticipate our argument a bit, we share the concern of many that such an identity system is inconsistent with American values and should not be undertaken in the absence of a national emergency. We also have reservations about the wisdom of placing a greater burden of immigration law enforcement on employers, rather than on the appropriate government authorities. Finally, employer screening of all newly hired workers to determine their legal right to work would raise the relative cost of low-wage workers, particularly in high-turnover jobs. This would further exacerbate the employment difficulties of many youths, women reentering the labor market, and other workers, including the disadvantaged minorities. It is not obvious that the favorable effect on their employment of reducing the supply of illegal aliens would outweigh the added costs.

The Student

Students are currently admitted to the United States upon proof of admission to an accredited institution, proof of financial support (either from the institution or from other sources), and on the condition that they not seek work. We see no reason to change the substantive provisions of this program. Encouraging students to study in the United States is advantageous in a number of ways: it provides a multicultural dimension to our institutions of higher learning, it assists the development of the Third World by training professionals, and it introduces the future elites of many countries to the United States.

The provision that the schools be accredited is needed to prevent the establishment of fake "trade schools" whose chief purpose is to provide "on-the-job" training—that is, whose purpose is to provide workers.

The requirement for financial support is designed to ensure that students are adequately maintained, especially given the requirement that they not work. The proof of financial support would include medical insurance and a round-trip ticket to the home country in addition to funds for tuition and living expenses.

The requirement that students not work is designed to ensure that student visas are not used to evade the temporary worker programs. Moreover, students who do not have extensive work experience in the United States are less likely to become immediate contributors to the "brain drain." There are two problems with this restriction. The first problem is that students, especially graduate students, are deprived of useful off-campus work-related experiences; problems might also arise with positions as interns or residents. These positions are normally compensated, although the level of compensation tends to be low. The second problem is with postgraduate jobs. These are now considered a routine part of training in some scientific fields, and, once again, they are compensated at a low level. The current accommodation for these exceptions is to permit students to work on campus in certain jobs and to permit students to remain in the United States for one year after degree completion to gain work experience related to their fields of study. We would continue such programs with the stipulation that exceptions be requested by bona fide educational, medical, scientific, or government agencies.

A different problem is the expectation that foreign students will be "full-time" students during their stay. "Full-time" does not imply that the student does not work; many native students are full-time students and still work. The term "full-time" usually has a financial definition rather than a definition based on the student's allocation of time: "full-time" refers to the amount of tuition that is being paid to a school. A requirement that a student remain a full-time student may penalize graduate students during crucial points in their studies, particularly when they are involved in degree-related research. We suggest instead that student visas be issued for a four-year period, with three one-year extensions easily granted upon the petition of the student and the educational institution. After the seven-year period, however, the student and the institution would have to justify the continuation of the student visa. This procedure is designed to prevent the "perpetual student" from unduly delaying the completion of the degree. The requirement for "full-time" status would then be eliminated for those in degree-related research programs.

The principal criticism of foreign student programs is that they increase the brain drain. The usual solution is to require the student to return home. With the exception of the job-related experience, as mentioned above, we propose that students be required to return home. The way to put teeth into this requirement is to insist that student visas cannot be converted into other kinds of visas (either temporary worker visas or permanent resident visas). A former holder of a student visa could apply for another visa only after a twelve-month stay in the home country or another country outside of North America (with the exemption of Mexican and Canadian students, who could return home). The request for a change of visa status would have to be made from the American embassy or consulate in the home country. This would prevent the temporary exodus of students from the United States to Canada to await permanent resident status. The one exception we propose is that students who marry American citizens be required to wait only three months before applying for a change of status. This three-month delay would have some inhibiting effect on marriages of convenience, but it is consistent with the admission of family members. Students who wished to convert their visas to refugee visas could apply to do so within the United States.

Provisions should be made for the admission of spouses and dependent children with the student. Their visas would not permit them to work, and they would have to be covered by the medical insurance and return ticket policy under which the student was admitted. Adjustment of status for student spouses and dependents could also be made only from the American embassy in the home country and with the same waiting period.

The Refugee

The Refugee Act of 1980 sets an annual quota of 50,000 resident alien visas a year, but it gives the President authority to admit additional refugees. The term "refugee" is in practice defined in response to political or other considerations as they arise. This allows maximum flexibility in responding to crises.

The Refugee Act tried to anticipate manipulation by foreign leaders who would presume on our humanitarian instincts by allowing admission only of refugees who had selected the United States as a country of second asylum. While another country had to be chosen by the refugee as the country of first asylum, it is always possible that no country will wish to serve as the asylum country.

In addition to our efforts to work through diplomatic channels to influence other governments not to create refugee streams, it is incumbent upon us to set our own policy for admitting refugees. Because there will probably be many more refugees than there are places for them in the United States for the foreseeable future, the U.S. will have to set up a system of priorities and preferences, much like that for resident aliens, for refugees. We outline our proposal for such a priority system in the paragraphs that follow.

The gravest danger and the closest ties. We suggest that the highest priority in admitting refugees be given to those who are judged to be in the greatest physical danger of starvation or annihilation and whose persecution is most closely related to U.S. policy or principles. This point can perhaps be better illustrated by examples than by an elaboration on the principle. The employees of the U.S. embassy in Saigon had a greater claim on our refugee admission program than do the victims of an earthquake. The claims on the U.S. refugee program by political prisoners, by members of outlawed political parties, or by losers in military conflicts would be measured by the degree to which their operations were financed by us or their political ideals approximated those of our system of government.

The great problem with this system of priorities is that it could encourage every petty dictator to threaten to exterminate those who oppose him rather than jail them. The threat to execute dissidents could be used to coerce the United States into accepting the dissidents as refugees. There are two stumbling-blocks for any dictator with this kind of blackmail in mind. First, the refugees given asylum in the United States would have a permanent soapbox for announcing their dissent. They could become more of a problem abroad than they were at home. Second, every other dictator in the world might have the same plan in mind. The potential number of refugees so created would force the United States to make decisions about whose dissidents it would accept. Every dictator would run the risk of receiving adverse publicity without successfully expelling any dissidents.

The United States could discourage the creation of refugees by threatening economic reprisals. For example, any rebate of the United States immigration tax could be withheld. Legislation could provide that, for every refugee admitted from a given country, the rebates for two resident aliens would be withheld. Consequences for foreign aid, trade treaties, and other relationships are also possiblities. However, none of these sanctions will be effective against the country that considers the United States its enemy.

The innocent. As a second priority in the refugee program, innocent bystanders and families of refugees should be admitted. When the families of political refugees were themselves in danger, they would be admitted under the first priority. This priority would include persons displaced in wars, widows of executed dissidents, and others whose only "crime" is a relationship or ascriptive characteristic rather than an affirmative act. Included in this group would be persecuted religious or ethnic groups. Again, if the persecution were violent—as in Germany under Hitler—the first priority would apply.

International agreement. The third priority for admission would be refugees admitted through agreements with other nations. These agreements might be multilateral, involving the U.S. and a number of other hospitable nations, or bilateral, involving the U.S. and one other country, perhaps a country already serving as a country of first asylum.

Other provisions for refugees. Because the number of potential refugees will always exceed the available openings, the United States must also aggressively pursue other means for resettling refugees. Among the methods that should be considered are financial aid to countries of first asylum and direct services to refugees in other countries. Medical care, the building of housing, and food are practical direct aids that could be given to countries of first asylum, and to resettlement agencies in other countries. To the extent that these are provided to victims of natural disasters—who might also be considered refugees—a model already exists for providing such aid.

Even all of these points do not fully solve the problems of identifying and defining refugees. However, based on these proposals, and the assumptions underlying them, we can state a definition and operating principle that should be helpful: Refugees migrate involuntarily. It is the degree of coercion, in the context of national responsibility and interest, that should determine which refugees are admitted.

Tourists and Other Temporary Visitors

It is in the interest of the United States to encourage tourism. Because of the concern with illegal immigration, however, obtaining a tourist visa to enter the United States has become onerous to the casual visitor. In some U.S. embassies the scrutiny of potential tourists is embarrassing and almost certainly discourages travel. In some ports of entry in the United States, inspectors have refused to honor the visas granted by embassy personnel abroad. Occasionally this has occurred because of suspected fraud, but in other cases it appears to stem only from the persistent fear of abuse, especially by persons of particular nationalities. In sum, the current system of tourist visas is prone to stereotyping and discrimination of the worst kind. This discrimination, although based on national origin, is not illegal under current legislation; antidiscrimination legislation takes effect only when the person has been admitted to the country.

We suggest several changes in procedures. First, acquiring a visa should be relatively easy, but tourists should be required to show proof of an ongoing, prepaid, nonrefundable ticket to a country other than the United States. Second, far more could be done to welcome tourists. The current inspection system by immigration and customs at most international airports is unpleasant for both the returning citizen and the tourist. Third, much more effort is needed in the enforcement of tourist visa deadlines and restrictions. Visa overstayers and visa abusers (i.e., those who work while holding a tourist visa) are major contributors to the volume of illegal immigration. Penalities for overstaying one's visa could range from denial of future visas to fines and imprisonment.

Summary

Many wish to come to the United States for a temporary stay, but current immigration policies make this difficult, if not impossible, for the majority of entrants. We propose that temporary workers, students, and visitors be considered under policies different from those governing permanent immigrants. The policies we propose have been designed to facilitate this kind of temporary immigration, with its benefits for both visitors and host country, while protecting participants against possible abuses of the programs.

Effective policies to regulate the flow of temporary entrants can be implemented with relative ease. It is far more difficult to regulate the flow of refugees. Because not every individual or group that wishes to come to the United States claiming refugee status can be admitted, policies governing refugees must reflect both humanitarian and national-interest criteria.

11
Rethinking the Administration of Immigration Policies

Throughout the public discussions on immigration, remarkably little has been said about the current administration of immigration policies. The final report of the Select Commission on Immigration and Refugee Policy (1981), for example, devoted little attention to the subject and had little to offer in recommendations for administrative changes. Yet even a cursory glance at immigration history shows that the administrative mechanisms of immigration are themselves an indicator of the true intent or effect of the legislation. Legislation enacted by Congress can be sabotaged by a stubborn bureaucracy; or a Congress that poses for its constituents with tough legislation can at the same time emasculate enforcement with niggardly appropriations. Cabinet-level agencies can fight for control of the administrative apparatus, and interest groups can exercise political pressure in a variety of ways, depending on the organization of the immigration agency. Throughout American immigration history, all of these things have happened.

Administrative Issues

A number of problems seem to be inevitable in any consideration of United States immigration policy. These include tensions between federal and state government jurisdictions, loopholes in the legislation, interagency conflict and other administrative problems, and the competing interests of various groups.

Federal-State Tensions

These tensions were particularly pronounced during the 1800s, when some states tried to limit immigration or to enforce additional state requirements, while other states established offices in Europe to recruit immigrants. The issue was definitively settled by the Supreme Court in its ruling that the federal government has the sole responsibility for admitting immigrants. The continuing tension is caused by the fact that state and local agencies are often used as settlement agencies for the immigrants. In addition, there is a strong preference among immigrants to settle in a relatively few cities and states so that these bear the burden of international migration.

Legislative Loopholes

Immigration legislation is passed by the Congress. But what Congress can do, Congress can undo. An annual quota system established by one piece of legislation can easily be amended in subsequent legislation, with possible contradictions going unnoticed or simply being ignored. This is most likely to happen when one piece of legislation sets a quota and subsequent legislation admits additional refugees or other persons. The result can be a crazyquilt of regulations and requirements, often proceeding from noble intent. As a last recourse, members of Congress can introduce private bills for individuals who ask for exceptions to legislation or who get caught in the administrative gears.

Administrative Discretion

Administrative discretion is inevitable in any enforcement system with finite resources. A decision to admit Cuban refugees will necessarily draw some personnel from a search for illegal aliens; a search for illegal aliens conducted in Cleveland may not be as fruitful, in terms of numbers apprehended, as one conducted in San Antonio, but it is less likely to be perceived as directed toward Mexicans and may be more effective in deterring further illegal migration than would increasing the revolving-door apprehensions at the border. Discretion enters at many points in the immigration process: in the decision at the border to honor a visa issued in an American consulate or embassy abroad; in the decision to search the trunk of one car at the border and not that of another car; in the decision to adjust the status of some illegal entrants rather easily, or to deport others immediately; in the decision to seek to strip citizenship from one suspected war criminal and not another. Many criticisms of the Immigration and Naturalization Service are really criticisms of the administrative priorities implicit in these discretionary decisions.

Interagency Conflict

Immigration is ultimately bound up with virtually every function of government, although some agencies are obviously more involved than others. Historically, the Departments of State, Justice, and Labor have been most involved, as has the Public Health Service. It is also easy to understand the concerns of other agencies: the Department of Health and Human Services, as well as the Departments of Defense, Treasury, Transportation, Commerce, and Housing and Urban Development. The immigration service has been administratively "housed," at various times, in the Departments of State, the Treasury, Commerce, and Labor. Its current location in the Justice Department emphasizes its role as an enforcement agency, but critics have argued that its many other functions do not lie within the area of expertise of the Justice Department. Indeed, the State Department is involved in issuing visas at its embassies and consulates abroad, and also in the admission of refugees. The Labor Department is involved in the labor certification of immigrants who seek to enter under the current third and sixth preferences, or as non-preference immigrants.

The Role of Private Agencies

Historically, family members already in the U.S. have played the major role in helping new immigrants adjust to the United States. However, local social service agencies and individual volunteers have also played an important role in welcoming immigrants to their communities and helping them get settled. From time to time the federal government seeks a specific relationship with these agencies; this was the case with the post–World War II displaced persons program, with the Cuban refugee program following Castro's rise, and with the most recent program for Indochinese and Cuban refugees. The concept of private "sponsorship" of refugees, done either by individuals or local groups, expresses this kind of relationship. At other times, however, the federal government has tended to ignore the existence of private efforts to help immigrants. There has been relatively little discussion of the role of the volunteer and the private social agencies in immigration.

The Role of Interest Groups

The testimony before the Congress demonstrates that many organizations and associations continue to have a deep and continuing interest in immigration. In many cases these groups are ethnic, national, language, or religious associations, but their explicit areas of interest range from civil rights and patterns of discrimination to native sports and cuisine.

Most of the ethnic-based interest groups favor easier immigration, particularly for persons of the same ethnicity. More recently, "environmentally" oriented interest groups have arisen, and have replaced the previous "nativist" interest groups in opposing immigration. The American Committee on Italian Migration and the Mexican-American Legal Defense and Education Fund are but two of the many examples of ethnic interest groups. The Federation for American Immigration Reform (FAIR), an environmentalist group opposed to increased immigration, is another.

A different set of lobbyists are those whose economic interests are directly or indirectly threatened by immigration. A number of labor groups and professional associations have brought heavy pressure to bear on the Department of Labor regarding occupational licenses, asking for declarations that their particular specialities are filled and that the domestic labor supply for the occupation is sufficient, and hence for reductions in the number of labor certificates and occupational-preference immigrants. During the late 1970s physicians and dieticians were successful in getting the Department of Labor to reduce the favorable treatment of these professions in the issuing of immigration visas. Other groups with obvious interests in immigration include immigration lawyers, colleges and universities with large numbers of foreign students and foreign professors, the travel industry, and many businesses with overseas trade interests.

An Immigration Commission

We propose the establishment of a commission, the National Immigration Administration (NIA), to replace the existing Immigration and Naturalization Service. While this new commission could not resolve all of the tensions inherent in administering immigration policies, it would be better equipped to deal with them than the current administrative framework.

The commission would be independent of the existing cabinet departments, but would not have cabinet status. The commission would be headed by five commissioners, appointed by the President and confirmed by the Senate for staggered five-year terms with a maximum of two consecutive terms. The length and the staggering of terms would reduce the likelihood of partisan control of the commission. The chairman of the commission would serve at the pleasure of the President of the United States. The chairman would act as administrator for the commission, would report directly to the President, and would be responsible for an annual report to both the President and the Congress. The new commission would be partially funded through the immigration tax and visa revenues, although these probably would not be adequate to cover the full cost of the agency, and some general revenues would be required for its support.

Because immigration intersects so many areas of public interest, it has never fit neatly into any single executive branch agency. Making the commission independent, and not tying it to any cabinet-level agency, would further reduce the influence of direct partisanship. The proposed commission's independence and status would permit it to take on all immigration-related tasks, from the issuing of visas to enforcement, without needing to rely on other agencies to perform part of its primary duties. Although this does mean that all of the interest groups and agencies would center their concerns on this one commission, the existence of the commission could ensure a sort of "equalized pressure." What happens today is that labor certification, for example, is delegated to a Labor Department that is partially "captured" by labor interests, while the pro-immigration groups focus their attentions on the Immigration and Naturalization Service.

As noted, this new commission would address all of the immigration-related tasks of the federal government. Some of these are discussed in further detail below.

The Issuing of Visas

The NIA would have personnel stationed in American embassies and consulates. In practice, most of these would be State Department personnel detailed to the NIA and part of whose salary would come from NIA appropriations. These foreign-duty officers of the NIA would be permitted to inspect documents of prospective visitors and to issue tourist visas, temporary worker visas, student visas, and visas to persons in immigrant categories exempt from numerical limitation. They would review the documentation and help determine the standing, under the "point system," of potential permanent residents, whose admission would be subject to numerical limitation. These documents would be forwarded to NIA headquarters in the United States. The decision to admit permanent residents, because it would be subject to an annual worldwide quota, would have to be made from a centralized location; permission to issue the permanent residence visas would then be cabled to the NIA personnel abroad. Foreign-duty officers would also cooperate in certifying applicants for temporary worker programs and in facilitating their entry to the United States.

Issuing visas from a centralized location suggests an obvious administrative efficiency: keeping visa applications and other pertinent file information "online" in a computerized system. Current technology makes this entirely feasible and would considerably aid the enforcement function. The present INS has an unfortunate reputation for losing visa applications and other documents. Computerized systems are certainly not foolproof, but they do offer the possibility of fewer misplaced or misfiled documents. Files on immigrants or visitors could be updated when a visitor leaves or when a permanent resident files an annual tax form. This has an obvious advantage for determining numbers of visa overstayers, allocating federal revenue-sharing to the locales where the immigrants actually live, and reducing fraud in the system. It would necessitate assigning a unique number (such as a Social Security number) to every visa applicant. However, safeguards have already been initiated in other government data programs to prevent any threat to privacy from using Social Security numbers for other purposes, and similar safeguards could be initiated for immigrants as well. It does seem that a link to the Internal Revenue Service will be inevitable, in part at least to recover the immigration tax from permanent residents and the various tax payments from the participants in the temporary worker program.

Gatekeeping Functions

NIA agents would perform services similar to those of the INS personnel at ports of entry. More funds should be sought, however, to provide extra personnel at busy airports and at particularly busy times. Returning citizens, tourists, and businessmen should not be subjected to the lengthy waits common in many airports. NIA agents would have access to the computerized file of information on immigrants. This should help curtail the occasional embarrassment and harrassment of immigrants whose visas are issued by the State Department and are challenged by the Immigration and Naturalization Service. Another advantage of the computerized check is its time-saving potential; instead of peering at cumbersome books with long lists of the names of undesirables, agents could merely key in the visa number and receive the file of information on the potential immigrant. A few discreet questions could be asked if fraud were suspected—with the answers already displayed on the computer screen. Cooperation between NIA officials and customs officials in the Treasury Department should be encouraged.

Immigration Magistrates

Because there are occasional disputes at the border about suspected fraudulent entries, even consolidating the international and domestic visa checks will not be sufficient. Provisions already exist for hearings to be held for potential entrants who might be barred, or for apprehended illegal entrants. We propose that the system of magistrates be enlarged so that a hearing within twenty-four hours can be granted in every such dispute. The NIA, every potential entrant at the border, and apprehended illegal aliens should have the right to appeal. In addition, immigrants already admitted to the United States should have an additional route of appeal to the United States courts. Persons not yet admitted to the United States do not have, in a strict sense, any constitutional rights. But denial of any sort of due process to these people seems to be such a violation of our intuitive sense of fair play that it should be avoided even if it is "legal."

The magistrate's hearing could also be the forum for the adjustment-of-status hearings for illegal entrants who were in the United States prior to the creation of the new temporary worker program and wished to formalize their positions. This could be done in two ways. First, the undocumented worker could become "documented" by applying for the temporary worker program. In this case, the hearing before the magistrate would merely ensure that the undocumented worker was not wanted for any crime. Undocumented workers already in the United States should be given priority in the temporary worker program. Second, the undocumented worker could choose to petition for permanent resident status on the same basis as other applicants under the point system. Either of these choices would expose the illegal immigrant to the risk of being deported, but they would also offer the opportunity to regularize status. It should be noted, however, that this opportunity should not be treated as a back-door amnesty policy. (Amnesty is discussed in the following chapter.)

Border Patrol and Area Control

If the magistrates serve as the judicial arm of the NIA, then the border patrol and area control inspectors (interior enforcement) could be thought of as the police arm. Even with the reforms we have suggested, it seems likely that many persons will have incentives to enter the United States illegally. Adopting a temporary worker program certainly does not mean that illegal immigration will end or that smugglers should be able to enter the country unchecked.

The greatest need of the border patrol today is for more resources, including personnel. Politicians and editorial writers who live in the Northeast often seem to have no conception of the vastness of the southwestern deserts, the length of the southern border, or the difficulty of an inhospitable terrain. As for the northern border, very little attention has been paid to it because of the perception that the "problem" is along the Mexican border. In fact, there is a well-organized pipeline for smuggling illegal Chinese entrants through British Columbia; the provinces of Ontario and Quebec are also reported to provide crossing points for many illegal entrants from Europe and the Caribbean.

After the land borders are secured, the border patrol's job will have just begun. The vast seacoasts of the United Sates offer many secluded spots for a small ship to come ashore; a small airplane may find many quiet landing strips and fly to them at such low altitudes that it is unlikely to be detected. Even in the busy and relatively well-patrolled seaports and airports, there are many opportunities to "jump ship" and merge with the crowd.

It should not be expected that the border patrol can seal the border and prohibit all illegal entries; the political and economic costs of attempting to do so would be prohibitive. In addition, there are visa overstayers and visa violators, as well as alien deportation cases. Hence, interior enforcement is as important as border enforcement. An important step would be the reversal of the trend in recent years of declining real resources for interior enforcement. Having allowed the problem to get out of hand through a policy that virtually offers de facto amnesty to those who successfully penetrate the border, the U.S. may have to provide a substantial increase in interior enforcement resources for several years. In addition, Justice Department regulations limiting the extent to which state and local police and welfare agencies can report suspected illegal aliens to the immigration authorities should be reviewed.

The deterrent effect of the resources currently devoted to border and interior enforcement is smaller than it might be because of the virtual absence of penalties against apprehended illegal aliens. Illegal aliens apprehended at the border are simply returned to the other side, free to try again. The revolving door at the border may have little net deterrent effect in spite of the impressive number of apprehensions. An apprehension and deportation in the interior imposes greater costs, and increased interior enforcement may therefore have much greater deterrent effects per apprehension. In addition, we endorse the introduction of a policy of fines and imprisonment for apprehended illegal aliens, particularly those who are repeat offenders. The implementation of these policies will require more enforcement and detention resources. Without these policies we do not know whether it is impossible to control illegal migration, as some believe, or whether the resources have been too meager to control it, as we believe is the case.

Refugee Unit

Unlike other immigrants, refugees are provided with basic subsistence and with resettlement aid. This implies a need for interagency collaboration on refugees, but new waves of refugees are usually greeted with ad hoc administrative structures that must try to coordinate the work of state and federal agencies, public and private agencies, and group and individual sponsors. Since there is now a greater number of refugees in the world than at any time since the end of World War II, and since new waves of refugees can be expected from several quarters, it seems likely that refugee settlement in some form will be a continuing objective of the United States. This in turn suggests that a set of prearranged procedures is needed to provide guidance in the reception and care of refugees. The insensitive handling of the 1980 wave of Cuban refugees—with what appeared to be concentration camps set up to receive them—must not be repeated.

No coordinated, advance planning for refugees has been possible because of a sense that it is somehow inviting trouble to plan for refugees—as if the act of planning could create the refugees. But this is superstititous thinking of the genre, "if we ignore it, it will go away." Even if the United

States does not have a thought-out plan for receiving refugees, events abroad are likely to continue to produce them. If we do have a plan for receiving them, then events abroad will be less likely to provoke a second crisis within the United States. But no planning for refugees can go forth until there is an agency specifically charged with that task. That would be the first responsibility of the refugee unit of the NIA.

The refugee unit would coordinate federal, state, local, and private agencies in the resettlement process. The idea of sponsorship needs careful scrutiny; sponsorships of previous refugees must be analyzed to learn where they have been successful and where they have failed. The refugee unit will need to seek supplemental appropriations when there is an unanticipated flow. But the unit will be able to provide the leadership to petition Congress. Refugee administration can then be removed from the category of crisis management.

NIA will receive refugees, provide them with temporary credentials, and see that basic subsistence is provided for some period of time. If large-scale relocation is planned, the NIA will take responsibility for that. Depending on the group, job training, English lessons, short courses in American history and culture, other education, medical attention, and personal counseling might be offered. NIA need not offer any of these programs; some might not be required, while others could be better supplied by local agencies or private citizens.

Statistical and Research Unit

One of the pervasive criticisms of the INS has been its inability to provide reliable data on immigration, both legal and illegal. Even the publication of annual reports and basic statistical data takes much longer than in other government agencies. Defenders of the agency have noted that it is principally an enforcement agency, not a statistical or research agency. Yet no other agency has taken on major responsibility for immigration data or research. Researchers have long noted the scarcity of data on immigrants; most extant research has been done using U.S. Census data (available only once a decade) or expensive custom-designed surveys.

It would be most helpful to legislators and to the executive agencies if there were more resources devoted to the statistical and research unit within the immigration agency, allowing the collection of more accurate and reliable data on immigrants, illegal aliens, other border crossers, and the administration of the agency. The agency need not do all of this research itself. It could make the data available to other agencies and nongovernment (academic and other) researchers. The current pattern of funding for research on immigration is scattershot. A few agencies (notably the Department of Labor) fund studies based on their need to learn more about Hispanics and other minorities or to learn about the impact of immigration on particular labor markets, although apparently not for determining labor "shortages" for the implementation of the labor certification program. Other seemingly unlikely sources of research interest have been the National Institute for Child Health and Human Development and several private foundations. The INS, which might be said to be interested in all aspects of immigration, did not have funds for research until 1977 and has yet to establish an adequate research section.

Realistic Expectations for the National Immigration Agency

If we return now to the areas of tension in immigration policy, we can examine the extent to which the NIA could alleviate the situation.

Federal-State Tensions

The NIA could not by itself eliminate federal-state tensions, but it could alleviate them in several ways. First, it would keep records of the location of immigrants. This would make it possible for a portion of the immigration tax to be rebated to the states and localities as revenue-sharing. Second, because it would take the leadership role in coordinating refugee programs, states would have specific NIA personnel to consult and specific offices to call. This would perhaps lessen the sense that one's state is being used as a "dumping ground" for refugees, or the feeling of a local community that a refugee settlement camp poses a community threat.

Legislative Loopholes

Congress would still be able to admit immigrants through private bills, and Congress would still be able to mandate large programs without providing funds for them. But the NIA would create an executive branch constituency that could propose legislation, point out needs for additional appropriations, and testify on the impact of proposed laws. The research unit could provide detailed information on the level of absorption of immigrants in the country, lessening the need for periodic special commissions and reviews that are in such haste to issue recommendations that they have little interest in the long-term research required for an understanding of the issues. The refugee unit, through a process of planning, could help move refugee programs from the area of crisis management to the area of controlled policy.

Administrative Discretion

No reform can entirely remove administrative discretion, nor would that be desirable. But a single immigration agency could remove some of the hazards of administrative discretion. For example, visas issued abroad would be issued by personnel of the NIA, the same agency that would scrutinize documents on entry. Suspicious entrants could be checked more efficiently through a more coordinated information system, and there would be less chance of capricious decisions. More important, a single agency would be better equipped to set priorities and regulations for its personnel because the centralized operation would handle all aspects of immigration.

Interagency Conflict

Interagency contention thrives where cooperation is mandated but no single agency has the obvious, manifest responsibility. Fragmented responsibility leads to a power vacuum, and this in turn leads to jockeying for position, subtle sabotage, and other games. The conflict in immigration has actually been rather muted compared to that in other areas, but the current system encourages further agency rivalry. A central immigration commission, in contrast, would create a clear mandate and an obvious mechanism for coordination of efforts. This would not eliminate conflicts, and certainly the new immigration commission would continue to need the cooperation of other agencies. But the creation of the commission would clearly pinpoint the responsibility for getting things done.

The Role of Private Agencies

It would be unwise either to force private agencies out of immigration issues or to narrowly circumscribe their roles. It is far wiser to let events dictate an appropriate role for them. But this implies that the role of the private agencies will change with circumstances, and a good deal of continuing liaison will be needed to preserve this flexibility. A permanent independent commission would have both the stability and the prominence to do this. Relations with private agencies could be made and nurtured even when there is no immediate crisis of refugees, or other crisis. The ongoing relations would ensure that there would be a network ready to respond when the inevitable shocks to the immigration program occurred.

The Role of Interest Groups

A central immigration commission would not eliminate the role of lobbyists in shaping immigration legislation. It would, however, provide a central target for all interest groups, those concerned with labor market issues as well as those concerned with specific nationality groups, those concerned with specific personnel problems as well as those worried about refugees. With every interest group dealing with a single commission, it seems less likely that any single group would come to "capture" the commission.

Enforcement of Immigration Law

It is easy to conceive of multiple tasks that the immigration commission should perform. The degree to which these tasks can be performed well will obviously depend upon the resources the commission has at its disposal. In particular, if Congress wants to put a high priority on enforcement, then the commission must have the personnel and the appropriations to enforce the law. To do a good job of patrolling the U.S. borders will require far more resources than we have so far been willing to commit to the project. Virtually no student of United States immigration problems is satisfied with the current state of illegal immigration. As long as the American economy continues to exert a strong "pull" relative to circumstances in other countries, no amount of enforcement will be sufficient to end illegal immigration. One can only devise systems that will make illegal immigration more difficult, that is, more costly for the illegal entrant. A number of measures to discourage illegal immigration have been proposed, but no measure is likely to succeed without a determined enforcement effort both at the border and in the interior.

Social scientists have studied the importance of enforcement and punishment as deterrents to crime (Becker, 1968). Illegal immigration is likely to be similar to other crime in terms of the structure of deterrence. While the last word on deterrence has certainly not been written, the current consensus seems to be that both the probability of being caught and the severity of the penalty are relevant. Arrests that involve virtually no penalty, such as the current revolving door at the border, have little or no deterrent effect. Stiff penalties without enforcement also have no deterrent effect. The greater efforts at border and interior enforcement discussed above need to be supplemented by penalties against illegal aliens. Fines and brief imprisonment for apprehended illegal aliens may have a substantial deterrent effect. At the very least, they are worth trying.

Summary

Reorganization of the immigration bureaucracy is not a panacea for American immigration problems; indeed, there is a great risk that it could become a cosmetic device that disguises a lack of real effort to deal with the problems. More fundamentally, American immigration problems do not have a single executive, legislative, or judicial solution. A simple problem-solving approach will always overlook the complexities inherent in immigration policy, including the enforcement of immigration law.

Yet the current administration of immigration law is not designed to promote consistent policy and efficient enforcement. In addition to the Immigration and Naturalization Service in the Department of Justice, the Department of Labor administers the labor certification programs for temporary workers and immigrants, and the State Department administers the issuance of visas. We propose that all immigration and naturalization services be performed by a single commission, the National Immigration Agency (NIA). The NIA would be independent of the cabinet agencies but would not have cabinet status. It would have five commissioners appointed by the President and confirmed by the Senate, with a chairman who acts as the administrator. A more coherent and efficient enforcement of immigration policy is more likely to emerge in the proposed administrative structure.

To be effective in enforcing immigration law, the immigration authorities need more resources than have been made available in recent years for both border and interior enforcement. Indeed, the recent focus on border enforcement at the expense of interior enforcement has reduced the overall deterrent effect of enforcement resources. Fines and brief imprisonment for apprehended illegal aliens may have a significant deterrent effect. More cooperation between state and local government agencies in reporting suspected illegal aliens to the immigration authorities would also enhance the enforcement of immigration law.

12
Recommendations

In this book, we have examined the U.S. immigration experience and developed a set of policy recommendations. These recommendations were based on the assumption that the primary purpose of U.S. immigration policy (as of any U.S. policy) is the promotion of the interests of the United States, given domestic and foreign policy concerns and the institutional framework within which immigration policy must operate. We have, however, viewed immigration policy as subject to complete review.

Our recommendations include retaining some features of current policy and sharply altering the thrust of other features. The primary change in focus is the reduction of the current overwhelming role of kinship in the rationing of immigration visas, with sharply increased emphasis to be given to the impact of immigrants on the U.S. economy. This is to be done through a skill-based point system for rationing immigration visas that are subject to numerical limitation, and a temporary worker program. Those with kinsmen who would no longer be able to immigrate, primarily low-skilled non-immediate relatives of resident aliens and recent naturalized citizens, would feel they lost by the change in focus. But the U.S. population as a whole, and particularly those with low levels of skills, would gain from the change in rationing criteria.

The recommendations constitute a complete reform of immigration policy. We believe that the time is ripe for such reform and that we offer a package that would attract very wide political consensus. This chapter recapitulates the major policy recommendations. It then discusses some recommendations made by others that we reject. This puts into sharper focus the features of our proposed program.

A Recapitulation of the Recommendations

Exempt Categories

We recommend retaining the current policy of numerically unlimited immigration by the immediate relatives of adult U.S. citizens, and we suggest adding an exemption for orphans adopted by American parents through a licensed U.S. social service agency. We recommend expanding the term "immediate relative" to include grandparents as well as parents, spouses, and dependent children of adult citizens, but we would require the citizen-sponsors to be adults and to guarantee the financial support and medical insurance for their relatives for the first five years in the U.S., unless an unanticipated disability arises after immigration. We do not recommend expanding the exempt category to include brothers, sisters, or collateral relatives, and we do not recommend a similar exemption for the relatives of resident aliens.

Quotas

Because a return to unrestricted immigration is not a realistic alternative, it is necessary to consider how we ration immigration beyond the immediate relatives of U.S. citizens. Rationing on the basis of racial or national origin is not consistent with American political beliefs. Rationing primarily on the basis of relationship to persons already in the United States makes little economic sense and may perpetuate the racial and national discrimination of the past. We recommend instead two devices for rationing places: a point system that would heavily weight training and skills, but would also give some advantage to relatives of citizens and resident aliens; and an immigration tax surcharge.

We recommend abolishing the current annual country ceilings but retaining the worldwide quota for immigrants other than those in the exempt category. The most important determinant in setting the numbers is the question of how many immigrants American society is able—or willing—to absorb. We propose 0.2 percent of the population—or two per thousand—as the basis for determining the number of numerically limited resident alien visas to be issued annually. This number is justified by the historical proportion of immigrants to the total population that continues to be easily absorbed and at the same time allows a realistic number of admissions. This implies about 500,000 visas subject to numerical limitation each year. Adjustment of the annual quota to the business cycle is not necessary, because economic immigration tends to be partly self-regulating, and because in the past four decades economic fluctuations have been difficult to predict and of relatively short duration.

Point System

Applicants with the highest number of points would be first in the queue for immigrant visas. Visas would be made available to the spouses and minor children of successful visa applicants. Points would be awarded primarily on the basis of characteristics that are likely to enhance the person's productivity in the U.S., including schooling, vocational training, on-the-job training, knowledge of English, and prearranged employment.

A smaller number of points would be awarded to applicants who have relatives in the U.S., as citizens or resident aliens, who agree to serve as sponsors. Those to be awarded such points would include the unmarried adult siblings of U.S. citizens and the spouses and dependent children of resident aliens who did not accompany them at immigration, as well as the parents and grandparents of resident aliens. Like the immediate relatives of U.S. citizens, the sponsors would have to be adults and would be responsible for the financial support of the immigrant for a period of at least five years.

Immigration Tax

The purpose of the immigration tax or surcharge is to enable others to share with the immigrant some of the "economic rent" (i.e., income gains greater than needed to induce immigration) that arises from the limitation on immigration. The immigration tax would be levied on all foreign workers, including immigrants, refugees, and temporary workers. The tax rate would be significant but not overwhelming, such as a 5 percent tax on earned income to be paid in addition to the federal income tax. Immigrants who earned no income would still have to file. This filing for tax purposes would be a substitute for the useful but recently abolished requirement of annual registration by aliens. Failure to file and pay the immigrant tax would be grounds for deportation. The tax would end if the immigrant became a naturalized citizen.

Revenues from the immigrant tax could help defray the expenses of processing immigrants, provide assistance to social overhead capital projects (e.g., roads, schools, hospitals) in local areas disproportionately affected by immigrants, and help to develop a "foreign-aid" program for countries of origin that lose investments in human capital to the U.S. through voluntary migrations.

Temporary Worker Program

We recommend a temporary worker program, enacted by bilateral agreements with the governments of the sending countries. Prospective employers would be required to provide medical insurance, Social Security tax payments, and guaranteed return transportation for their workers, in addition to a wage at least equal to the federal minimum wage and not less than the prevailing wage for that type of job. Temporary workers would be permitted to change jobs if new employers agreed to abide by the regulations. Temporary workers could bring their families (spouses and minor children) if their families were also covered by medical insurance, and would not become public charges, but their families could work only if they also were enrolled in the program. The employer would have to demonstrate to the immigration authorities why temporary workers were required and would have to pay the prevailing wage or the legal minimum wage for that job, whichever is higher. Temporary workers would also be subject to the immigration tax. The purpose of this plan is to make temporary workers available but no cheaper than indigenous labor.

Temporary worker visas would be for one year but could be renewed for a total of three consecutive years. Temporary workers would then have to return to their home countries for a period no less than half of the duration of their previous stay before they could again be admitted. Although they could not apply for resident alien visas until they returned to the homelands, those who did not violate the conditions of the agreement would be given additional points under the point system since they would have proven their ability to contribute to the American economy by participating in the labor market. The number of such points would have to be kept small, however, to prevent the temporary worker program from becoming a back-door immigration policy. Illegal aliens already in the United States would be given preference in applying for a temporary worker program.

Refugee Programs

We recommend that careful thought be given to the way in which refugees are defined. We suggest that the refugees' links to the United States and the nature of the threat to them in their native lands be the principal criteria used for admission. We recommend that major responsibility for the cost of resettling refugees be placed with the federal government.

United States immigration policy should not encourage other governments to "create" refugee movements as a means of either blackmailing the United States or eliminating undesirable nationals. United States immigration policy must be seen as only one aspect of our position on refugees. Greater resources devoted to the financing of third-country resettlement may help reduce opposition to refugee resettlement in the U.S. Much more work needs to be done in forecasting political situations likely to create refugees, as well as the connections between United States foreign policy and the creation of refugees.

Students, Business Travelers, and Tourists

Strong encouragement should be given to such temporary foreign visitors as students, businessmen, and tourists. One useful form this encouragement can take is minimizing the red tape required for a short-term visa. But a computerized system for checking visa numbers as visitors leave the country is necessary to keep some track of visa overstayers and reduce this mechanism for illegal entry.

Social Services

One important source of friction in the immigration controversy is the provision of social services to immigrants, especially illegal aliens. To make matters worse, these services are often provided by state and local governments, although only the federal government has jurisdiction over immigration. The provision of medical services seems to be a major issue. We recommend that all classes of immigrants and foreign visitors (with the exception of visitors with visas for less than six months) be admitted only with proof of medical insurance. In the case of relatives admitted under the exempt category and point-system immigrants who received points as a result of kinship to a U.S. sponsor, the sponsor would be responsible for the proof of coverage; in the case of temporary workers, the employer would be responsible for the proof of coverage. We do not advocate a new federal health insurance program, but provision of insurance through private insurance carriers.

Insurance coverage is not a substitute for the current provision that immigrants be free from contagious diseases. The fact that most immigrants are healthy and are relatively young should make the cost of health insurance reasonable. In the infrequent cases of persons being admitted to the United States specifically for medical treatment, there are already provisions for ensuring their financial responsibility.

Immigrants would not be eligible for the regular income-contingent transfer programs (Food Stamps, AFDC, Medicaid, Supplemental Security Income) during their first five years in the U.S., unless an unanticipated disability arose after immigration. Sponsors would be responsible for the immigrant's support. In emergency situations, however, short-term assistance would be made available from the state general assistance program, with a federal-state sharing of expenses.

In the case of the social insurance programs (worker's compensation, unemployment compensation), workers who met state requirements would be eligible regardless of immigrant status. Presumably, their employers would have paid the necessary premiums. Similarly, because temporary workers and other immigrants will have Social Security tax withheld, they should be eligible for Social Security benefits on the same basis as U.S. citizens.

Administrative Provisions

We recommend the formation of a single independent commission, the National Immigration Agency, which would take on all aspects of immigrant admission and enforcement of immigration laws. The five-member commission would be appointed by the President and confirmed by the Senate, with the chairman acting as head of the agency.

We recommend the creation of a nationwide, computerized system, based on visa numbers, to document both the entry and the exit of immigrants, temporary workers, and short-term foreign visitors. Embassy personnel who issue visas should be formally employed by the new immigration commission, so that the granting of visas would be more centralized.

Enforcement

We recommend that greater resources be made available to enforce immigration law both at the border and in the interior. Border enforcement with little interior enforcement, a policy trend of recent years, has created a virtual revolving door; with no cost attached to apprehension, the apprehended are encouraged to try again. Greater coordination among federal, state, and local authorities in identifying illegal aliens would aid the enforcement effort. Fines and brief imprisonment for apprehended illegal aliens would further increase the cost of apprehension to them and thus would tend to deter illegal entry and violation of the provisions of legally obtained visas.

Proposals for Reform that We Reject

We have spelled out in considerable detail, in the preceding chapters, the reasons for the recommendations summarized in this chapter. There are proposals for immigration reform that have been made from time to time that we have not endorsed. We turn now to our reasons for not endorsing them.

Employer Sanctions

Probably the most frequently advocated measure for reducing illegal immigration is sanctions against employers for knowingly hiring illegal aliens. This proposal appears to be attractive because most undocumented workers have entered the United States to work; thus, the one person with whom they must have contact is the employer. But to delegate the responsibility for enforcing immigration laws to the employer seems neither fair nor wise. It is certainly not fair that the employer, rather than the landlord, the grocer, the utility companies, or the other persons in contact with illegal aliens, be made responsible for their detection. The proposal is part of a growing trend to shift the burden of enforcing social policy to the private sector of the economy, and in particular the employer.

The obvious effect of employer sanctions would be to require employers to spend more time and money in their hiring decisions—something employers are reluctant to do. Verification of legal status would raise the relative cost of labor in low-wage and high-turnover jobs, thereby reducing job opportunities for many low-skilled native workers. Whether this would be offset by reduced competition with illegal aliens is not clear.

To reduce their information costs, employers would look for simplified ways of determining someone's status. Passports would probably be the easiest means of doing so: they are difficult to counterfeit, they have photographs, and they are issued periodically by government agencies. But the visas in foreign passports can be confusing, and an employer may fear that they have been counterfeited. Furthermore, millions of Americans who do not have passports would be forced to obtain them because most would have no other means of proving to employers that they had a legal right to work in this country. Other types of government identification are much less satisfactory. One need not be a citizen or resident alien to hold a driver's license, and voter registration cards and even Social Security cards are easy to counterfeit or obtain fraudulently. (Some illegal aliens have been able to receive bona fide Social Security cards, despite a tightening of procedures, because birth certificates can be counterfeited or fraudulently obtained, and it is not uncommon for more than one illegal alien to use one Social Security number.) Nonofficial documents, such as baptismal certificates, would not be acceptable. Alternatively, an employer could use an even cheaper method for avoiding undocumented workers: simple stereotyping. Employers might fear to "take a chance" that even a fifth-generation Mexican-American or Asian-American was a citizen. "Looking" Hispanic or Asian-origin or having a Spanish or Asian surname might be sufficient to disqualify citizens and legal resident aliens from jobs.

Although we do not recommend new sanctions of the sort under discussion, we do recommend that the government be diligent in enforcing existing regulations on employers. Employers who break the provisions of the Fair Labor Standards Act (minimum wage, overtime provisions) should expect sanctions, whether or not they employ illegal aliens. Enforcement of laws already on the books is the best guarantee that immigrants will not have their wages unlawfully withheld, be paid less than the minimum wage, be excluded from the Social Security fund, and so on.

Employers are already burdened with many requirements that they serve as links between the government and the citizen. The red tape required to hire workers has led, and if increased will continue to lead, to a contraction in employment opportunities, particularly for workers with low skills and high job turnover rates, for whom these added costs of employment are large relative to their wages. Employer sanctions share this general problem along with the specific problem of enhancing employment discrimination.

A National Identity Card

The national identity card has often been proposed as an adjunct to the employer-sanction plan. Under this proposal, a difficult-to-forge, federally issued identification card would be given to every citizen and to every legal foreign entrant. Employers could merely check the cards of job applicants. One objection raised to this system is that it could be linked to Social Security Administration and Internal Revenue Service records and form the basis for a national system of internal passports. A more immediate objection to the national identity card is that it would create an administrative nightmare. Computerizing a system for keeping track of several million visa numbers is one thing; providing identity cards for over 230 million Americans in addition to the several million immigrants, temporary workers, and tourists is quite another. It is a disproportionate response to the problem of illegal immigration. Civil libertarians may be right in fearing that an inappropriate policy response could be made to seem more appropriate by having the national identity card serve additional functions.

Amnesty

It is proposed from time to time that we should "wipe the slate clean" with a general amnesty for illegal aliens currently in the country. For a variety of related reasons we do not advocate an amnesty. First, even the rumor of an amnesty is likely to temporarily increase the volume of illegal immigration; after President Carter's election, and his suggestion of an amnesty, there was an increase in illegal immigration across the Mexican border. Second, an amnesty has the effect of rewarding lawbreakers at the expense of those who have waited, often for many years, for legal entry. It is difficult to think of hard-working, ambitious people as lawbreakers, and we have tended to treat illegal immigration as a minor offense. Nevertheless, a major social problem has arisen because of the cumulation of these "minor" offenses. It seems unwise to endorse these actions, in effect, by granting an amnesty. Third, an amnesty creates expectations of future amnesties. Rather than "wiping the slate clean" and letting a new immigration policy take effect, an amnesty would encourage still more to cross the border, keep a low profile, and wait for the next amnesty. Fourth, the negative effects of an amnesty would be intensified if recipients of amnesty, or the relatives they sponsored with their new resident alien status, were charged to the quotas. This would reduce immigration opportunities for those who wish to immigrate but have chosen to obey U.S. law and wait for visas.

Finally, there are reasons why the immigration of those who become illegal aliens is not sanctioned by immigration law. Illegal aliens are disporportionately low-skilled workers and this tendency will persist. Granting amnesty awards illegal aliens legal access to the income-transfer and social services (e.g., schooling, public medical care) systems, permits the immigration of immediate family members, and gives other family members priority for immigration. As a result, the former illegal aliens are less likely to return home during periods of seasonal or cyclical slack in economic activity, and they are more likely to bring their dependents to the United States. The result of an amnesty, therefore, would be a greater burden on the income transfer and social service systems, which could constitute a significant net drain on the income of the native population. The burden would be felt most strongly by low-skilled native workers, who would be faced with increased competition for scarce income tranfer and social service resources as well as increased competition in the labor market.

Occupation-Specific Labor Certification

The Office of Labor Certification in the Department of Labor designates certain occupations or professions as in short supply, either in the country as a whole or in a given labor market. These designations are used in implementing the labor-shortage requirements involved in obtaining the labor certificates that are required for entry under the third and sixth preferences. The other third- and sixth-preference visa petitions involve both the applicant and the prospective U.S. employer (who must demonstrate a "need" for an immigrant worker that cannot be satisfied by workers already in the country) before a labor certification is issued. Once the visa is obtained, the immigrant is not legally bound to the employer or the occupation for which the labor certificate was obtained. Many would retain the current approach of a job-specific or skill-specific labor certification program. We have rejected such a labor certification program in favor of a broader skill-based policy that does not focus on specific skills or specific employers.

We reject the labor-certification approach because it is subject to too much abuse. Labor unions, professional associations, and other interest groups with a protectionist bias pressure the Labor Department to certify that their occupations are overcrowded. For example, foreign-born physicians were removed from the most favored occupational classification for receiving labor certification because of pressure from American physicians asserting that there were "too many" doctors, and because of the government's concern that more doctors would mean higher Medicare and Medicaid expenditures. A "shortage" of doctors in inner-city and rural hospitals then resulted in changes in the regulations to permit labor certifications for doctors who intend to go to areas that the Department of Health and Human Services certifies as having a physician shortage. Of course, once a physician receives a resident alien visa he is not bound to work for the hospital or in the area for which the labor certificate was obtained. The American medical profession has renewed its campaign against the "flood" of foreign doctors. As another example, physical therapists and dieticians with advanced degrees were included in the most favored category because the U.S. was the only country in which such advanced degrees could be obtained, and the U.S. universities offering these programs supported the special treatment as a means of attracting students. Dieticians were subsequently removed, however, when the American Dietetics Association complained about an "oversupply" in the profession. Analyses of labor market conditions apparently play no role in the current rule-making process.

The problem is not that those currently administering the labor certification program are not up to the task, but rather that the system encourages substantial pressure from single-occupation interest groups without countervailing pressure from the widely dispersed consumers who are ultimately affected by the decisions. This problem would be defused if broad skill levels were used as the rationing mechanism (as in our proposed point system) rather than occupation-by-occupation rationing.

The occupation-specific or job-specific labor certification approach could, in principle, be more successful if there were a stagnant labor market with little opportunity for mobility of workers. Then "shortage" occupations could be identified. In the dynamic U.S. labor market, however, efforts by government and private sector economists to forecast future labor demands by specific occupation have not been successful, and the more narrowly defined the occupation and the longer the time horizon for the forecast, the lower their success rate. This approach also ignores the substantial occupational adjustments of the native-born and of immigrants with duration of U.S. residence (Chiswick, 1978b). These adjustments permit fairly rapid corrections for shortages that might develop. Indeed, granting a labor certification is not even a guarantee that the immigrant will work in the designated job or occupation.

A more appropriate way to address the concern about attracting skilled workers is through the "point system" we have proposed. Points would be issued primarily on the basis of skill, and more highly skilled workers would be more successful in their visa applications. Occupations with labor shortages would presumably pay higher wages, thereby attracting more U.S. workers and more foreign-born workers, who could enter under the exempt categories or under the point system. Efforts to tailor points to narrowly defined occupational interests will result in intense lobbying by narrow occupational interests, with each claiming their occupation needs special treatment—protection if the lobbying is by workers, easier entry if it is by employers.

Independent Immigrants

A proposal made by some that a certain number of visas be set aside for "independent immigrants" is a reaction to the emphasis on family reunification in current immigration policy. The independent immigrant would be one who has no family already in the United States and who does not otherwise qualify. Our proposals carry this view one step further by sharply reducing the role of kinship in rationing immigration visas. However, we would not also reject productivity criteria for rationing immigration visas, a step implied in some "independent immigrant" proposals. An independent immigrant could enter under the skill-based point system without any relatives already here. Or, if his country were part of a bilateral agreement, he could be part of a temporary worker program. While we agree that people should have the right to leave their countries of origin, they do not at the same time have the right to enter any country of their choosing.

Further Family Reunification

A number of proposals have been made to extend the current emphasis on family reunification, both by increasing the kinds of relationships that qualify and by treating the relatives of permanent residents on the same basis as the relatives of citizens. While we would provide a small number of points under the point system for nonimmediate relatives with a U.S. sponsor, and while we do extend the current "exempt" category to include grandparents of adult U.S. citizens, we do not favor the extended family reunification proposals. Without further safeguards, family reunification poses the possibility of an enormous expansion of the size of the immigrant population, with little regard for their skills and their impact on the U.S. labor market and with the possibility for greatly increasing the number of dependents—young and old—in the immigrant population. This in turn is likely to increase the strain on income tranfers and social services and to increase the level of tension in the U.S. over immigration. Family reunification is politically comfortable—it satisfies the interest groups of immigrants already in the United States—and it has an appealing humanitarian sound. But it also has costs: it raises the effective annual quota by a large number and it may prevent the entry of more valuable workers who happen not yet to have any American relatives or any access to lobbyists. Indeed the benefits of a kinship program that includes extended family members are received largely by the resident aliens and recent citizens who presumably like having their distant relatives in the U.S., but the economic cost of accepting less productive immigrants is paid for by the rest of the population.

Foreign Aid for Mexico

Some of the students of illegal immigration have claimed that greater employment opportunities within Mexico would stem illegal immigration. United States investment, it is claimed, could make Mexico more attractive to its potential emigrants. Although a considerable amount of light industry has already settled in Mexico near the border, the motivation has been productive labor rather than immigration relief. But other critics have argued that the border development program, rather than keeping potential emigrants in Mexico, has given them a taste of American industrial life and of the border towns. And by encouraging migration from the more remote areas of Mexico to the border, these programs may actually have encouraged illegal immigration to the U.S. Indeed, since these industries have been predominantly female-intensive, it has been alleged that after families move from the interior to the border because of these programs, the wife works in the border industries and the husband illegally enters the U.S. for temporary work (see, for example, Cross and Sandos, 1981).

We do not recommend the border industrialization program as an immigration policy. First, it is not obvious that it has retarded rather than enhanced illegal immigration from Mexico. Second, even if the current small programs have discouraged such immigration, to implement them on the scale necessary to significantly reduce illegal immigration would require a massive infusion of funds—substantially more than one job would have to be created to reduce illegal immigration by one person. Third, it is not certain that the Mexican government wishes to pursue such a policy. Fourth, Mexico's economic development is more likely to be enhanced if development policy focuses on this issue, rather than combining it with immigration policies.

A New Bracero Program

The temporary worker program we have recommended differs in important respects from the Bracero Program of 1942 to 1964. First, the Bracero Program was limited to young, single men; our proposed program is not. Second, the Bracero Program withheld part of the men's wages to ensure their return to Mexico; our program requires that the employer place return fare in an escrow account. Third, the Bracero Program sharply limited the occupation and industry the bracero could pursue. Our policy contains no such limits, providing the employer is willing to go to the trouble of joining the temporary worker program and can demonstrate why temporary workers are warranted. Fourth, the Bracero Program specified the quality of housing and other living necessities to be provided the workers. Our program permits workers to purchase these commodities for themselves, with the provision that the employer pay the prevailing wage or the minimum wage, whichever is greater, provide medical insurance, and pay the applicable Social Security and other taxes.

Greater Restrictions on Citizenship

Partly because of the return migration of some Hispanics, and partly because of the importance and complexity of the issues facing the electorate on election day, some observers have suggested that naturalization be made much more difficult for immigrants. Ways of doing this would include instituting more rigorous tests of English proficiency, but the most frequent suggestion is lengthening the period of residence in the United States from five years to ten years, fourteen years, or even longer. We have not advocated such a change; instead, some of our recommendations would encourage citizenship, but only at the discretion of the immigrant (e.g., the waiver of the immigrant tax when an alien becomes a citizen). Forced citizenship is not desirable, but citizenship can certainly be rewarded by giving citizens an advantage in serving as sponsors for immigrants, and by an immigration tax that ends when a person is naturalized.

The five-year residence requirement can be justified as ensuring that the immigrant is adjusted to the United States and will not regret the change of citizenship. Recent studies, for example, have suggested that as many as 10 percent of legally admitted Mexicans returned to Mexico within three years (e.g., Cornelius, 1976).

Encouraging citizenship is an important difference between United States immigration programs and those of European countries. Where citizenship is not encouraged, an antagonistic "we-they" relationship can arise between the immigrants and the native-born. The possibility of becoming a citizen is a central part of the American creed; while it is true that most immigration proceeds from economic motives, it is also true that the United States gains strength from the political allegiance of naturalized citizens.

Because we leave the possibility of citizenship open to the immigrant, we do not suggest that immigrants be allowed to vote in local or state elections as they do in some European countries and as they did in some parts of the United States until as recently as 1920.

Epilogue

In the coming decades, new generations of immigrants will come to the United States, and new generations of Americans will question the wisdom of admitting them. And yet, in spite of our fears and our doubts, they will continue to come. In capital cities all over the world, daybreak will show that long lines have already formed in the United States embassies. In little restaurants and in luxury hotels, in taxis and on assembly lines, in research laboratories and hospitals, and even in Ft. Chaffee, Arkansas, each immigrant affirms the American creed. On every national holiday, in federal courts all over the country, men and women, born in countries all over the globe, will stand to affirm that their new country is the United States. There is little economic incentive and there is no political pressure to acquire citizenship. At a time when American citizens question the meaning of the American creed and doubt the promise of the American dream, each successive generation of immigrants presents both affirmation and a challenge.

This is perhaps the contemporary twist in the perennial dilemma of immigration in America. Underlying the fears of cheap foreign labor competing unfairly with native workers and of linguistic divisiveness and of environmental degradation is the suspicion that the nation is somehow weakened by having all these strangers in our midst. In a time when America is unsure of its stature among nations, and when patriotism is somewhat suspect, if not ridiculed, we find it difficult to define what an American—this "new man"—is except in the most primordial terms: "This is my own, my native land." When the vision of our greatness is most tenuous, our fear of the stranger is most intense. And so we need an immigration policy that is designed to preserve the society and values of Americans while contributing to the economic promise of America. We need a policy that can provide a rational assurance that it will promote economic growth while being true to the traditions of a nation of immigrants. We need an immigration policy that responds to the realities of the international community at the end of the twentieth century. To fashion such a policy we must be mindful of myths while examining them in the harsh light of political and economic realities. The dilemma of immigration in America will continue, but it can be addressed in the context of the experience of the last two hundred years.

References

Bean, Frank D., King, Allan G., and Passel, Jeffrey. 1983. "The Number of Illegal Migrants of Mexican Origin in the United States: Sex Ratio-Based Estimates for 1980." *Demography* 20 (February)

Bean, Frank D., and Swicegood, Gray. 1982. "Generation, Female Education and Mexican American Fertility." *Social Science Quarterly* 63 (March): 131-144.

Becker, Gary S. 1968. "Crime and Punishment: An Economic Approach." *Journal of Political Economy* (March): 169-217.

Bennett, Marion T. 1963. *American Immigration Policies: A History.* Washington: Public Affairs Press.

Blau, Francine D. 1980. "Immigration and Labor Earnings in Early Twentieth Century America." In *Research in Population Economics*, Vol. 2, ed. Julian L. Simon and Julie DaVanzo. Greenwich, CT: Jai Press.

———. 1982. "The Use of Transfers by Immigrants." University of Illinois at Urbana-Champaign, mimeographed.

Bloch, Louis. 1921. "Occupations of Immigrants Before and After Coming to the United States." *Journal of the American Statistical Association* 17: 750-64.

Bonacich, Edna. 1972. "A Theory of Ethnic Antagonism: The Split Labor Market." *American Sociological Review* 37 (October): 547-59.

———. 1973. "A Theory of Middleman Minorities." *American Sociological Review* 38 (October): 583-594.

Bouvier, Leon S. 1977. "International Migration: Yesterday, Today, and Tomorrow." *Population Bulletin* 32 (September).

———. 1981. "The Impact of Immigration on United States Population Size." *Population Trends and Public Policy*, Washington D.C.: Population Reference Bureau.

Briggs, Vernon. 1975. *Mexican Migration and the United States Labor Market.* Austin: University of Texas Press.

Bryce-Laporte, R. S. 1977. "Visibility of the New Immigrants." *Society* 14 (September/October): 18-33.

———. 1980. *Sourcebook on The New Immigration: Implications for the United States and the International Community.* New Brunswick, N.J.: Transaction Books.

Bustamante, Jorge. 1976. "Structural and Ideological Conditions of Undocumented Mexican Immigration to the U.S." In *Current Issues in Social Policy*, ed. W. Boyd Lettrell and Gideon Sjoberg. Beverly Hills, California: Sage Publications.

Carliner, David. 1977. *The Rights of Aliens: The Basic ACLU Guide to an Alien's Rights*. New York: Avon Books.

Chicago Public Library Omnibus Project. 1942. *The Chicago Foreign Language Press Survey*. Chicago, Illinois: Chicago Public Library.

Chicago Tribune, September 5, 1920, Sec. 1, p. 6.

Chiswick, Barry R. 1977a. "The Income Transfer System: Impact, Viability and Proposals for Reform." In *Contemporary Economic Problems, 1977*, ed. William Fellner, pp. 347-428. Washington: American Enterprise Institute.

_____. 1977b. "Sons of Immigrants: Are They At An Earnings Disadvantage?" *American Economic Review* (February): 376-380 (Errata, *AER*, September 1977, p. 775).

_____. 1978a. "The Effect of Americanization on the Earnings of Foreign-Born Men." *Journal of Political Economy* 86 (October): 897-922.

_____. 1978b. "A Longitudinal Analysis of the Occupational Mobility of Immigrants." In *Proceedings of the 30th Annual Winter Meeting, Industrial Relations Research Association*, ed. Barbara D. Dennis, pp. 20-27. Madison: I.R.R.A.

_____. 1979. "The Economic Progress of Immigrants: Some Apparently Universal Patterns." In *Contemporary Economic Problems, 1979*, ed. William Fellner, pp. 359-399. Washington: American Enterprise Institute.

_____. 1980. *An Analysis of the Economic Progress and Impact of Immigrants*. Report prepared under contract number 21-06-78-20, Employment and Training Administration, U.S. Department of Labor, mimeographed (NTIS PB80-200454).

_____. 1981. "Guidelines for the Reform of Immigration Policy." In *Essays in Contemporary Economic Problems, 1981/1982*, ed. William Fellner, pp. 309-347. Washington: American Enterprise Institute.

_____. 1982a. "Differences in Educational Attainment Among Racial and Ethnic Groups: Patterns and Preliminary Hypotheses." Paper presented at National Academy of Education Conference on the State of Education, Chicago, May 1982. Abstracted in *Academy Notes*, 13 (1): 13-14.

_____. 1982b. *The Employment of Immigrants in the United States*. Washington: American Enterprise Institute.

_____, ed. 1982c. *The Gateway: U.S. Immigration Issues and Policies*. Washington: American Enterprise Institute.

_____. 1982d. "The Impact of Immigration on the Level and Distribution of Economic Well-Being." In *The Gateway: U.S. Immigration Issues and Policies*, ed. Barry R. Chiswick, pp. 289-314. Washington: American Enterprise Institute.

_____. 1983a. "An Analysis of the Earnings and Employment of Asian-American Men." *Journal of Labor Economics* 1 (April).

———. 1983b. "The Earnings and Human Capital of American Jews." *Journal of Human Resources*, 18 (Summer).

———. In press. "Illegal Aliens in the U.S. Labor Market." *Proceedings of the International Economic Association 6th World Congress.*

Coale, Ansley J. 1972. "Alternative Paths to a Stationary Population." In *Commission on Population Growth and the American Future, Research Reports* Vol. 1, ed. Charles F.Westoff and Robert Parke Jr., pp. 591-603. Washington D.C.: U.S. Government Printing Office.

Congressional Research Service. 1979. *U.S. Immigration Law and Policy: 1952-1979.* Washington, D.C.: Library of Congress.

Cornelius, Wayne A. 1976. "Mexican Migration to the United States: The View from Rural Sending Communities." Cambridge, MA: Migration and Development Study Group of M.I.T., mimeographed.

———. 1978. "Mexican Migration to the United States: Causes, Consequences and U.S. Responses." Cambridge, Mass.: Migration and Development Study Group of M.I.T., mimeographed.

Crevecoeur, Hector St. John de. 1963. *Letters from an American Farmer.* New York: The New American Library of World Literature.

Cross, Harry E., and Sandos, James A. 1981. *Across the Border: Rural Development in Mexico and Recent Migration to the United States.* Berkeley: University of California Press.

Dagodag, Tim W. 1975. "Source Region and Composition of Illegal Mexican Immigration to California." *International Migration Review* 9 (Winter): 499-511.

Dinnerstein, Leon, and Reimers, David. 1975. *Ethnic Americans: A History of Immigration and Assimilation.* New York: Harper and Row.

Douglas, Paul H. 1919. "Is the New Immigration More Unskilled than the Old?" *Journal of the American Statistical Association* (June): 393-403.

Dunne, Finley P. 1898. "On the Anglo-Saxon." *Mr. Dooley in Peace and in War.* Boston: Small, Maynard & Co., p. 55.

Easterlin, Richard A. 1980. "Economic and Social Characteristics of the Immigrants." In *Immigration*, ed. R. Easterlin, D. Ward, W.S. Bernard, and R. Ueda, pp. 1-34. Cambridge, MA: Belknap Press.

Ehrlich, Paul R., Bilderback, Loy, and Ehrlich, Anne. 1979. *The Golden Door: International Migration, Mexico and the United States.* New York and Toronto: Ballantine Books.

Featherman, David L., and Hauser, Robert M. 1978. *Opportunity and Change.* New York: Academic Press.

Feingold, Henry. 1970. *The Politics of Rescue: The Roosevelt Administration and the Holocaust, 1938-1945.* New Brunswick: Rutgers University Press.

Fox, Robert W. 1980. "Latin America: Population and Urbanization." *The International Population News Magazine*, Vol. 8, No. 10 (October).

Garcia, Robert. July 1980. "Census Undercount: Time to Adjust." In Conference
on Census Undercount: Proceedings of the 1980 Conference, pp. 12-24,
Washington: U.S. Bureau of the Census.

Gerking, Shelby D., and Mutti, John H. 1980. "Costs and Benefits of Illegal Immigration: Key Issues for Government Policy." *Social Science Quarterly* Vol.
61, No. 1 (June): pp. 71-85.

Gilford, Leon, and Lansey, Beverly. 1981. "The Effect of Undercount Adjustment
on Apportionment." Washington: U.S. Bureau of the Census (mimeographed).

Glaser, William A. 1978. *The Brain Drain: Emigration and Return*. Oxford: Perga-
mon Press.

Goldfarb, Robert A. 1982. "Occupational Preferences in U.S. Economic Law: An
Economic Analysis." In *The Gateway: U.S. Immigration Issues and Policies*,
ed. Barry R. Chiswick. Washington: American Enterprise Institute.

Gordon, Linda W. 1980. "Settlement Patterns of Indochinese Refugees in the
United States." *INS Reporter* (Spring): 8-10.

Graham, Otis. 1980. "Illegal Immigration and the New Reform Movement." *Immigration Papers II*. Federation for American Immigration Reform (February).

Grebler, Leo. 1966. "The Naturalization of Mexican Immigrants in the U.S."
International Migration Review 1: 17-32.

Greeley, Andrew M. 1974. *Ethnicity in the United States: A Preliminary Reconnais-
sance*. New York: John Wiley and Sons.

_____. 1976. *Ethnicity, Denomination, and Inequality*. Beverly Hills, CA: Sage.

_____. 1977. *The American Catholic: A Social Portrait*. New York: Basic Books.

_____. 1981. "Immigration and Religion-Ethnic Group: A Sociological Reapprais-
al." In *The Gateway: U.S. Immigration Issues and Policies*, edited by Barry
R. Chiswick, pp. 159-192. Washington, D.C.: American Enterprise Institute.

_____, McCready, William, and Theisen, Gary. 1980. *Ethnic Drinking Subcultures*.
New York: Praeger Publishers.

Guest, Avery M. 1982. "Fertility Variation Among the U.S. Foreign Stock Population in 1900." *International Migration Review* 16 (Fall): 577-594.

Hansen, Marcus Lee. 1940. *The Immigrant in American History*. Cambridge, MA:
Harvard University Press.

Harper, Elizabeth J. 1975. *Immigration Laws of the United States*. 3rd edition.
Indianapolis: Bobbs-Merrill Co., Inc.

Hauser, Philip M. 1979. "Introduction and Overview." In *World Population and
Development: Challenges and Prospects*, edited by Philip M. Hauser, p. 1-62,
Syracuse, New York: Syracuse University Press.

Heer, David. 1979. "What Is the Annual Net Flow of Undocumented Mexican
Immigrants to the United States?" *Demography* 16 (August): 417-23.

Hernandez, Jose, et al. 1973. "Census Data and the Problem of Conceptually Defining the Mexican-American Population." *Social Science Quarterly* 53 (March): 671-687.

Hirschman, Charles. June 1978. "Prior U.S. Residence Among Mexican Immigrants." *Social Forces* 56: 1179-1202.

_____. and Wong, Morrison G. 1981. "Trends in Socioeconomic Achievements Among Immigrant and Native-Born Asian Americans, 1960-1976." *The Sociological Quarterly* 22 (Autumn): 495-523.

Hutchinson, E.P. 1956. *Immigrants and Their Children, 1850-1950.* New York: John Wiley.

_____. 1981. *Legislative History of American Immigration Policy, 1798-1965.* Philadelphia: University of Pennsylvania Press.

"Iran Sending Teams to Western Europe to Recruit Doctors." *New York Times*, 13 February 1983, Section 1, p.8.

Kammen, Michael. 1972. *People of Paradox: An Inquiry Concerning The Origins of American Civilization.* New York: Knopf.

Keely, Charles B. 1971. "Effects of the Immigration Act of 1965 on Selected Population Characteristics of Immigrants to the United States." *Demography* 8 (May): 157-69.

_____. 1975. "Effects of U.S. Immigration Laws on Manpower Characteristics of Immigrants." *Demography* 12 (May): 179-91.

Knowles, Malcolm S. 1962. *The Adult Education Movement in the United States.* New York: Holt, Rinehard, & Winston.

Kraly, Ellen Percy. 1982. "Emigration from the U.S. Among the Elderly." Paper presented at the annual meeting of the Population Association of America.

Kramer, Jane. 1980. *Unsettling Europe.* New York: Random House Inc.

Kubat, Daniel. 1979. *The Politics of Migration Policies.* New York: Center for Migration Studies.

Landes, Elisabeth E. 1980. "The Effect of State Maximum Hours Laws on the Employment of Women in 1920." *Journal of Political Economy* 88.

Lieberson, Stanley. 1980. *A Piece of the Pie: Blacks and White Immigrants Since 1880.* Berkeley, CA: University of California Press.

Light, Ivan. 1972. *Ethnic Enterprise in America: Business and Welfare Among Chinese, Japanese, and Blacks.* Berkeley: University of California Press.

Lightbourne, Robert, Jr., and Singh, Susheela. 1982. "The World Fertility Survey: Charting Global Childbearing." *Population Bulletin* 37 (March): 1-54.

Los Angeles Times. 1979. "Illegal Aliens Cost U.S. Jobs — Marshall." December 2, part 1, p. 1.

Martin, Philip L., and Richards, Alan. 1980. "International Migration of Labor: Boon or Bane." *The Monthly Labor Review* (October): 49.

Martin, Walter T., and Poston, Dudley L. Jr. 1977. "Differentials in the Ability to Convert Education into Income: The Case of the European Ethnics." *International Migration Review* Vol. II, No. 2: 215-231.

Martin, Walter T., Poston, Dudley L., Jr., and Goodman, Jerry D. 1980. "Converting Education into Income and Occupational Status: Another Look at the European Ethnics." *Pacific Sociological Review* 23 (July): 297-314.

McLemore, S. Dale. 1973. "The Origins of Mexican-American Subordination in Texas." *Social Science Quarterly* 53 (March): 656-670.

Morse, Arthur D. 1968. *While Six Million Died: A Chronicle of American Apathy.* New York: Random House.

Myrdal, Gunnar. 1944. *An American Dilemma.* New York, London: Harper Brothers.

New York Times, September 1, 1919, p. 6.

New York Times, October 19, 1919, p. 14.

North, David S. 1978. *Seven Years Later: The Experience of the 1970 Cohort of Immigrants in the U.S. Labor Market.* Washington: Linton & Co.

_____.1981. "Enforcing the Immigration Law: A Review of the Options." In *U.S. Immigration Policy and the National Interest*, Appendix E, Papers on Illegal Aliens, Select Commission on Immigration and Refugee Policy.

_____, and Houstoun, Marion F. 1976. *The Characteristics and Role of Illegal Aliens in the U.S. Labor Market: An Exploratory Study.* Washington: Linton and Co., Inc.

Parai, Louis. 1975. "Canada's Immigration Policy: 1962-1974." *International Migration Review* 9 (Winter): 470-471.

Pedraza-Bailey, Silvia. 1980. "Political and Economic Migrants in America: Cubans and Mexicans." Unpublished Ph.D. dissertation, Department of Sociology, University of Chicago.

Pedraza-Bailey, Silvia, and Sullivan, Teresa A. 1979. "Bilingual Education in the Reception of Political Immigrants." In *Ethnoperspectives in Bilingual Education.* Research Series Vol. I., ed. Raymond V. Padilla, pp. 376-394. Ypsilanti, MI: Eastern Michigan University.

Penalosa, Fernando. 1969. "Education-Income Discrepancies Between Second and Later Generation Mexican-Americans in the Southwest." *Sociology and Social Research* 53 (July): 448-454.

Piore, Michael J. 1979. *Birds of Passage: Migrant Labor and Industrial Societies.* New York: Cambridge University Press.

Portes, Alejandro. 1982. "Immigrants' Attainment: An Analysis of Occupation and Earnings Among Cuban Exiles in the United States." In *Social Structure and Behavior: Essays in Honor of William Hamilton Sewell*, ed. R.M. Hauser, D. Mechanic, A.D. Haller, and T.S. Hauser, pp. 91-111. New York: Academic Press.

———.Clark, Juan M., and Bach, Robert L. 1977. "The New Wave: A Statistical Profile of Recent Cuban Exiles to the United States." *Cuban Studies* 7 (January): 1-32.

Poston, Dudley L. Jr., Martin, Walter T., and Goodman, Jerry D. 1982. "Earnings Differences Between Old and New U.S. Immigrants." *Pacific Sociological Reivew* 25 (January): 97-106.

Reimers, David. 1982. "Recent Immigraton Policy: An Analysis." In *The Gateway: U.S. Immigration Issues and Policies,* edited by Barry R. Chiswick, pp. 13-53. Washington: American Enterprise Institute.

Rindfuss, Ronald R., and Sweet, James A. 1977. *Postwar Fertility Trends and Differentials in the United States.* New York: Academic Press.

Rist, Ray. 1978. *Guestworkers in Germany: The Prospects for Pluralism.* New York: Praeger.

Robinson, J. G. 1980. "Estimating the Approximate Size of the Illegal Alien Population in the United States by the Comparative Trend Analysis of Age-Specific Death Rates." *Demography* 17 (May): 159-176.

Rottenberg, Simon, ed. 1981. *The Economics of the Legal Minimum Wage.* Washington, D.C.: American Enterprise Institute.

San Antonio Express, February 16, 1920, p. 1.

Select Commission on Immigration and Refugee Policy. 1981. *U.S. Immigration Policy and the National Interest: Staff Report.* Washington.

Siegel, Jacob S., Passel, Jeffrey S., Rives, Norfleet W. Jr., and Robinson, J. Gregory. 1977. "Development Estimates of the Coverage of the Population of States in the 1970 Census: Demographic Analysis." *Current Population Reports.* Series P-23, No. 65. Washington: U.S. Bureau of the Census.

Siegel, Jacob S., Passel, Jeffrey S., and Robinson, J. Gregory. 1981. "Preliminary Review of Existing Studies of the Number of Illegal Residents in the United States." In Select Commission on Immigration and Refugee Policy, *U.S. Immigration Policy and the National Interest,* Appendix E, Papers on Illegal Migration to the United States. Washington.

Simon, Julian. 1981. "What Immigrants Take From and Give To the Public Coffers." In Select Commission on Immigration and Refugee Policy, *U.S. Immigration Policy and the National Interest,* Appendix D, Papers on Legal Immigration to the United States. Washington, DC.

Smith, Richard Ferree. 1966. "Refugees." *The Annals* 367 (September): 43-52.

Stolnitz, George. 1978. "International Migration Policies: Some Demographic and Economic Contexts." In *Migration: Patterns and Policies,* edited by William H. McNeil and Ruth S. Adams. Bloomington: Indiana University Press.

Sullivan, Teresa A., and Pedraza-Bailey, Silvia. 1979. "Differential Success Among Cuban-American and Mexican-American Immigrants: The Role of Policy and Community." Washington, D.C.: National Technical Information Service.

Tanton, John. 1979. "Rethinking Immigration Policy." *Immigration Papers I*. U.S.A.: Federation for American Immigration Reform (January).

Tienda, Marta, and Neidert, Lisa. 1981. "Language Education, and the Socioeconomic Achievement of Hispanic Origin Men." In *Hispanic Origin Workers in the U.S. Labor Market*, ed. Marta Tienda, pp. 258-288. Washington: National Technical Information Services.

Ueda, Reed. 1980. "Naturalization and Citizenship." In *Immigration*, ed. R. Easterlin, D. Ward, W. S. Bernard, and R. Ueda, pp. 106-154. Cambridge, MA: Belknap Press.

United Nations. 1973. "The Determinants and Consequences of Population Trends." Volume I. *Department of Economics and Social Affairs Population Studies* No. 50. New York.

U.S. Bureau of the Census. 1965. *Census of Population: 1960*. Subject Reports. National Origin and Language. Washington.

_____. 1965. *Census of Population: 1960*. Subject Reports, Nativity and Parentage. Washington.

_____. 1972. *Public Use Samples of Basic Records from the 1970 Census: Descriptions and Technical Documentation*. Washington.

_____. 1973. *1970 Census of Population*. Subject Reports. National Origin and Language. Washington.

_____. 1975. *Historical Statistics of the United States, Colonial Times to 1970*. Washington.

_____. 1980. "Comparison of Current Trends with the 1977 Population Projections of the United States: August 1980." *Current Population Reports* Ser. P-25, No. 889. Washington D.C.: U.S. Government Printing Office.

U.S. Commission on Civil Rights. 1980. *The Tarnished Golden Door: Civil Rights Issues in Immigration*. (A Report of the United States Commission on Civil Rights, September 1980, pp. 7-22). Washington D.C.: U.S. Government Printing Office.

U.S. Congress, House. Congressional Record, 67th Cong., 1st sess., 510 (remarks of Representative Huddleston).

U.S. Congress, House. Congressional Record, 67th Cong., 1st sess., 501 (remarks of Representative Johnson).

U.S. Congressional Research Service. 1980. "Temporary Worker Programs: Background and Issues," p. 5.

U.S. Department of Commerce, Bureau of the Census. 1980. "Preliminary Review of Existing Studies of the Number of Illegal Residents in the United States."

U.S. Department of Justice. 1976. *Preliminary Report: Domestic Council Committee on Illegal Aliens*. Washington: Department of Justice. (December)

_____. 1978. *Naturalization Requirements and General Information*. Washington. (January)

_____. 1980. *The 1978 Statistical Yearbook: Immigration and Naturalization Service*. Washington D.C.: U.S. Government Printing Office.

_____. Various years. *Annual Report: Immigration and Naturalization Service*. Washington.

_____. Various years. *Statistical Yearbook: Immigration and Naturalization Service*. Washington.

U.S. Department of Labor. 1979. "Profile of Labor Conditions (Mexico) 1979." Washington D.C.: U.S. Government Printing Office.

U.S. Department of State. 1980. "Immigrant Numbers for December 1980." Bureau of Consular Affairs, Vol. V, No. 3. Washington D.C.: U.S. Government Printing Office.

_____. Bureau of Consular Affairs, Visa Office. February 1983. "Immigrant Numbers for February 1983." (Issued monthly).

U.S. House of Representatives, Select Committee on Population. 1978. *Legal and Illegal Immigration to the United States*. Washington. (December)

U.S. Immigration Commission. 1911. *Reports of the Immigration Commission*. Washington: Government Printing Office.

U.S. News and World Report. 1974. "Silent 'Invasion' That Takes Millions of American Jobs." December 9, pp. 77-78.

Usher, Dan. 1977. "Public Property and the Effects of Migration Upon Other Residents of the Migrant's Countries of Origin and Destination." *Journal of Political Economy* 85 (October): 1001-20.

VanArsdol, Maurice Jr., et al. 1978. "Non-Apprehended and Apprehended Undocumented Residents in the Los Angeles Labor Market: An Exploratory Study." University of Southern California, mimeographed.

Wachter, Michael L. 1978. "Second Thoughts About Illegal Immigrants." *Fortune Magazine*, May 22, 1978.

Ward, David. 1980. "Settlement Patterns and Spatial Distribution." In *Immigration*, ed. R. Easterlin, D. Ward, W. S. Bernard, and R. Ueda, pp. 35-74. Cambridge, MA: Belknap Press.

Williamson, Jeffrey G. 1980. "Immigrant-Inequality Trade-Offs in the Promised Land: Income Distribution and Absorptive Capacity Prior to the Quotas." Economic History, Discussion Papers Series. Madison: University of Wisconsin Press.

Wilson, Kenneth, and Martin, W. Allen. 1982. "Ethnic Enclaves: A Comparison of the Cuban and Black Economies in Miami." *American Journal of Sociology* 88 (July): 135-160.

_____. and Portes, Alejandro. 1980. "Immigrant Enclaves: An Analysis of the Labor Market Experiences of Cubans in Miami." *American Journal of Sociology* 86 (September): 295-319.

"World Population Plan of Action." 1975. *Population and Development Review* 1 (September): 163-182.

Zelinsky, Wilbur. 1973. *Immigration Settlement Patterns, The Cultural Geography of the U.S.* Englewood Cliffs, NJ: Prentice-Hall.

Index